Best Practices in
Trade Policy Reform

A World Bank Publication

Best Practices in Trade Policy Reform

Vinod Thomas and John Nash

with
Sebastian Edwards
Thomas Hutcheson
Donald Keesing
Kazi Matin
Garry Pursell
Alexander Yeats

Published for The World Bank
Oxford University Press

Oxford University Press

OXFORD NEW YORK TORONTO DELHI
BOMBAY CALCUTTA MADRAS KARACHI
PETALING JAYA SINGAPORE HONG KONG
TOKYO NAIROBI DAR ES SALAAM
CAPE TOWN MELBOURNE AUCKLAND
and associated companies in
BERLIN IBADAN

© 1991 The International Bank for
Reconstruction and Development / THE WORLD BANK
1818 H Street, N.W., Washington, D.C. 20433, U.S.A.

Library of Congress Cataloging-in-Publication Data

Thomas, Vinod, 1949–
    Best practices in trade policy reform / Vinod Thomas and John Nash
with Sebastian Edwards . . . [et al.].
        p.   cm.
    Includes bibliographical references and index.
    ISBN 0-19-520871-4
    1. Developing countries—Commercial policy. 2. Developing
countries—Economic policy. 3. Economic stabilization—Developing
countries.   I. Nash, John D., 1953–   . II. Title.
    HF1413.T518   1991
382'.3'091724—dc20   91-27502
                                                                      CIP

Foreword

Trade policy was high on the agenda of reform in many developing countries in the 1980s, a decade marked by reform efforts on several fronts. The gains from integration into the world economy were known to be substantial. Yet barriers to imports and exports had proliferated and were impeding that integration—and retarding growth. Many countries also found that access to the rapidly changing technologies needed for competitiveness in world markets depended on increasing their openness. For many of these same reasons, trade policy reform was frequently central to the adjustment programs supported by World Bank loans and International Monetary Fund programs in the 1980s.

Despite the gains promised from trade liberalization, serious objections and skepticism about its effectiveness nonetheless remained. This book examines how much liberalization has actually taken place and how effective it has been in promoting economic growth. It highlights practical problems and constraints, both economic and political. The analysis draws on the experience of developing countries with trade policy design and implementation to suggest how they can obtain stronger and more sustainable results.

The study finds that where reforms have been significant and credible, economic growth and the balance of payments have improved. Developing countries are more open and their trade regimes more efficient today than they were a decade ago. Yet many countries have held back, implementing less extensive liberalization of foreign trade than anticipated and needed. The outcomes have also often fallen short of expectations. Macroeconomic instability and lack of complementary actions to reinforce positive responses to reform are the primary reasons.

Drawing on its review of worldwide experience, the book recommends three important departures from current practice or changes in emphasis, with a view to improving the effectiveness of trade reforms.

v

• First, sharper reductions in the effective protection afforded to domestic producers are needed to boost competition and efficiency. Many countries have switched from quantitative restrictions on imports to tariffs; while that indicates progress, lowering of protection also requires a substantial tariff reform.

• Second, successful trade reforms must have the support of macro-economic policies that achieve and maintain stability in the economy. The budgetary consequences of trade liberalization need to receive more thoughtful attention. And countries with high and variable rates of inflation need to stabilize their economy before a major liberalization.

• Third, domestic regulation, inadequate investment, and institutional weaknesses in many countries block the benefits of trade reform programs. To obtain substantial benefits in these cases, it is crucial to deregulate, to increase investments, and to carry out institutional reforms together with the liberalization of foreign trade.

With these and other recommendations, the book reaffirms the rationale for trade policy reforms and solidly endorses their continuation under adjustment programs. By applying the lessons of wide-ranging experience, countries should be able to improve the acceptability and the effectiveness of further liberalization.

Stanley Fischer was Vice President of Development Economics and Chief Economist at the World Bank during the preparation of this study. He provided the critical guidance and overall direction for the inception, design, and implementation of the work. The book also drew inspiration from the extensive research on trade liberalization by Anne O. Krueger, Jagdish Bhagwati, and the late Bela Balassa.

Lawrence H. Summers
Vice President
Development Economics
    and Chief Economist
The World Bank

Contents

Foreword by Lawrence H. Summers　　v

Acknowledgments　　xi

Acronyms and Abbreviations　　xii

1　Framework for Trade Policy Issues　　1

Gains from Trade Policy Reform　　5
What Constitutes Trade Policy Reform?　　9
The Approach and Contribution of This Book　　14
Notes　　21

2　Implementation of Trade Policy Reforms　　25

Restrictiveness of Trade Regimes　　25
What Was Proposed?　　27
Implementation and Changes in Incentives　　31
Import Liberalization and Protection　　35
Progress and Constraints in Reform　　37
Summary and Conclusion　　42
Notes　　43

3　Trade Policy Reforms and Performance　　46

Trade Policy and Growth in the Long Term　　46
Trade Policy Reform and Economic Recovery in the 1980s　　54
Effects of Trade Policy Reform on Employment　　67
Constraints to a Stronger Supply Response　　74
Summary and Conclusion　　75
Notes　　76

4   The Political Economy of Trade Policy Reform   80

Obstacles to Reform   80
Implications for Reformers   87
Summary and Conclusion   93
Notes   94

5   Macroeconomic Environment and Trade Policy   96

Stabilization in the 1980s   96
Stabilization and the Effectiveness of Trade Policy Reform   97
Revenue Effects of Trade Policy Reform   109
Complications of the Debt Burden   116
Credibility, Investment, and Sustainability   117
Summary and Conclusion   118
Notes   119

6   Policies for Export Development   123

Export Performance in the 1980s   125
Practical Ways to Develop Manufactured Exports   128
Primary Sector Exports   142
Summary and Conclusion   147
Notes   150

7   Issues in Import Policy Reform   153

Comprehensiveness, Intensity, and Speed   155
Removal of Quantitative Restrictions   156
Tariff Reform   162
Import Policy Reforms and Domestic Reforms   169
Summary and Conclusion   176
Notes   177

8   External Constraints and Opportunities   179

External Factors Affecting Trade Policy   179
The GATT Negotiations and Unilateral Reform   184
Foreign Direct Investment   190
Trade Policy Issues in Regional Integration   191
Summary and Conclusion   197
Notes   198

9 Assessing the Experience of Trade Policy Reform   202

Trade Policy Reforms and Their Effects   202
The Sequencing and Timing of Trade Policy Reforms   204
Trade Policy Measures   208
Policies Complementary to Trade Policy Reform   212
Credibility and Sustainability   213
Implications for Trade Policy Reform   214
Notes   215

Index   217

Acknowledgments

Many people contributed in various ways to this volume and merit our sincere gratitude. Stanley Fischer and John Holsen provided guidance and support throughout its preparation. Nadav Halevi, Andras Inotai, and Ramon Lopez wrote background papers upon which some of the book's analysis is based. Francis Ng provided excellent statistical support, while Rebecca Sugui and Karla Cabana handled the word processing and logistics with great efficiency. Among the many who gave very helpful written comments on earlier drafts were Bela Balassa, Pedro Belli, Deepak Bhattasali, Colin Bradford, Patrick Conway, Robert Calderisi, Jaime de Melo, Dennis de Tray, Faezeh Foroutan, Gene Grossman, Ann Harrison, Brendan Horton, Fred Jaspersen, Daniel Kaufmann, Margaret Kelly, Raj Krishna, Rajiv Lall, Danny Leipziger, Robert Liebenthal, Johannes Linn, Paul Meo, Pradeep Mitra, Michael Michaely, Constantine Michalopoulos, Guy Pfeffermann, Chrik Poortman, Lant Pritchett, Sarath Rajapatirana, D. C. Rao, Neil Roger, Michael Sarris, Wendy Takacs, Irfan Ul Haque, Steve Webb, and Heng-Fu Zou. Reviews from staff meetings in all regions of the Bank were quite useful to the authors.

Acronyms and Abbreviations

ASEAN	Association of Southeast Asian Nations
CACM	Central American Common Market
CIF	Cost, insurance, and freight
COMTRADE	Commodity trade
EC	European Communities
EEC	European Economic Community
EFTA	European Free Trade Association
ERER	Equilibrium real exchange rate
ERP	Effective rate of protection
FDI	Foreign direct investment
FOB	Free on board
GATT	General Agreement on Tariffs and Trade
GDP	Gross domestic product
GNP	Gross national product
GSP	Generalized System of Preferences
IBRD	International Bank for Reconstruction and Development
IDA	International Development Association
IMF	International Monetary Fund
MUV	Manufacturing unit value
NBER	National Bureau of Economic Research
NIE	Newly industrialized economy
NRP	Nominal rate of protection
OECD	Organisation for Economic Co-operation and Development
QR	Quantitative restriction
RER	Real exchange rate
SAL	Structural adjustment loan
SDR	Special drawing right
SECAL	Sectoral adjustment loan
SITC	Standard International Trade Classification

TFP	Total factor productivity
UDEAC	Union douanière et économique d'Afrique centrale (Economic and Customs Union of Central Africa)
UNDP	United Nations Development Programme
UNCTAD	United Nations Conference on Trade and Development
VAT	Value added tax

1
Framework for Trade Policy Issues

Considerable evidence now indicates a strong positive association between trade policy reform and economic growth. Trade restrictions and domestic policy interventions create a bias against tradables, especially exports, that prevents achievement of internal and external balance and obstructs growth. Yet many countries continue to retain their highly restrictive trade regimes.

The developing countries generally began to feel the real force of the costs of trade and related domestic interventions in the late 1970s and early 1980s when they were hit by a series of severe external shocks—rising oil prices and interest rates and worsening terms of trade. Many countries initially responded to these shocks and mushrooming fiscal deficits and balance of payments problems by restricting imports even more. But as their problems persisted and even worsened, some began to recognize the need for structural adjustment, including the need for trade policy reforms that would make their economies more open and their production more competitive.

Consequently, trade policy reform has constituted a major part of the efforts toward structural adjustment made by many developing countries in the 1980s, often with the support of adjustment lending from the World Bank and arrangements with the International Monetary Fund (IMF).[1] These reforms, encompassing commercial and exchange rate policies, were intended to make the economies more open. Reductions in the restrictiveness of the trade regime (see box 1-1) were expected to shift incentives toward tradables, especially exportables, and thus lead to a more efficient allocation of resources and a rekindling of long-term economic growth.

External financing from the World Bank and the IMF in support of structural adjustment was intended to facilitate the policy change, especially since imports were likely to increase more than exports in the initial response to the reform. On average, countries that adopted structural adjustment programs have differed both in their initial con-

Box 1-1. *Measures of Trade Restrictiveness*

Trade policy reforms affect the price of tradables relative to nontradables. Such changes in the relative price are usually indicated by changes in the *real exchange rate* (RER), which is usually expressed as an index of the nominal exchange rate (with respect to the major trading partner or, preferably, a trade-weighted average of rates with all partners), deflated by the ratio of domestic and external price indexes, or the inverse. As an index, the real exchange rate is used to describe changes. To be used normatively, it should be combined with other information (such as the difference between the official and parallel rates) on whether the initial level is out of line (see box 5-1 in chapter 5).

Reductions in the number of commodities subject to quantitative restrictions are sometimes measured as the *share of the liberated commodities in the value of total imports (or exports)*. This can be misleading, however, because the more stringent the quantitative restrictions the smaller the shares, and prohibited goods have no weight at all. A more meaningful measure is the *share in national production of goods competing directly with the liberated imports*. A problem in measuring the economic effects of reductions in quantitative restrictions or tariffs is that only some tariffs and quantitative restrictions are binding. Nonbinding quantitative restrictions allow more imports than economic agents wish to import, so their elimination has no economic impact.[1] Some tariffs may be higher than the minimum level that would effectively prohibit imports (the so-called water in the tariff), so the reduction may have no economic impact. Furthermore, changes in quantitative restrictions and tariffs are often carried out simultaneously, which makes the effect even harder to measure.

One effort to resolve these difficulties has been to compare changes in the *nominal rates of protection* (NRPs), which summarize the net effect of all policy changes (both tariff and nontariff) on incentives for each product. The NRP of a product is the premium paid domestically because of trade restrictions. This may be calculated as $(P_D/P_W) - 1$, where P_D is the domestic price and P_W is the world or border price, converted to the domestic equivalent at the exchange rate applicable to the product and adjusted for differences in quality between the domestic product and the internationally traded product as well as in the cost of transporting them to a common point of sale. On the production side, the NRP is supposed to measure the extent to which protection causes resources to be pulled toward a protected sector, assuming there are no protected imported inputs. For consumers, the NRP measures the degree of distortion affecting their demand decisions. Alternatively, the NRP measures the difference between the undistorted value of a good—its border price—

1. On measuring the effects of nontariff barriers, see R. Baldwin, "Measuring the Effects of Nontariff Trade-Distorting Policies," in *Trade Theory and Economic Reform: North, South, and East: Essays in Honor of Bela Balassa* (Cambridge, Mass.: Basil Blackwell, 1991).

and the cost of producing a marginal unit domestically or the value placed on consuming a marginal unit, assuming markets are competitive. There are, however, problems in making the correct adjustments for quality differences and transport costs. Moreover, the presence of protected imported inputs appears to limit the usefulness of NRPs, because "protected" producers whose inputs are subject to higher (lower) protection than their products are protected less (more) than their NRPs would indicate. Also, when there are numerous protected outputs and inputs and the NRPs of several goods change simultaneously, the ranking of products by changes in output will not necessarily be the same as their ranking by changes in NRP.

Protected traded inputs are accounted for by the *effective rate of protection* (ERP), which measures the protection to net value added in an activity and thus the artificial pull of that activity on nontraded resources in production.[2] (The ERP is irrelevant in analyzing the effect of protection on consumers.) Intuitively, when the ERP of a protected activity decreases, the resources going to that activity should decrease as well, making ERPs a reasonable predictor of the impact of reform.[3] Flows of inputs can be netted out at either the industry level (where the ERP is an appropriate measure) or the economywide level to give trade flows (where the NRP is the correct measure). Both approaches are formally equivalent at the economywide level.[4]

Despite the difficulty of predicting changes in the allocation of resources, the pattern of NRPs and ERPs is a useful indicator of distortions and reforms.[5] For example, movement from high and highly dispersed protection among sectors to low and more uniform protection will increase the efficiency of resource allocation, at least when this is accomplished by lowering the highest rates (see chapter 7). Furthermore, when these measures are used as broad indicators, it usually makes little difference whether protection is measured by NRPs or ERPs. Both measures are likely to tell the same story in the aggregate. At the industry or sectoral level, ERPs can be useful indicators of resource pull

---

2. A closely related measure, *the domestic resource cost*, directly measures the cost of the domestic resources used to earn one dollar of foreign exchange by displacing imports or generating exports, on the margin, with domestic resources valued at shadow prices.

3. Such a prediction is valid only under a restrictive set of conditions, and it cannot be unambiguously proven, for example, that when more than one ERP change simultaneously, the activity whose ERP has increased relative to the others will necessarily attract the most resources. See J. N. Bhagwati and T. N. Srinivasan, "The General Equilibrium Theory of Effective Protection and Resource Allocation," *Journal of International Economics* 3 (1973):259–81.

4. A. Ray, "Welfare Significance of Nominal and Effective Rates of Protection," *Australian Economic Papers* 19 (June 1980):182–90.

5. Note, however, that the information necessary to calculate the NRP and ERP is difficult to obtain if quantitative restrictions are used or tariffs are redundant.

(Box continues on the following page.)

Box 1-1 *(continued)*

although different indexes of resource pull may require alternative measures of ERP whose degree of accuracy depends on a relatively strict set of conditions.[6] For one reasonable index—value added at world prices—ERP as usually defined is the appropriate measure.

Aggregate protection measures are sometimes summarized as *antiexport bias.* This approach groups tradable sectors into import-competing products and exportables. The bias is measured as $(1 + RP_I)/(1 + RP_E)$, where RP_I is the average net rate of protection to imports (as a percentage of import value) and RP_E is the average net rate of protection to exports (as a percentage of export value). A ratio greater than unity indicates an import-substituting or antiexport regime, a ratio of unity indicates neutrality (or, to some commentators, an export-promoting regime), and a ratio less than unity indicates an export-promoting (or ultra-export-promoting) bias.

6. See W. Ethier, "The Theory of Effective Protection in General Equilibrium: Effective Rate Analogues of Nominal Rates," *Canadian Journal of Economics* 10 (May 1977):233–45.

ditions and in the extent of changes in their trade policy from those not involved in these programs (see chapter 2). The severity of external sector problems in the early 1980s and the extent of subsequent trade policy reforms were greater for recipients of trade policy adjustment loans than for nonrecipients. Furthermore, the recovery in economic performance (measured by growth of gross domestic product, or GDP) in the mid- to late 1980s has been stronger in the former, on average, than in the latter (see table 1-1). These improvements in relative performance were attributable not only to greater external financing but also to reforms in policy (see chapter 3). Among economies that have adjusted, however, the extent and effectiveness of reform have varied substantially.

Economic distortions and the bias they create have been reduced by lowering import protection, by increasing export incentives, or by doing both. Successful approaches have included reforms involving a somewhat interventionist but relatively neutral policy as well as reforms entailing substantial liberalization. Some gave priority to policies for an adequate real exchange rate and the development of exports (the Republic of Korea and Taiwan); others concentrated on reducing interventions and lowering import protection (Chile and Mexico). Successful trade policy reform has comprised elements of a shift to greater neutrality in incentives and of liberalization through a reduction in distortions. Most economies with substantial trade restrictions have achieved gains from trade policy reforms when these reforms have been effectively complemented by macroeconomic and institutional reforms.

A considerable body of literature exists on the rationale for, and benefits of, trade policy reforms, and the next section of this chapter clarifies and assesses the nature of these benefits. Some observers, however, have expressed a variety of concerns about trade liberalization.[2] (The meaning of terms related to trade policy reform will be considered in the third section of this chapter.)

First, some argue that trade liberalization aggravates the balance of payments and fiscal problems that have afflicted many countries in the 1980s. Second, they dispute the benefits of liberalization and greater openness, contending that there are no firm grounds for believing that trade liberalization increases the growth rate of the economy. To the contrary, some observers argue that protecting infant industries will improve economic growth, while some also assert that world trade conditions prevent reforming economies from increasing their exports. Third, some observers express concern with the transitional problems associated with liberalization. In particular, they fear that liberalization produces unemployment and that devaluation increases inflation rates.

This book recognizes the possibility of conflicts between trade reforms and other reforms, but suggests actions that can help to avoid them. It demonstrates that trade reforms improve economic performance, and it also identifies complementary measures that will augment the supply response.

Gains from Trade Policy Reform

The main objectives of import controls have been to protect domestic industry, raise revenue, and improve the balance of payments. Some interventions have also been directed at promoting exports through special incentives. On balance, the effect of trade interventions has been to protect import substitutes and to create a bias against exports. The resource allocation costs of trade restrictions and the resulting protection are both direct and indirect.

Costs of Protection

Direct costs derive from the misallocation of resources in production and the reduction in consumer welfare caused by the misalignment of domestic and international prices (assuming that international prices are by and large the proper benchmark). In a static and partial equi-

Table 1-1. Selected Economic Indicators for Forty Recipients and Forty-seven Nonrecipients of World Bank Trade Adjustment Loans, 1965–72 to 1982–88

(unweighted averages, in percent)

Indicator	Group[a]	Period average				Recent experience						
		1965–72	1973–77	1978–81	1982–88[b]	1982	1983	1984	1985	1986	1987	1988[b]
Growth rate												
GDP (mp)	R	5.2	4.1	3.5	2.4	0.3	0.4	2.2	3.5	3.9	3.2	3.6
	NR	5.5	6.0	4.2	2.5	3.1	1.9	2.8	2.7	2.6	1.5	3.0
Exports (gnfs)	R	7.1	5.2	5.3	4.2	-0.8	1.6	6.5	2.1	7.1	6.3	6.8
	NR	7.4	4.9	6.5	3.4	-1.9	3.5	5.9	1.5	4.0	5.3	5.5
Imports (gnfs)	R	7.8	7.0	4.6	1.1	-6.6	-4.5	1.0	2.9	2.4	5.8	6.8
	NR	5.5	10.2	7.8	0.2	-1.3	-4.7	1.2	4.7	-1.8	2.1	0.9
Shares of GDP												
Exports (gnfs)	R	21.2	24.4	24.2	26.1	23.8	24.5	26.7	26.7	26.2	27.3	27.7
	NR	22.5	25.6	26.8	23.4	24.7	24.7	25.4	24.8	22.9	21.1	20.1
Imports (gnfs)	R	23.5	29.4	31.9	30.5	31.6	30.3	30.7	30.8	29.0	30.3	30.6
	NR	27.4	33.7	38.4	34.4	39.1	35.8	34.4	33.8	33.1	32.3	32.3
Resource balance[c]	R	-2.3	-4.9	-7.7	-4.4	-7.8	-5.8	-4.0	-4.1	-2.8	-2.9	-2.9
	NR	-4.9	-8.1	-11.6	-11.0	-14.4	-11.1	-9.0	-9.0	-10.2	-11.2	-12.2
Current account balance	R	-3.6	-4.2	-7.4	-5.3	-8.7	-6.6	-4.8	-5.3	-3.9	-4.2	-3.4
	NR	-4.4	-2.7	-5.6	-5.4	-8.5	-6.1	-3.9	-4.0	-5.5	-4.0	-6.1
Gross domestic investment	R	18.4	21.8	23.3	19.2	21.1	19.2	18.7	19.2	18.7	18.9	18.6
	NR	18.6	23.8	25.0	21.6	25.3	21.8	21.4	20.7	20.5	20.5	21.0
Debt-burden ratio[d]												
External debt/GDP	R	19.8[e]	24.5	37.2	66.9	48.1	55.2	61.1	70.9	74.3	86.0	72.3
	NR	19.1[e]	22.9	33.7	55.0	41.8	48.0	51.3	58.0	63.2	66.1	56.4

External debt/ exports (gs)	R	110.8[e]	115.7	154.6	281.7	215.2	250.7	238.6	288.5	328.6	350.5	299.7
	NR	102.3[e]	100.9	133.8	275.1	186.0	212.6	231.0	277.5	337.3	333.8	347.8
Debt service/ exports (gs)	R	13.6[e]	14.2	19.0	25.2	21.8	23.5	22.3	25.6	28.3	26.4	28.5
	NR	9.8[e]	9.2	11.8	18.7	15.4	15.3	16.3	19.0	21.4	19.7	24.0
Interest/ exports (gs)	R	3.9[e]	4.6	7.6	12.3	11.0	11.9	11.8	12.7	12.9	12.3	13.8
	NR	2.8[e]	2.8	4.4	7.5	6.5	6.6	6.8	7.4	8.3	7.2	9.5
Prices Consumer prices (percentage change)	R	8.3	30.3	25.2	35.1	23.9	33.9	40.9	40.1	23.3	29.5	54.4
	NR	3.4	13.4	14.5	22.4	18.1	22.9	18.8	26.3	26.4	23.6	21.0
Real exchange rate[f] (1980 = 100)	R	n.a.	n.a.	100.6	89.7	108.8	102.9	97.2	94.4	82.2	71.9	70.5
	NR	n.a.	n.a.	99.1	105.6	106.0	109.2	114.2	114.7	100.2	98.5	96.4
Terms of trade[g] (1980 = 100)	R	131.2	117.0	101.9	91.8	91.3	92.9	94.3	91.9	93.2	87.1	92.1
	NR	118.3	108.2	99.8	88.6	93.5	94.2	95.8	91.4	84.1	79.8	81.5

Note: mp = market prices, gnfs = goods and nonfactor services, gs = goods and services, n.a. = not available. Growth rates are measured in constant prices; shares of GDP are measured in current prices.
a. R = 40 recipients, NR = 47 nonrecipients. Forty-one countries received loans, but Guinea is excluded because its time-series trade data are unavailable. See table 1-2 for country groupings and box 1-3 for a discussion of the groupings.
b. Preliminary estimates. c. Resource balance = difference between exports and imports of goods and nonfactor services.
d. Debt = debt outstanding and disbursed, public and private, medium and long term. e. Data refer to 1970–72.
f. An increase indicates a real appreciation. g. Ratio of export to import price indexes of merchandise goods.
Source: Based on World Bank and IMF data.

7

librium framework, these direct costs are generally estimated to be about 1 or 2 percent of GDP a year. The costs are larger, however, when the likely effects of the market structure are also considered.[3] In some cases, protection has been linked to noncompetitive pricing. Protection has also been empirically linked to excessive market entry in the protected domestic markets in some countries, which means that firms are operating at a suboptimal scale. Furthermore, the existence of increasing returns to scale in some industries may magnify the gains from liberalization. One study estimated that the gains to Korea from liberalization would be 1 percent of GDP assuming constant returns to scale but would be as high as 10 percent if there were increasing returns to scale.[4]

Indirect costs include the waste of resources in income-generating but unproductive activities associated with protection—such as smuggling, lobbying, evading tariffs, and building plants with excess capacity to get import licenses.[5] These rent-seeking costs are significant in economies with severe restrictions. On the assumption that rents from the restrictions cause an equivalent use of real resources in these unproductive activities, the costs have been estimated at well over 6 percent of GDP in Turkey and India, for example.[6] The indirect costs of foreign exchange controls and nontariff barriers tend to be large because they involve allocations made by the authorities (for example, licensing organizations, state importing monopolies) on a discretionary basis rather than on efficiency grounds. Import controls and undesirable domestic interventions such as price controls and investment licensing are also mutually supportive. High tariffs—especially when they amount to de facto prohibitions—may also induce smuggling and lobbying activities.

The costs of trade and domestic restrictions become most visible when a country faces severe external shocks. Economies that maintain protectionist restrictions are largely divorced from the international price structure and fail to adjust production in response to changes in relative prices, such as higher oil prices. In many cases protective regimes also isolate the domestic economy from technological progress abroad, which ultimately hurts competitiveness. When the terms of trade shifted against developing countries in the past decade, many of them were unable to increase exports rapidly and had little scope for further efficient import substitution. Large trade deficits and macroeconomic imbalances were the result.

Growth Effects of Reform

Once-and-for-all gains from reduced protection show up in a temporarily higher rate of GDP growth as resources move to relatively more efficient production. The increase in GDP growth is affected by the way in which the economy adjusts to the price changes.[7] When the resource reallocation is complete, the economy is expected to be producing at a higher level of GDP, with the size of the increment depending on the initial distortion, the type and extent of reforms, and the extent of resource reallocation. These resource shifts alone do not necessarily increase the long-run rate of growth once the adjustment is complete, but the economy will maintain a higher level of GDP than before.

More difficult to demonstrate, but of great practical importance, are the dynamic effects of reforming the trade regime. There is an empirically established correlation between outward-oriented trade policies and the growth of total factor productivity in industry (see chapter 3).[8] Traditional theories of growth are inadequate for capturing this relation, but other approaches are more successful. If reforms help to improve investment and savings incentives continuously, they can also boost the long-run growth rate. Some recent growth models have replaced the traditional assumption of constant returns to scale with one of increasing returns to scale and different types of external economies. If the marginal return to capital does not decline, as it does in traditional models, the incentives to accumulate capital do not disappear automatically. So if trade policy reforms raise the marginal return to capital, they can generate a higher growth rate. Other models have focused on the role of technological change in generating a higher equilibrium growth rate. The fewer the trade restrictions, the greater an economy's ability to take advantage of a wider range of innovations and thereby increase its growth rate. One empirical study that developed a model based on this effect and tested for its significance in a sample of ninety countries found that such effects of economic openness encouraged growth.[9] Other research has shown that greater openness increases the size of the potential market. The resulting reward to innovation encourages technological progress at home.[10]

Some recent literature has pointed out a rationale for strategic trade policy—that is, for providing protection for certain key industries—based on the excess profits the protected industries are likely to earn in oligopolistic global markets or the external economies they create for other firms.[11] In practice, however, it is hard to target these interventions successfully. For this and other reasons, the conditions under which strategic trade policy can raise a country's welfare are unlikely to be met in developing countries (box 1-2).

What Constitutes Trade Policy Reform?

The terms *outward orientation* and *openness* say more about the consequences of policies than about the policies themselves.[12] Differences in

Box 1-2.   *The New Trade Theory and Strategic Trade Policy*

Can a government increase national welfare by providing assistance to domestic firms that compete in oligopolistic international markets? Until recently, most economists would have instinctively replied "no," with appropriate caveats regarding externalities of various sorts. But trade theorists have now identified a number of cases in which protection or subsidization of home-bred "national champions" can be an economically smart thing to do.

The argument for strategic trade policy applies to markets in which a handful of firms compete in oligopolistic fashion and receive excess profits or rents (a rate of return on investment that exceeds the normal, competitive return in more heavily contested markets). In such markets, the strategic use of government policy—through import tariffs or export subsidies, for example—can strengthen the home firm in relation to foreign firms and help it acquire a larger share of the industry's excess profits. Provided enough profits are shifted to the home firm, a tariff or subsidy can represent a good bargain overall despite its other costs. This profit shifting provides a rationale, at least in principle, for the use of aggressive trade policies.

In practice, the implementation of strategic trade policies is fraught with difficulties. For one thing, the government has to identify the appropriate industries for targeting. This requires an ability to spot markets in which excess profits (rents) are being made. An important obstacle here is the need to distinguish between ex post (realized) and ex ante (planned) profits. In risky industries, enterprises that emerge successful will appear to make large excess profits; what is much less observable is the fact that some firms do not succeed and go bankrupt. There is no economic case for targeting industries in which high profits simply serve to compensate firms for the large probability of failure.

In the developing world, the applicability of strategic trade policy is further reduced because few firms have established themselves in the kinds of industries in which these conditions arise. In the few instances that can be identi-

---

the type of policy reform can lead to differences in the degree of outward orientation that results. Some reforms emphasize liberalization, some a shift to more neutrality. Sometimes the terms are used interchangeably. Most objections to trade policy reform concern measures that are generally encompassed by the term *liberalization.* There is also a tendency when discussing issues of trade policy reform to speak of absolute dichotomies instead of gradations of change: outward orientation versus inward orientation, liberal versus interventionist, neutral versus biased.

fied, little evidence can be found that targeting has paid off by bringing about the desired shifting of profits.[1]

Even when appropriate industries can be identified with acceptable certainty, selecting the correct policy in support of home firms is difficult. For example, trade theorists have identified cases in which national income can be raised only by imposing a tax on domestic firms; subsidies can be inappropriate because in industries in which pricing behavior may have been too aggressive to begin with, they induce firms to reduce their prices. Hence, to ensure that strategic trade policy increases domestic welfare, the government has to be unrealistically knowledgeable about the nature of the strategic interactions between home and foreign firms.

Finally, strategic trade policy is a game that a country's trade partners can also play, to the detriment of all involved. A government's competitive support of national champions is likely to invite retaliation. In the ensuing trade war, all sides can end up losers.

Because of these and other limitations, the trade theorists who helped develop the arguments for strategic trade policy remain extremely skeptical about their relevance.[2] Most fear that, rather than being used to enhance national welfare, these new ideas will do damage in the hands of interventionists who take cover behind the intellectual respectability the ideas provide.

1. See the account of the Brazilian firm Embraer's EMB-120 commuter airplane in R. Baldwin, "High Technology Exports and Strategic Trade Policy in Developing Countries: The Case of Brazilian Aircraft," in G. K. Helleiner, ed., *New Trade Theory and Industrialization in Developing Countries* (New York: Oxford University Press, forthcoming).

2. See P. R. Krugman, "Is Free Trade Passé?" *Journal of Economic Perspectives* 1 (Fall 1987):131–44.

Source: Background note by Dani Rodrik, John F. Kennedy School, Harvard University.

A Shift toward Neutrality versus Liberalization

A *shift toward neutrality* is a change that makes the policy-induced effect on price incentives more nearly uniform—broadly speaking, among exportables, importables, and nontradables as well as between sales of a given product in the domestic and foreign markets. Because most economies have a substantial bias against exportables relative to importables and nontradables, moving toward neutrality means a reduction in anti-export bias. This reduction can be achieved by reducing import protection, by raising export incentives, or by doing both. *Liberalization* means a reduction in trade restrictions and an increase in the use of prices instead of discretionary intervention by bureaucrats and politicians. It implies a reduction in the welfare cost of government interventions—that is, a reduction in the direct costs or at least in some of the indirect costs.[13]

Two distinctions help in applying the terms *liberalization* and *neutrality* in policy reform. First, *trade policy reform,* as the term is used in this book, can be a move toward neutrality or a liberalization or both. Sometimes a reform is both a shift toward neutrality, with or without greater intervention, and a liberalization—for example, the elimination of an export restriction. A reform can also be a liberalization without being a shift toward neutrality, as, for example, the substitution of approximately equivalent tariffs for quantitative restrictions. Similarly, a reform involving more intervention can be a move toward neutrality—for example, an export incentive to offset some of the adverse effects of high import tariffs.

The second distinction is that both liberalization and a shift toward neutrality refer to a movement along a spectrum, not necessarily to a sudden shift from total control to free trade.[14] For example, a depreciation of the real exchange rate and the use of tariffs in place of quantitative restrictions reduce the welfare cost of protection and constitute some liberalization. A partially compensated devaluation, by combining a reduction in tariffs with devaluation, leads to greater neutrality in the incentive system while increasing welfare. These actions do not necessarily eliminate either the interventions or the protection, but they potentially lead to superior outcomes.

Trade policy reforms include such measures as the removal of export restrictions and export taxes, the introduction or improvement of duty drawback or temporary admission systems for imported inputs used in exports, the removal of quantitative import restrictions, and the reduction and simplification of import tariffs or the imposition of taxes on domestic production of protected items at rates equal to their tariffs. Devaluation can also be a reform. With an import regime dominated by quantitative restrictions, devaluation helps to cut the excess demand for imports and hence reduce the pressure on the quantitative restriction system in rationing imports, which in turn helps to reduce the indirect economic costs. Devaluation can also reduce antiexport bias, since the local-currency prices of exports rise by the full amount of the devaluation, whereas the prices of import substitutes (insulated from import competition) may rise only to the extent that devaluation increases their raw material and other costs and that the demand for their products permits.

Alternative Approaches for Promoting Trade and Growth

Success in promoting trade and growth can be found in liberal and liberalizing regimes, as well as in somewhat interventionist but relatively neutral policy regimes. Chile, for example, has recently achieved high rates of export and income growth with minimal policy intervention and a neutral incentive structure established over the course of a decade. Hong Kong has had successful laissez-faire policies for a very long time. But Korea and Taiwan experienced high rates of growth with significant, export-promoting market intervention or assistance during earlier stages of development. The intervention in these two cases was more nearly neutral and less distortionary than in most developing economies (see box 6-1 in chapter 6) and more effective than elsewhere. Moreover, in these cases and in others during the 1980s in which economic performance improved (such as Ghana, Indonesia, Mexico, and Turkey), the direction of reform has been toward liberalization.

A more outwardly oriented economy can thus be reached through a relatively hands-off approach or through selective and judicious government assistance. Reliance on noninterventionist and neutral policies supported by an adequate exchange rate and a stable macroeconomic environment has several merits. It avoids the susceptibility to misjudgment and abuse to which targeted investment policies are prone. It also avoids the practical problems that can arise because direct export-support mechanisms involving subsidies may become subject to countervailing duties under the General Agreement on Tariffs and Trade (GATT). Studies of large samples of economies—using many different time periods, measures of intervention, and combinations of countries—have indicated that less interventionist regimes have been more effective in promoting exports and growth (chapter 3).[15]

At the same time, studies of a number of economies bring out the positive role of well-designed government policies in supporting trade development (chapters 3, 5, 6, and 7). The most important policies complementary to trade policy reform are those that promote a stable macroeconomic environment and a sound legal framework. Without these conditions, and other policies that promote factor mobility, the reallocation of resources in response to trade reform is much reduced. Other beneficial complements to trade policy reform include an efficient and honest trade-related business and administrative environment (ports, customs regulations, customs agents, banks, telecommunications, and transport), as well as public and private institutions for collecting and disseminating export market information and developing links with international buyers.

Box 1-3.   *Country Groupings and Time Periods*

The full country sample used in this study comprises eighty-eight developing countries (table 1-2, column 1). These are the ninety-five countries defined as low- or middle-income in *World Development Report 1989* (New York: Oxford University Press, 1989), with the exception of ten countries for which data were lacking (Afghanistan, Bhutan, Islamic Republic of Iran, Iraq, Democratic Kampuchea, Lao People's Democratic Republic, Lebanon, Libya, Romania, and Viet Nam) and with the addition of three others, which received adjustment loans and for which data are available (The Gambia, Guinea-Bissau, and Guyana).

Among the eighty-eight countries, forty-one received adjustment loans with significant trade components between 1979 and 1987 (table 1-2, column 2). For lack of data, Guinea is excluded from our analysis, which leaves a group of forty loan recipients for consideration. By and large, these countries correspond to those that have made some efforts in trade reform. But this group also includes a few countries that effected little policy change (Guyana, Yugoslavia, Zambia, and Zimbabwe), and the group of forty-seven other countries (nonrecipients of adjustment loans) includes two that carried out substantial reforms although they did not receive trade adjustment loans (Bolivia and Haiti). In some cases we examine this group of thirty-eight trade reformers. In some discussions the focus narrows to the group of ten countries, among the forty trade loan recipients, that received three or more loans (the intensive trade adjustment loan recipients in column 4)—and on the twenty-six countries that received a loan long enough before 1986 to allow sufficient time for assessing implementation (column 5). Because precise data on policy implementation were not available for three of these twenty-six countries—Brazil,

The Approach and Contribution of This Book

The objective of this book is to assist in the design and implementation of trade policy reform. Its approach is to bring together a variety of evidence on the experience of various economies with reform and to draw policy implications. The analysis relies on country studies, cross-sectional data, and interviews with practitioners. The type of data and analysis varies from chapter to chapter according to the issues addressed, data requirements, and data availability. For example, chapters 2 and 3 use large samples of cross-country data, whereas chapters 4 and 7 necessarily rely more on illustrative examples and case studies.

The main focus is trade policy reform during structural adjustment, with an emphasis on the experience of the 1980s. Since the World Bank's adjustment lending has extensively supported trade policy reforms, we pay special attention to countries that received such lending

Costa Rica, and Tanzania—but were available for Bangladesh, which did not receive its first loan until 1987, the resulting group of twenty-four countries (column 6) was often used rather than the group of twenty-six.

In chapters 2 and 3 we compare the various groupings of adjustment loan recipients and trade policy reformers with the other developing countries, as well as with twenty-one industrial countries (column 7). To assess the link between policy and performance, in chapters 3 and 5 we subdivided the twenty-four countries into performance categories—low, medium, and high—on the basis of implementation data. We also use other country groupings in the analysis—low-income versus middle-income countries, Sub-Saharan Africa, highly indebted countries, exporters of manufactures, oil-exporting countries, and nonoil- and nonmanufactures-exporting countries (columns 8 through 14, respectively).

Changes in performance during the 1980s are the main focus of analysis, although we also look at long-term trends in performance. In some of the comparisons we focus on time periods before and after adjustment lending to a particular country. Because most of the trade adjustment lending was initiated around 1983–84, we pay particular attention to the periods before and after these years (1980–82 and 1981–83 compared with 1984–86 and 1985–87, respectively). Most of the quantitative analysis ends with 1987, although preliminary data for 1988 are also often presented.

Source: Statistical analysis by Francis Ng, Trade Policy Division, Country Economics Department, World Bank.

(see box 1-3 and table 1-2). Closely related is the experience of economies with adjustment programs supported by the IMF. The broader implications of the findings, however, concern trade policy reform more than adjustment lending as such.

Chapter Outlines

This chapter began by clarifying what is meant by policy reform and what it is expected to accomplish. Other topics covered are the extent and types of policy changes aimed for in adjustment programs, the flexibility of program design in adapting to conditions found in individual economies, and success in implementation (chapter 2). The effectiveness of trade liberalization in increasing economic efficiency and growth is examined both through comparisons of countries that did and countries that did not implement reforms and through country studies (chapter 3).

Table 1-2.   *Country Groupings Used in Trade Reform Analysis*

88 developing countries[a]		41 trade adjustment loan recipients[a]	47 nonrecipients of adjustment lending	10 intensive trade adjustment loan countries	26 pre-1986 trade adjustment loan countries
(1)		*(2)*	*(3)*	*(4)*	*(5)*
Algeria	Mozambique	Argentina	Algeria	Chile	Brazil
Argentina	Myanmar	Bangladesh	Benin	Côte d'Ivoire	Chile
Bangladesh	Nepal	Brazil	Bolivia	Ghana	Colombia
Benin	Nicaragua	Burundi	Botswana	Jamaica	Costa Rica
Bolivia	Niger	Central	Burkina Faso	Malawi	Côte d'Ivoire
Botswana	Nigeria	African Rep.	Cameroon	Mauritius	Ghana
Brazil	Oman	Chile	Chad	Mexico	Guyana
Burkina Faso	Pakistan	Colombia	China	Philippines	Jamaica
Burundi	Panama	Costa Rica	Congo	Senegal	Kenya
Cameroon	Papua New	Côte d'Ivoire	Dominican Rep.	Turkey	Korea,
Central	Guinea	Ghana	Ecuador		Rep. of
African Rep.	Paraguay	Guinea[a]	Egypt		Madagascar
Chad	Peru	Guinea-Bissau	El Salvador		Malawi
Chile	Philippines	Guyana	Ethiopia		Mauritius
China	Poland	Hungary	Gabon		Mexico
Colombia	Portugal	Indonesia	Gambia, The		Morocco
Congo	Rwanda	Jamaica	Greece		Pakistan
Costa Rica	Senegal	Kenya	Guatemala		Panama
Côte d'Ivoire	Sierra Leone	Korea, Rep. of	Haiti		Philippines
Dominican Rep.	Somalia	Madagascar	Honduras		Senegal
Ecuador	South Africa	Malawi	India		Tanzania
Egypt	Sri Lanka	Mauritania	Jordan		Thailand
El Salvador	Sudan	Mauritius	Lesotho		Togo
Ethiopia	Syria	Mexico	Liberia		Turkey
Gabon	Tanzania	Morocco	Malaysia		Yugoslavia
Gambia, The	Thailand	Nepal	Mali		Zambia
Ghana	Togo	Niger	Mozambique		Zimbabwe
Greece	Trinidad and	Nigeria	Myanmar		
Guatemala	Tobago	Pakistan	Nicaragua		
Guinea[a]	Tunisia	Panama	Oman		
Guinea-Bissau	Turkey	Philippines	Papua New		
Guyana	Uganda	Senegal	Guinea		
Haiti	Uruguay	Tanzania	Paraguay		
Honduras	Venezuela	Thailand	Peru		
Hungary	Yemen Arab	Togo	Poland		
India	Rep.	Tunisia	Portugal		
Indonesia	Yemen, People's	Turkey	Rwanda		
Jamaica	Dem. Rep. of	Uruguay	Sierra Leone		
Jordan	Yugoslavia	Yugoslavia	Somalia		
Kenya	Zaire	Zaire	South Africa		
Korea, Rep. of	Zambia	Zambia	Sri Lanka		
Lesotho	Zimbabwe	Zimbabwe	Sudan		
Liberia			Syria		
Madagascar			Trinidad and		
Malawi			Tobago		
Malaysia			Uganda		
Mali			Venezuela		
Mauritania			Yemen Arab		
Mauritius			Rep.		
Mexico			Yemen, People's		
Morocco			Dem. Rep. of		

24 trade adjustment loan countries (6)	21 industrial countries (7)	40 low-income countries[a,b] (8)	48 middle-income countries[c] (9)	37 Sub-Saharan African countries[d] (10)	17 highly indebted countries[d] (11)
Bangladesh	Australia	Bangladesh	Algeria	Benin	Argentina
Chile	Austria	Benin	Argentina	Botswana	Bolivia
Colombia	Belgium	Burkina Faso	Bolivia	Burkina Faso	Brazil
Côte d'Ivoire	Canada	Burundi	Botswana	Burundi	Chile
Ghana	Denmark	Central	Brazil	Cameroon	Colombia
Guyana	Finland	African Rep.	Cameroon	Central	Costa Rica
Jamaica	France	Chad	Chile	African Rep.	Côte d'Ivoire
Kenya	Germany, Fed.	China	Colombia	Chad	Ecuador
Korea, Rep. of	Rep. of	Ethiopia	Congo	Congo	Jamaica
Madagascar	Iceland	Gambia, The	Costa Rica	Côte d'Ivoire	Mexico
Malawi	Ireland	Ghana	Côte d'Ivoire	Ethiopia	Morocco
Mauritius	Italy	Guinea[a]	Dominican Rep.	Gabon	Nigeria
Mexico	Japan	Guinea-Bissau	Ecuador	Gambia, The	Peru
Morocco	Luxembourg	Guyana	Egypt	Ghana	Philippines
Pakistan	Netherlands	Haiti	El Salvador	Guinea[a]	Uruguay
Panama	New Zealand	India	Gabon	Guinea-Bissau	Venezuela
Philippines	Norway	Indonesia	Greece	Kenya	Yugoslavia
Senegal	Spain	Kenya	Guatemala	Lesotho	
Thailand	Sweden	Lesotho	Honduras	Liberia	
Togo	Switzerland	Liberia	Hungary	Madagascar	
Turkey	United	Madagascar	Jamaica	Malawi	
Yugoslavia	Kingdom	Malawi	Jordan	Mali	
Zambia	United	Mali	Korea, Rep. of	Mauritania	
Zimbabwe	States	Mauritania	Malaysia	Mauritius	
		Mozambique	Mauritius	Mozambique	
		Myanmar	Mexico	Niger	
		Nepal	Morocco	Nigeria	
		Niger	Nicaragua	Rwanda	
		Nigeria	Oman	Senegal	
		Pakistan	Panama	Sierra Leone	
		Rwanda	Papua New	Somalia	
		Sierra Leone	Guinea	Sudan	
		Somalia	Paraguay	Tanzania	
		Sri Lanka	Peru	Togo	
		Sudan	Philippines	Uganda	
		Tanzania	Poland	Zaire	
		Togo	Portugal	Zambia	
		Uganda	Senegal	Zimbabwe	
		Yemen, People's	South Africa		
		Dem. Rep. of	Syrian Arab Rep.		
		Zaire	Thailand		
		Zambia	Trinidad and		
			Tobago		
			Tunisia		
			Turkey		
			Uruguay		
			Venezuela		
			Yemen Arab Rep.		
			Yugoslavia		
			Zimbabwe		

(Table continues on the following page.)

Table 1-2   *(continued)*

20 manufactures-exporting countries[e] (12)	13 oil-exporting countries[d] (13)	55 Nonoil-, nonmanufactures-exporting countries[f] (14)	
Bangladesh	Algeria	Argentina	Nicaragua
Brazil	Cameroon	Benin	Niger
China	Congo	Bolivia	Panama
Greece	Ecuador	Botswana	Papua New
Hungary	Egypt	Burkina Faso	Guinea
India	Gabon	Burundi	Paraguay
Jordan	Indonesia	Central	Peru
Korea, Rep. of	Mexico	African Rep.	Philippines
Malaysia	Nigeria	Chad	Rwanda
Morocco	Oman	Chile	Senegal
Nepal	Syrian Arab Rep.	Colombia	Sierra Leone
Pakistan	Trinidad and	Costa Rica	Somalia
Poland	Tobago	Côte d'Ivoire	South Africa
Portugal	Venezuela	Dominican Rep.	Sudan
Sri Lanka		El Salvador	Tanzania
Thailand		Ethiopia	Togo
Tunisia		Gambia, The	Uganda
Turkey		Ghana	Yemen Arab Rep.
Uruguay		Guatemala	Yemen, People's
Yugoslavia		Guinea[a]	Dem. Rep. of
		Guinea-Bissau	Zaire
		Guyana	Zambia
		Haiti	Zimbabwe
		Honduras	
		Kenya	
		Jamaica	
		Lesotho	
		Liberia	
		Madagascar	
		Malawi	
		Mali	
		Mauritania	
		Mauritius	
		Mozambique	
		Myanmar	

Note: Any reference to trade adjustment lending implies only that the countries received a trade adjustment loan and not that policy reforms were necessarily implemented (see box 1-3).

a. Although Guinea received a trade adjustment loan, it is excluded from the statistical analysis because time-series trade data are unavailable.

b. GNP per capita in 1987 of US$480 or less. Data for Myanmar and Guinea are incomplete or not available.

c. GNP per capita in 1987 of US$481–$5,999.

d. *World Development Report 1989* classification.

e. Manufacturing exports exceed 35 percent of merchandise exports (based on 1987 or the most recent year). As in *World Development Report 1988,* manufacturing exports are defined as Standard International Trade Classification (SITC) 5, 6, 7 and 8, excluding 68, 651, 652, 654, 655, and 667 in the COMTRADE database of the United Nations. Data for Botswana, The Gambia, Haiti, Lesotho, and Mozambique are incomplete or not available.

f. Nonmanufactures exporters are those countries whose manufacturing exports do not exceed 35 percent of merchandise exports.

The political dynamics of domestic interest groups affected by reforms often determine the eventual fate of the program and thus are also explored (chapter 4). Drawing on the theory of public choice and examples of successful and failed liberalization attempts, chapter 4 provides recommendations on the timing and pace of a trade reform program, the preparation necessary for its enactment and implementation, its design and institutional affiliation, and compensation of losers.

Both the inconsistencies and the complementarities between trade policy reforms and budget stabilization measures are examined (chapter 5). Certain types of trade reform may increase the budget deficit if not compensated for by other measures. Also, in countries with very high inflation, efforts to reduce inflation that are based on the use of the nominal exchange rate as a price anchor, rather than on adequate macroeconomic policies, can lead to an appreciation in the real exchange rate. Furthermore, the real interest rate often rises under programs of disinflation. Such circumstances call into question the sustainability and credibility of trade policy reforms under severe macroeconomic instability, which suggests that priority in sequencing might sometimes be given to effective stabilization.

In most circumstances there are strong arguments for having trade policy reforms accompany or precede stabilization. The new investment that accompanies stabilization may flow to the wrong sectors if incentives are distorted by trade (or other) policies. In addition, a commitment to integrate into the world economy can help a country to maintain a sound macroeconomic policy. Furthermore, many types of trade policy reforms may not only improve the incentive structure but also reduce the fiscal deficit. The appropriate sequence of stabilization and reform thus depends on the initial conditions and the types of reform being considered.

What is an appropriate and supportive menu of price measures and nonprice measures (for example, institutional support) for an effective export policy? Chapter 6 reviews the export performance, especially for manufactured exports, of developing countries. Specific policy measures are analyzed to determine what problems have been encountered and why relatively few countries have sustained their export growth. Price measures—especially a realistic exchange rate—and specific institutional and administrative reforms are found to be essential in assisting exporters.

Aside from exchange rate reform, the most common first step in import reform (discussed in chapter 7) is to reduce the coverage of quantitative restrictions, often by converting them to tariffs. At a later stage, the level of protective tariffs is usually lowered by various methods. The analysis shows why the conversion of quotas to tariffs is beneficial even if the level of protection remains unchanged. With respect to issues of tariff reduction, the most relevant questions concern the achievement of greater uniformity of tariffs, which may require increases in some tariff rates on imported inputs; both the merits and the limitations of greater uniformity are set out. Another design issue concerns the ways in which domestic sector characteristics and policies (market concentration, labor market rigidities, institutional characteristics, and regulatory policies) interact with trade policy and complement or impede its effectiveness.

In the course of examining external opportunities and constraints, chapter 8 considers the opportunities available to developing countries for improving their position in international trade through multilateral trade negotiations. One issue is how countries should evaluate the options of immediate unilateral reform versus eventual multilateral reform under the auspices of the GATT. The importance of an unambiguous commitment by the GATT to the granting of credit for unilateral reform is underscored. The benefits and costs of regional integration are also considered. While pointing out the limited potential of trade policy in aiding regional coordination schemes, the chapter highlights other measures that may be more effective. The chapter also discusses the role of foreign direct investment and the policies that have proven to be most effective in attracting and using it to enhance development.

Common Themes

One issue that is implicit in the discussion throughout the book is the diversity of experience. The analysis shows that trade policy reform has helped to boost economic performance. But the design and implementation of reform have depended on the extent of trade distortions, macroeconomic stability, and required complementary actions. Accordingly, the application of various country taxonomies is useful. First, differences in initial trade restrictiveness call for different sequences of reforms: exchange rate depreciation and the elimination of export restrictions first in some cases, reduction of export and import restrictions simultaneously in others, and a lowering of protection in yet others. Second, trade liberalization under macroeconomic instability, debt overhang, and high inflation faces quite distinct constraints. Third, Sub-Saharan countries, and low-income countries in general, have been burdened in addition by underdeveloped institutions and infrastructure that limit the supply response to price changes.

The key and multiple roles played by macroeconomic and exchange rate policy in trade policy reform are examined from several perspectives. Chapter 4 discusses the role of devaluation in signaling the credibility of reforms. Chapter 5 looks at the exchange rate as a macroeconomic variable and investigates the conditions under which its role in inflation stabilization programs might conflict with trade policy reform. Chapter 6 stresses the importance for exporters of macroeconomic stability and a devalued and stable exchange rate. Chapter 7, in contrast, shows that the exchange rate can also determine relative prices among tradable goods when quantitative restrictions on imports are binding and that it thus plays a crucial role in programs involving the removal of quantitative restrictions.

Another issue relates to the constraints to reform and the constraints to the supply response. Chapter 2 discusses the constraints to reform implementation under adjustment lending, and chapter 4 highlights the political economy of the reform process. Several chapters discuss the constraints to a stronger supply response to reform. The constraints are identified in chapter 3, while other chapters discuss specific constraints in more detail. The role of credibility is highlighted in chapters 4 and 5. Chapter 6 identifies institutional constraints to the export response, while chapter 7 shows how domestic market rigidities, inappropriate public sector policies, and infrastructural weaknesses limit the response to import liberalization. Constraints imposed by external protectionism are discussed in chapter 8.

Finally, the sequencing of trade policy reform is addressed in several chapters. The interaction between macroeconomic stabilization and liberalization is dealt with in chapter 5. Complementarities between trade liberalization and domestic liberalization are considered in chapter 7, which also addresses the sequencing and pacing of various import liberalization measures. The book's main conclusions and their implications for future trade reform programs are pulled together in chapter 9.

Notes

1. Trade policy reform has accounted for about 30 percent of the conditions in adjustment lending. For details, see World Bank, *Adjustment Lending: An Evaluation of Ten Years of Experience,* Policy and Research Series no. 1 (Washington, D.C., 1989).

2. For an analysis of the rationale for trade policy reforms, see W. M. Corden, *Trade Policy and Economic Welfare* (Oxford: Clarendon Press, 1974). For discussions of concerns regarding trade liberalization, see, for example, Jeffrey Sachs, "Trade and Exchange Rate Policies in Growth-Oriented Adjustment Programs," Department of Economics, Harvard University (Cambridge, Mass., 1987); Lance Taylor, *Economic Openness: Problems to the Century's End* (Helsinki: World Institute for Development Economics Research, 1988); and United Nations Conference on Trade and Development, *Trade and Development Report 1989* (Geneva, 1989).

3. When the initial distortions are very large, conventionally estimated gains in resource allocation from reforms may turn out to be 5 to 7 percentage points of GDP. See J. Bergsman, "Commercial Policy, Allocative Efficiency, and X-Efficiency," *Quarterly Journal of Economics* 88 (August 1974): 409–33. Under severe distortions, parallel markets may provide more realistic price signals than official prices, in which case the calculations based on official prices would overstate the gains from reforms. On protection and domestic markets, see Timothy Condon and Jaime de Melo, "Industrial Organization Implications of QR Trade Regimes: Evidence and Welfare Costs," Development Research Department, World Bank (Washington, D.C., 1986).

4. Jaime de Melo and David Roland-Holst, "Industrial Organization and Trade Liberalization: Evidence from Korea," Trade Policy Division, Country Economics Department, World Bank (Washington, D.C., 1989).

5. A former Undersecretary of the Economy in Argentina has noted that "it is more profitable to spend time in these corridors [of the Ministry of the Economy and the Central Bank] than in the manufacturing plant" (Julio Nogués, "Latin America's Experience with Export Subsidies," Policy, Planning, and Research Working Paper no. 182, International Economics Department, World Bank [Washington, D.C., 1989] p. 23).

6. For some examples, see W. Grais, J. de Melo, and S. Urata, "A General Equilibrium Estimation of the Effects of Reductions in Tariffs and Quantitative Restrictions in Turkey in 1978," in T. N. Srinivasan and John Whalley, eds., *General Equilibrium Trade Policy Modeling* (Cambridge, Mass.: MIT Press, 1986); A. O. Krueger, "The Political Economy of the Rent-Seeking Society," *American Economic Review* 64 (June 1974):291–303; and Sharif Mohammad and John Whalley, "Rent-Seeking in India: Its Costs and Policy Significance," *Kyklos* 37, fasc. 3 (1984):387–413.

7. Taking factor market rigidities and underemployment of factors into account can introduce two opposing effects into the analysis. First, if labor or other factors are immobile in the short term, the reform can produce adjustment costs. Second, the impact on growth can be stronger if underemployed factors take advantage of improved trading opportunities.

8. For evidence, see Hollis Chenery, Sherman Robinson, and Moshe Syrquin, *Industrialization and Growth: A Comparative Study* (New York: Oxford University Press, 1986); M. Kim Mahnje, "Korea's Adjustment Policies and Their Implications for Other Countries," in Vittorio Corbo, Morris Goldstein, and Mohsin S. Khan, eds., *Growth-Oriented Adjustment Programs* (Washington, D.C.: IMF and World Bank, 1987); A. O. Krueger and Baran Tuncer, "An Empirical Test of the Infant Industry Argument," *American Economic Review* 72 (December 1982):1142–55; Mieko Nishimizu and J. M. Page, Jr., "Total Factor Productivity Growth, Technological Progress, and Technical Efficiency Change: Yugoslavia 1965–78," *Economic Journal* 92 (December 1982):920–36; Oli Havrylyshyn, "Yugoslavia: The Experience of Trade Policy Reform, 1965–1975," in "Trade Liberalization: The Lessons of Experience," LAC Regional Series Report no. IDP14, Latin America and the Caribbean Region, World Bank (Washington, D.C., 1988). For a review, see H. Pack, "Industrialization and Trade," in Hollis Chenery and T. N.

Srinivasan, eds., *Handbook of Development Economics* (Amsterdam: North-Holland, 1988).

9. P. M. Romer, "What Determines the Rate of Growth and Technological Change?" Policy, Planning, and Research Working Paper no. 279, Country Economics Department, World Bank (Washington, D.C., 1989).

10. See, for example, G. M. Grossman, "Promoting New Industrial Activities: A Survey of Recent Arguments and Evidence" (paper prepared for Economics and Statistics Department, Organisation for Economic Co-operation and Development, Paris, 1989) and G. M. Grossman and Elhanan Helpman, *Comparative Advantage and Long-run Growth*, NBER Working Paper 2809 (Cambridge, Mass.: National Bureau of Economic Research, 1989).

11. See, for example, P. R. Krugman, ed., *Strategic Trade Policy and the New International Economics* (Cambridge, Mass.: MIT Press, 1987); B. J. Spencer and J. A. Brander, "International R&D Rivalry and Industrial Strategy," *Review of Economic Studies* 50 (1983):707–22; and Arvind Panagariya, "Variable Returns to Scale in General Equilibrium Theory Once Again," *Journal of International Economics* 10 (November 1980):499–526.

12. Policy, of course, is not the only determinant of the share of trade in GDP. Trade's share is also determined by a country's size, its proximity to other markets, and the similarity of its factor endowments to those of the rest of the world, among other things. For this reason, changes in the trade share may be a reasonably good measure of the effect of a change in policy in a given country, but a cross-country comparison of trade shares is not a good measure of the policy orientation of the countries in the comparison. Thus, the ratio of the sum of exports plus imports to GDP was about 21 percent on average during 1985–88 for the United States, a country with a relatively liberal trade regime, but about 50 percent for Kenya, Malawi, and Yugoslavia, which have restrictive regimes.

13. A shift toward neutrality or a liberalization does not always represent a beneficial reform, however. For example, some types of partial liberalization in the face of pervasive distortions might reduce welfare. Similarly, a poorly designed export subsidy may promote neutrality but raise the welfare cost.

14. Colin I. Bradford and William H. Branson have developed a useful scheme for classifying trade regimes along a spectrum. See their *Trade and Structural Change in Pacific Asia* (Chicago: University of Chicago Press for National Bureau of Economic Research, 1987).

15. G. W. Scully, for example, studied the effect of intervention on income growth in a worldwide sample. See Scully, "The Political Economy of Free Trade and Protectionism" (paper prepared for conference on the Political Economy of Neo-mercantilism and Free Trade, Big Sky, Montana, June 9–11, 1988). Bela Balassa examined the effect on agricultural and manufactured exports in Sub-Saharan Africa in his "Incentive Policies and Agricultural Performance in Sub-Saharan Africa," Policy, Planning, and Research Working Paper no. 77, Development Economics Department, World Bank (Washington, D.C., 1988). Other studies include W. R. Easterly and D. L. Wetzel, "Determinants of Growth: Survey of Theory and Evidence," Policy, Planning, and Research Working Paper no. 343, Country Economics Department, World Bank (Washington, D.C., 1989); D. Landau, "Government Expendi-

ture and Economic Growth: A Cross-Country Study," *Southern Economic Journal* 49 (January 1983):783–92; and Keith Marsden, *Links between Taxes and Economic Growth: Some Empirical Evidence,* World Bank Staff Working Paper no. 605 (Washington, D.C., 1983).

2

Implementation of Trade Policy Reforms

This chapter focuses on the implementation of trade policy reform in the 1980s.[1] The success of the trade policy reforms is evaluated by means of cross-country data and country studies prepared or assembled for this study. The detailed empirical findings are based on proposals for changes in commercial policy and exchange rate policy in forty developing countries that received trade adjustment loans during 1980–87 (see box 2-1) and on implementation data available for twenty-four of the forty countries.[2]

Restrictiveness of Trade Regimes

Six measures of the initial level of trade restrictiveness for these developing countries are considered: export impediments,[3] import impediments on inputs used in the production of exports, quantitative restrictions[4] on noncompetitive imports, quantitative restrictions on competitive imports, tariff rates,[5] and tariff rate dispersion (that is, the extent to which the tariffs differ across product categories). Based on reviews of the evidence,[6] the forty countries were grouped into three broad categories according to the average antiexport bias of each group relative to the others at the outset of adjustment lending: low, medium, or high. Although the measurement is somewhat subjective, the differences among the groups were sufficiently large to permit such a classification. Only Chile and Korea had a relatively low level of restrictiveness. Sixty percent of the countries had a high level, and 35 percent had a medium level prior to receiving adjustment lending (the early 1980s in most cases).

Comparing the trade restrictions in developing countries with those in industrial countries helps to put the reform measures in clearer perspective.[7] First, the average tariff rate for fifty developing countries, weighted by the imports of each, was 26 percent at the end of 1985.[8] Adding other import charges raises the figure to 34 per-

Box 2-1. *Adjustment Lending and Trade Policy*

From 1979 to 1988, a total of 155 adjustment loans were made to fifty-seven countries. Of these, ninety-four loans to forty-two countries had significant trade policy components.[1] Among the ninety-four trade loans, fifty-five were structural adjustment loans (SALs) and thirty-nine were sectoral adjustment loans (SECALs). In addition, there were two program loans (see table). More than one-third of these operations included technical assistance components or were accompanied by technical assistance loans in support of trade reforms.

World Bank Loans with Trade Policy Components, by Lending Instrument, 1979–88

Year	SALs		SECALs		Total		Program loans	
	N	A	N	A	N	A	N	A
1979	0	0.0	1	31.5	1	31.5	0	0.0
1980	4	590.0	0	0.0	4	590	0	0.0
1981	6	782.0	2	87.0	8	869	0	0.0
1982	5	801.6	0	0.0	5	801.6	1	110.0
1983	11	1,859.7	6[a]	1,130.9	17	2,990.6	0	0.0
1984	2	431.0	3	301.4	5	732.4	1	140.0
1985	4	387.8	4	560.0	8	947.8	0	0.0
1986	7	669.0	7	1,420.5	14	2,089.5	0	0.0
1987	8	539.0	9	2,021.0	17	2,560.0	0	0.0
1988	8	725.0	7	1,607.0	15	2,332.0	0	0.0
1979–88	55	6,785.1	39	7,159.3	94	1,3944.4	2	250.0

N = number of loans; A = amount in millions of U.S. dollars.

a. Includes the Export Development III loan to Jamaica, although the program was discontinued.

Source: World Bank data.

For this study we reviewed the loans approved during 1979–87—seventy-nine trade loans to forty countries. Forty-two percent of the operations (thirty-three loans) were in eighteen Sub-Saharan countries, 13 percent (ten loans) in six Asian countries, 30 percent (twenty-four loans) in ten Latin American or Caribbean countries, and 15 percent (twelve loans) in six countries in the Europe, Middle East, and North Africa region. Together, 63 percent (fifty loans) went to the twenty-three middle-income countries in the sample and 37 percent (twenty-nine loans) to the seventeen low-income countries (GNP per capita below $480 in 1987). Thirty-one operations were in thirteen highly indebted countries, and twenty-one loans went to twelve exporters of manufactures (countries whose manufactured exports constituted more than 35 percent of their total merchandise exports in 1987).

---

1. Through June 1989, there were ninety-six loans with significant trade policy components to forty-four countries.

cent. For many countries, average rates were much higher (about 90 percent in Bangladesh, Costa Rica, and Pakistan), and within each country rates were very dispersed, with top rates much higher than the average. Most of the World Bank's major borrowers had average tariff rates over 25 percent in 1987–88, and the highest (India's) was 118 percent. By contrast, average tariffs on industrial goods in the Organisation for Economic Co-operation and Development (OECD) countries were estimated to be about 5 percent in a 1980 GATT report and are roughly of that order today.[9]

The coverage of nontariff barriers—usually a more serious restriction than tariffs—in the fifty developing countries was estimated to be 40 percent (unweighted) of import items corresponding to all tariff positions at the end of 1985. Using a different measure of coverage, a World Bank study of eight developing countries for which data were available found that six had nontariff barriers covering products representing 35 percent or more of production. Another study gives a similar estimate for thirty-eight developing countries in 1982.[10] The same study estimates that 15 percent of the industrial product categories of the eleven industrial countries in the sample were subject to nontariff barriers in 1984. Another study provides a similar figure (15.9 percent) for all products in fourteen industrial countries in 1986.[11] Thus, these countries, like the developing countries, restricted trade more strongly using nontariff barriers than using tariffs, although the restrictions using both measures were considerably weaker in industrial than in developing countries.

According to these estimates, developing countries, on the whole, have much more restrictive trade regimes than do industrial countries. Furthermore, protection tends to be highest against trade from other developing countries.[12] Exchange rates were also severely misaligned in many developing countries in the early 1980s, as indicated by country studies carried out by the World Bank and the IMF. Despite the greater levels of restrictiveness in trade policy, however, developing countries have exhibited a stronger tendency toward increasing openness than industrial countries in the 1980s.

What Was Proposed?

In more than half the countries that received trade adjustment loans during 1979–87, the targeted reforms were deemed adequate using the criteria of whether the reform proposals addressed the specific problems of each country and would, if implemented, significantly reduce the antiexport bias. This judgment was based on a comparative review of evidence in World Bank reports.

Proposals to reform commercial policy were strong in twelve of the twenty-four countries with *high initial restrictiveness* (as in Ghana, Jamaica, Mexico, and Turkey). Mexico in the early 1980s, for example, had a regime biased strongly against exports, with ineffective export development measures (such as duty drawbacks) and a highly restrictive import regime (quantitative restrictions covered virtually all imports). The reform proposals in a series of loans to Mexico improved the environment for exports directly, reduced the coverage of quantitative restrictions and other nontariff barriers on imports to very low levels, and created a structure of relatively low and uniform tariff rates. In six of the twenty-four cases, reform proposals were considered only moderate (as in Bangladesh and Yugoslavia). In Bangladesh, in spite of very severe import restrictions (as well as ineffective export development measures), the proposals concentrated exclusively on developing exports by introducing drawbacks, exchange retention, and other schemes. And in six others, the proposals were mild or nil (as in Brazil, Guyana, and Pakistan).

Among the fourteen countries with *moderate initial restrictiveness,* nine had moderate or strong proposals. Mauritius, for example, began its adjustment process with very high protection on imports through licensing and taxes as high as 600 percent, but imposed few direct impediments to exports and had a functioning duty drawback system. Its proposals called for a significant reduction in import protection and improvements in the drawback scheme. For the fourteen countries, the strength of export policy proposals generally corresponded more closely to the degree of initial restrictiveness than did that of import policy proposals. Also, the intensity of the proposals (mild, moderate, or strong) was greater in Latin America than in the other regions.

Sequencing of actions in the export and import areas is another important dimension of trade reform.[13] By and large, reductions in export impediments, together with realignment of the real exchange rate, have received priority in reform proposals under adjustment lending. These reforms have been accompanied or followed by a switch from quantitative restrictions to tariffs. Either in parallel or subsequently, a reduction in protection levels has often been proposed.

Most policy packages included a reduction in restrictions on exports and imports and a greater reliance on exchange rate depreciation and the use of tariffs in place of quantitative restrictions (see table 2-1). Reform of exchange rate policy was almost always an important goal, whether stated or implicit, and was often carried out in conjunction with an IMF arrangement. In Colombia, for example, exchange rate reform and fiscal reform were the most notable improvements associated with adjustment lending. Other price and nonprice export incentives were also proposed in various loans. Almost all loans supported greater

Table 2-1. *Intensity and Distribution of Major Trade Policy Reform Proposals among Forty Countries Receiving World Bank Trade Adjustment Loans, 1979–87*

(number of countries)

	Distribution		Intensity		
Area of reform	Present	Not present	Strong	Moderate	Mild or absent
Exchange rate[a]	38	2			
Export development[b]	33	7			
Studies of protection	28	12			
Overall export policy			15	15	10
Imports for exports			17	15	8
Overall import policy			14	15	11
Nonprotective quantitative restrictions			14	16	10
Protective quantitative restrictions[c]			14	15	11
Tariff level[c]			7	21	12
Tariff dispersion			7	24	9
Schedule of future action			6	29	5
Overall reduction in antiexport bias			17	12	11

a. Often these were not explicit conditions, but understandings under the program.

b. Removal of restrictions, provision of export credits, insurance, guarantees, institutional development, and the like.

c. Where reforms include a replacement of quantitative restrictions by tariffs, they are counted in both these categories.

Source: World Bank data.

use of tariffs in place of quantitative restrictions, or reductions in the level and dispersion of tariff rates.[14] Proposed reductions in the coverage of quantitative restrictions were large in some cases, but modest on average across countries in the case of both items competing with domestic production and noncompetitive items (luxuries, for example).

An area that has received inadequate attention is policy reform affecting domestic competition (on its importance, see box 2-2 on Poland). Price and wage controls, entry and exit barriers, and other regulatory constraints prevent the economy from adapting to the changes in incentives that accompany trade policy reforms (see chapter 7). Yet reform of these domestic policies has seldom been addressed in adjustment lending. One study found that only 2 percent of adjustment lending conditions were related directly to entry and exit barriers and 3 percent to other nonprice regulatory policies.[15]

Box 2-2. *Poland: Policies for Trade Promotion*

In 1987, Poland began to implement the second stage of the economic reform program initiated in 1981. The thrust of the reform is to continue de-
centralization, simplify administrative procedures, and permit freer play of
market forces. Its spirit is most succinctly captured in the frequently expressed principle: "Everything is allowed that is not explicitly forbidden by
law." Specific elements include more automaticity of procedures, increased
transparency and growing uniformity of trade instruments, gradual lowering
of protection to bring prices closer to world levels, demonopolization of trade
privileges, and increased use of the exchange rate as an instrument of trade
promotion. Under the auspices of the UNDP/World Bank Trade Expansion
Program, a mission visited Poland to evaluate the reforms and recommend
steps to enhance Poland's opportunities for greater trade. Some of the
mission's conclusions, which may be relevant to other reforming socialist
economies, are summarized below.

Three problem areas remain: continuing macroeconomic disequilibrium,
central regulation of prices and quantity allocations, and distorted trade incentives. Internal macroeconomic imbalance—in the form of shortages and
excess domestic demand and liquidity fed by budgetary excesses—is a major
factor that inhibits export expansion by absorbing much of production. The
planning mechanisms of price control and materials allocation continue to be
used to deal with this imbalance, thus inhibiting the flexible price and resource allocation adjustments needed for the transition to efficient trading
patterns. Progress has been made on trade policy measures through devaluation, increased foreign exchange retention rights for enterprises, tax relief
measures, and substantial demonopolization of trading rights. But two unfavorable characteristics of the trade regime persist: incentives discriminate by
sector and favor the less efficient producers. Foreign exchange allocation is
the keystone of export policy, but in the context of goods shortages and excess domestic currency (zloty) liquidity, attempts to use foreign exchange allocations to motivate exporters have resulted in a multiplicity of foreign
exchange allocation mechanisms and "markets" and in high premiums in the
markets that are not strictly controlled.

Several recommendations were made. First, the macroeconomic disequilibrium must be resolved. Successful trade promotion requires solving generalized shortages through the elimination of excess zloty liquidity, the
imposition of greater budget discipline, and a reduction in price and wage
controls. To the extent that rationing persists because of the macroeconomic
disequilibrium, it should be implemented in ways that ensure that exports receive comparable incentives through access to foreign exchange and materials and through the flexible application of wage and price adjustments.

Second, the coverage of central planning and allocation mechanisms needs
to be reduced more rapidly to prevent the planning mechanisms (which re-

main administratively strong) from being applied in favor of domestic market needs at the expense of exports. Two shortcomings of price reform merit remediation. First, price liberalization has been limited largely to internationally traded goods, particularly exports, and should be extended. Second, and more fundamental, price reform has not led to the dissolution of traditional price-setting mechanisms and a new reliance on market forces but rather to the use of the price-setting mechanism to more closely simulate market-clearing prices. Retention of this administrative mechanism makes it very easy to reverse the progress of the reform. Although wages and profits are not directly controlled, the application of various taxation mechanisms, including the "excess wage bill" tax, limits enterprise flexibility in setting wages. Until deeper fiscal reform brings increased reliance on taxation of personal and enterprise incomes, the restrictive effect on wage flexibility of the excess wage bill tax should be reduced or eliminated. The very high tax rates on profits also impede efficient resource reallocation, particularly the comparatively higher rate for export enterprises. Also needed is a rapid move to positive interest rates to improve incentives for efficient investment. This increase in rates would reduce the demand for credit and help the move to tighter monetary policies.

Third, export incentives should be simplified and made more uniform and transparent. The price equalization account, which subsidizes inefficient exporters at the expense of efficient ones, should be reduced in scope. Any subsidy should be received by all exporters of a given product, regardless of their level of profitability; ceiling rates should be established; and rates should be reduced as the zloty is devalued. Allowing exporters to retain foreign exchange is the strongest direct incentive for exporters. The system should be simplified and move toward greater uniformity as soon as possible. The role of fiscal incentives should decline as real devaluation, greater retention rights, and less administrative intervention stimulate exports.

Source: Oli Havrylyshyn, *Poland: Policies for Trade Promotion,* UNDP/World Bank Trade Expansion Program (Washington, D.C.: Trade Policy Division, World Bank, 1989).

Implementation and Changes in Incentives

Among the twenty-four countries with data on implementation of reform policies, only two had a low level of restrictiveness (Chile) or antiexport bias (Korea) at the beginning of the 1980s. Implementation was judged to be good for both. For the eight countries judged to have had a moderate level of restrictiveness, implementation judgments varied from poor (for example, Malawi, where quantitative restrictions on imports were raised after balance of payments problems arose), through medium (Panama), to good (Mauritius, where most proposals were implemented and the antiexport bias was reduced). Among the remaining fourteen countries that had high initial levels of restrictiveness, six of the nine countries with strong commercial policy reform proposals had relatively good implementation records (Ghana, Madagascar, Mexico, the Philippines, Senegal, and Turkey).

Substantial action has been taken to reduce restrictions on exports (licensing, prohibitions, and export taxes). Restrictions on imported inputs used in the production of exports have also been significantly reduced. On the import side, several countries have made substantial progress in switching from quantitative restrictions to tariffs. Many countries have adopted tariff reform programs. Notable progress has been made in reducing maximum tariff rates, limiting the number of tariff classes, establishing a (low) minimum tariff (which usually means raising input tariffs, thereby reducing the effective protection of final goods and making protection more uniform), and reducing tariff exemptions.

The lowering of protection levels, especially for products that compete with domestic industry, has been modest on average. Most trade regimes continue to maintain escalated tariff structures, with higher tariffs (and stronger quantitative restrictions) on final goods than on capital goods and lower rates (and more numerous exemptions) for intermediate and raw materials. Tariff dispersion has usually been reduced, but dispersions in effective protection are still large. This experience demonstrates that commercial liberalization is a drawn-out process. For instance, only four countries (Jamaica, Mexico, Senegal, and Turkey) of the fourteen with highly restrictive regimes in the early 1980s had achieved a high degree of commercial liberalization by 1987–88. Guinea, a country not in the sample for want of time-series data, also had a highly restrictive regime that was substantially liberalized in 1986–87.[16]

A larger depreciation in the real exchange rate has occurred in countries receiving trade adjustment loans than in others. In part this reflected the recipient countries' higher debt and significantly greater external shocks, which made larger depreciations necessary. The larger depreciation was also the result of exchange rate reform, macroeconomic stabilization, and trade liberalization (see chapter 5). Few countries, however, floated their exchange rates. In the presence of binding quantitative restrictions on some imports, a real devaluation increases the price not only of tradables relative to nontradables but also of exportables relative to some importables, thereby reducing

Table 2-2.   *Intensity of Reforms in Trade Regimes in Twenty-four Countries during 1980–87*

Exchange rate depreciation[a]	Reduction in antiexport bias through commercial (export and import) policy		
	Mild	Moderate	Substantial
Mild (appreciation or no change)	Guyana[b]	Côte d'Ivoire Senegal	
Moderate (less than 20 percent)	Kenya Malawi Togo Yugoslavia[b] Zimbabwe[b]	Bangladesh Madagascar Morocco Panama Philippines Thailand	Jamaica Korea[c] Mauritius
Substantial (20 percent or more)	Pakistan Zambia[b]	Colombia Ghana	Chile[c] Mexico Turkey

Note: The table indicates changes after reform compared with the prereform situation. In the case of commercial policy, the judgment of the prereform situation is derived from accounts in Bank reports. In the case of the exchange rate, the judgment is based on trends in purchasing power parity over the long term. In some countries, there have been important changes since 1987 that are not captured in this table: improvements in Morocco and reversals in Turkey are cases in point. In some instances major improvements occurred in 1986–87 that are emphasized in the table (for example, Mexico and Jamaica in commercial policy). There are also important reformers that are not included in this sample because adjustment lending for trade policy was too recent (Indonesia and Uruguay) or because the reform was not implemented in connection with adjustment lending (Bolivia and Haiti).

a. Based on a measure of the average change in real effective exchange rate (trade-weighted average of exchange rate vis-à-vis trading partners) during the period after the first loan compared to the period from 1965 to the year before the first loan.

b. Aborted, reversed, or no commercial policy reform.

c. Chile and Korea had already achieved substantial reforms by the early 1980s.

Source: World Bank and IMF data.

antiexport bias. Moreover, a large depreciation, by raising the border price of imports (in domestic currency), can eventually make some quantitative restrictions redundant, thereby resulting in a liberalization of the import regime (chapter 7).

Table 2-2 indicates the extent of exchange rate depreciation and the intensity of commercial policy reforms among the twenty-four countries. By comparing the changes in the period after the trade loan with the trend prior to the loan, it suggests the extent of reductions in the antiexport bias. The table does not fully capture the extent of the initial problem, however. For example, both Korea and the Philippines

Figure 2-1. *Real Exchange Rate Indexes for Selected*
Country Groupings, 1978-88
(1980 = 100)

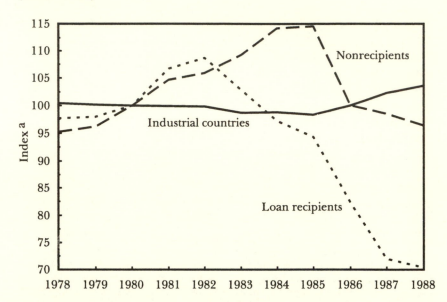

Note: Data are unweighted averages for the twenty-one industrial countries, forty trade
adjustment loan recipients, and forty-seven nonrecipients of trade adjustment lending
listed in table 1-2 in chapter 1.

a. Multilateral index of the real exchange rate measured against a basket of currencies
of trading partners. An increase in the index indicates a real appreciation.

Source: Based on IMF data.

depreciated their real exchange rate "moderately" compared with
their long-term levels, but Korea's long-term level was clearly more
"adequate" (see box 5-1 on the real exchange rate in chapter 5). Subject to this caveat, the table distinguishes the degree of reform in the
twenty-four countries in the 1980s. Korea, Mexico, and Turkey are
three of the most substantial commercial policy reformers. Chile, Colombia, Ghana, Pakistan, and Zambia sustained the largest depreciation in the real exchange rate in the period following the loan
compared with their previous long-term trend rates.

Adjustments in real exchange rates were substantial in many of the
countries that received trade adjustment loans (see box 5-1 in chapter
5). The adjustments involved a series of devaluations or the institution
of a crawling peg, supported by macroeconomic adjustments. Figure
2-1 compares changes in a trade-weighted multilateral real exchange
rate in relation to major trading partners for twenty-one industrial

countries, forty recipients of trade adjustment loans, and forty-seven nonrecipients. The domestic currency depreciated in real terms by 22 percent between the periods 1981–83 and 1985–87 among the forty trade loan recipients, in contrast to 2 percent in the nonrecipient countries, and depreciated only very slightly in the industrial countries (table 2-3). This implies that the price of traded goods relative to the price of nontraded goods increased in the trade adjustment loan countries.

Although economywide measures of the real exchange rate can indicate a change in bias against tradable goods, these measures seldom show the changes that may occur in relative prices between exportable commodities and import substitutes.[17] A partial distinction can be made by using separate export and import weights to calculate the real exchange rate. To make a full distinction, however, measures of changes in effective protection for the different sectors, or measures of real effective exchange rates for exporting activities versus import-substituting activities, would be needed. Although individual country studies of import protection and its effects exist for Argentina, Chile, Colombia, Kenya, Korea, Mexico, Morocco, Pakistan, the Philippines, Thailand, and Turkey, the results are not comparable across countries and are rarely based on time-series data. Comparisons of even nominal protection rates or the coverage of quantitative restrictions are difficult. There is an urgent need to build a database to enable comparisons of nominal and effective protection rates over time and across developing countries.

Import Liberalization and Protection

Import-GDP ratios can reflect both the availability of external financing and import liberalization. During the 1980s, import levels in developing countries declined (in current and constant prices) on average because of balance of payments problems, as did import-GDP ratios. The ratio of nonfuel imports to GDP declined as well, although the extent of the fall was less than for total imports. The reduction in the import-GDP ratio was significantly less for countries associated with trade reforms and adjustment lending (table 2-4), but from this evidence alone, it is not clear whether this was due to reduced protection, or increased financial flows, or both.

Import protection on average has fallen modestly (rather than substantially) in most of the countries studied. By and large, tariff structures remain escalated, with the highest protection afforded to final goods. This seems consistent with the evidence on changes in the composition of nonfuel imports since 1980. If protection of the most highly protected goods (consumer goods) had been reduced substantially,

Table 2-3. Real Exchange Rate Indexes for Selected Country Groupings, 1980–88
(unweighted averages)

| | | | | | | | | | | Percentage change | |
| | | | | | | | | | | 1984–86/ 1980–82 | 1985–87/ 1981–83 |
Sample group	1980	1981	1982	1983	1984	1985	1986	1987	1988ᵃ		
10 intensive trade loan recipients	100.0	114.0	113.2	98.6	84.0	81.2	73.2	69.4	69.8	−27.1[b]	−31.3[c]
26 trade loan recipients	100.0	107.7	110.4	103.5	96.2	93.4	81.9	72.1	71.5	−14.6[b]	−23.1[c]
40 trade loan recipients	100.0	106.8	108.8	102.9	97.2	94.4	82.2	71.9	70.5	−13.3[b]	−22.0[c]
47 non-recipients	100.0	104.7	106.0	109.2	114.2	114.7	100.2	98.5	96.4	5.9	−2.0
Developing countries	100.0	105.8	107.4	106.1	105.7	104.5	91.2	85.2	83.4	−3.8[c]	−12.0
Industrial countries	100.0	99.9	99.8	98.7	98.8	98.4	100.1	102.7	103.7	0.8	−0.5

Note: See box 1-3 in chapter 1 for a description of the sample groupings. An increase in the index indicates a real appreciation.
a. Preliminary estimates.
b. The difference in means of depreciation between the loan recipients and nonrecipients is significant at the 1 percent level.
c. The difference in means of depreciation between the loan recipients and nonrecipients is significant at the 5 percent level.
Source: Based on IMF data.

they would have increased as a percentage of imports, and intermediates used in their domestic production would have decreased their share in the total. Instead, intermediate goods, and capital goods to a lesser extent, have increased relative to consumer goods in the total (table 2-5).

For most countries, detailed quantitative measures of the direct effects of the reforms are not available. The limited information that is available on individual countries shows considerable variation in changes in import impediments (see table 3-7 in chapter 3). Chile, Korea, Mexico, the Philippines, and Turkey are among the countries that undertook broad import reform.

Chile rapidly replaced its quantitative restrictions with virtually uniform tariff rates of 10 percent by mid-1979. The uniform rate has been changed several times but has been stable at 15 percent for the past several years. Commercial policy reversals were corrected and coupled with a substantial devaluation during 1983–85. Since 1983 the export-GDP ratio has nearly doubled. Mexico implemented a major reduction in import restrictions in the mid-1980s, together with a large devaluation, substantially reducing antiexport bias and achieving a large increase in nonoil exports. Korea has sustained liberalization and export development over a long period of time. Turkey carried out a major trade reform and provided substantial export incentives in the first half of the 1980s, transforming an inward-oriented economy to a more outward-looking one and nearly tripling its export-GDP ratio during 1980–87.

The Philippines began with tariff reform in the early 1980s and, after some delay, followed up with substantial reductions in quantitative restrictions in the mid-1980s. Its export-GDP ratio increased modestly, from about 19 percent in 1978–81 to 23 percent in 1987. Colombia, whose trade regime has been characterized by remarkable stability over the past thirty years, undertook some export promotion along with modest import reform in the 1980s. Kenya and Pakistan, among many others, undertook only mild reforms although their trade regimes are quite restrictive. Yugoslavia and Zambia implemented reforms, only to abandon or reverse them later. Overall, the effect of import reform on antiexport bias has varied, ranging from very significant reduction in Mexico to little change in Pakistan. For most countries, there is not enough information to measure any change in bias.

Progress and Constraints in Reform

Many instances can be found of abandonment, reversals, and flip-flops of policy reforms. Despite modest goals, Yugoslavia, for example, abandoned its reforms. Kenya and Côte d'Ivoire made slow progress,

Table 2-4. *Imports of Goods and Nonfactor Services as a Percentage of GDP for Selected Country Groupings, 1980–88*
(unweighted averages)

										Percentage change	
										1984–86/	*1985–87/*
Sample group	*1980*	*1981*	*1982*	*1983*	*1984*	*1985*	*1986*	*1987*	*1988[a]*	*1980–82*	*1981–83*
10 intensive trade loan recipients	32.7	31.9	27.9	27.8	28.6	29.0	28.4	31.6	28.0	−7.2[b]	1.5[b]
26 trade loan recipients	34.3	32.5	29.1	28.1	27.9	28.5	28.5	29.6	26.1	−11.4[b]	−3.5[b]
40 trade loan recipients	33.4	32.3	30.5	29.4	29.1	29.3	28.7	29.1	26.2	−9.5[b]	−5.6[b]
47 non-recipients	39.9	40.9	39.7	37.1	32.9	32.9	30.9	30.1	31.2	19.8	−20.2
Developing countries	36.9	36.9	35.4	33.5	31.1	31.1	29.8	29.6	28.4	−15.7[c]	−14.3[c]
Industrial countries	35.5	34.9	34.7	34.5	36.4	37.1	38.0	37.7	40.1	6.0	8.2

Note: These data are in constant prices. Very similar results are obtained using current prices.

a. Preliminary estimates.

b. The difference in means between the loan recipients and nonrecipients is significant at the 5 percent level.

c. The difference in means between the loan recipients and nonrecipients is significant at the 10 percent level.

Source: World Bank estimates based on national account statistics.

Table 2-5. *Composition of Nonfuel Imports at Current Prices in the Trade Adjustment Countries, 1980–87*

Component	*1980*	*1982*	*1983*	*1984*	*1985*	*1986*	*1987*
Composition (percent)							
Consumer goods	22.4	20.4	20.2	19.7	18.0	17.9	16.5
Capital goods	31.0	32.6	33.7	32.7	33.1	32.2	32.2
Intermediate goods	46.6	47.0	46.1	47.6	48.9	49.9	51.3
Total nonfuel imports	100.0	100.0	100.0	100.0	100.0	100.0	100.0
Average value (millions of U.S. dollars)	4,260	3,871	3,492	3,568	3,517	3,818	4,379

Note: Data are averages for the thirty-seven countries for which data were available.

Source: World Bank estimates based on balance of payments data.

while Morocco and Thailand partially reversed their tariff reform. Argentina reversed its reform of quantitative restrictions. Sierra Leone, Somalia, Uganda, and Zambia abandoned their use of exchange rate auctions. If policy changes are not sustainable and credible, the supply response to the reforms is also likely to be limited.[18]

Constraints to Policy Reform

Four factors can be identified as constraints to more thorough implementation of reforms.[19] One impediment is poor macroeconomic performance and conflicts between trade policy reform and stabilization goals. Recession, continuing high inflation rates, and real appreciation of the currency inhibited earlier reforms in Costa Rica, Jamaica, and the Philippines. Balance of payments problems resulting from a fall in copper prices and faulty exchange rate management contributed to Zambia's policy reversal. In a few cases, trade reforms have been curtailed because a fall in trade tax revenues worsened the fiscal deficit and no compensatory measures were introduced to reduce spending or raise revenue in other ways. For fiscal reasons, Morocco partially reimposed the import surcharges it had reduced in an earlier phase of reform. In the Philippines, customs duties and tariff surtaxes imposed to increase revenues for stabilization purposes have conflicted with attempts to liberalize imports. Although these conflicts may sometimes be unavoidable, less distorting means of generating revenue (or reducing expenditures) are preferable to trade taxes, which themselves create distortions (chapter 7). When a country has a weak tax system, however, some trade taxes may remain necessary in the short term to generate sufficient revenue (see chapter 5).

Second, a weak short-term supply response has impeded reform by limiting its effectiveness. A strong and rapid increase in output from export and efficient import-substitution industries helps the sustainability of reforms by quickly absorbing resources released from the previously highly protected sectors. Rapid export response also helps avert a balance of payments crisis. Slow export expansion contributed to Kenya's failure to liberalize. Costa Rica and Côte d'Ivoire, which made more rapid progress in commercial policy reform, were vulnerable to declining terms of trade, and their export diversification is only just beginning. Even Chile, with its unusually high commitment to reform, has been helped by a strong export response, which has increased the availability of foreign exchange and has thereby helped prevent a balance of payments crisis and the consequent policy reversals. In Jamaica, the availability of financing has been crucial for maintaining the liberalization effort in the face of a worsening current account balance.

A third constraint is inadequate government commitment to the reform program. Inadequate commitment has limited the sustainability of reforms, particularly in the highly indebted countries and in Sub-Saharan Africa. In a number of cases in which the government has not adopted the program as its own, with full commitment (Kenya, Malawi, and Zambia), implementation has been weak. The slow pace of reform has in turn sometimes hurt the credibility of the program for the private sector, further diminishing its sustainability. Changes in political regime and leadership often compound these problems and have led to policy reversals. A related constraint is internal opposition to reform (see chapter 4). Resistance from those who stand to lose from policy changes has often delayed or reversed reductions in protection, as was the case in Zimbabwe. In Yugoslavia, despite modest goals related to trade and the foreign exchange regime, political opposition (in addition to macroeconomic instability) led to dilution or reversal of reforms in the period under review—although, more recently, further progress has been made.

A fourth constraint relates to institutional or administrative weaknesses. Progress in reform of trade-related institutions such as customs services has been particularly slow. Sometimes a country's limited administrative capacity has been a critical constraint, as in the case of the slow progress made in Bangladesh and Côte d'Ivoire. The introduction of tariff reforms, export tax rebates, duty drawback systems, and bonded warehouses has been subject to administrative delays in many cases. Often, changes in policy require accompanying changes in administrative arrangements and capabilities if they are to be successfully implemented—for example, import administration may need to be reorganized to implement tariff reforms. Sometimes policy changes have been predicated on the completion of studies, which were delayed for various reasons (for example, in Colombia and Kenya). In many cases, a general problem is the absence of a medium-term economic policy planning framework within which trade reforms can be discussed, coordinated, and implemented. Planning ministries and departments in many countries (Colombia, India, and Pakistan, for example) are well organized to conduct medium-term physical and financial planning, and many finance ministries and monetary authorities are well equipped to deal with short-term macroeconomic policies, but none of these entities are designed to formulate trade policies for the medium term.

New Sectoral Reform Programs

Almost all seventeen of the adjustment loans with significant trade policy reform components introduced during calendar years 1988 and

1989 were follow-up loans. Ten were in Sub-Saharan Africa, four in the Latin America and Caribbean region, one in Asia, and two in the Europe, Middle East, and North Africa region. The great variance across programs in the actions prescribed emphasizes both how far some countries have progressed and how little reform has been undertaken by others. It also underscores the multiplicity and multiple layers of trade and domestic regulations that have insulated economies and that must be removed to open them to international competition and to encourage exports.

Many countries still have import licensing requirements and high and widely dispersed tariff rates. For several countries, especially in Sub-Saharan Africa, the real binding constraint to imports is foreign exchange rationing, with other barriers being redundant. Thus, many of these countries must begin by reducing foreign exchange rationing, in conjunction with devaluation and unification of rates. But to reduce the divergence between domestic and world price structures, nontariff barriers must also be relaxed and tariffs lowered. Some of the reform programs in Sub-Saharan African countries that have already received multiple trade policy loans are still at a very early stage, at least on the import side, and are a long way from significantly reducing protection. A number of programs call for a reduction in the coverage of nontariff barriers but for little reduction in tariffs (Honduras, Nigeria, Togo, and Tunisia).

Other countries continued to implement long-running trade policy reforms in 1988–89 and are now getting into relatively advanced issues. Mexico, for example, has already eliminated almost all nontariff barriers to manufactured imports and has one of the lowest and most uniform tariff structures in the developing world. Mexico is now revising its antidumping policy because of concern that it was providing unjustified protection. In addition, bottlenecks created by regulations in the Mexican transport sector and inefficiencies in the customs service have impeded efficient adjustment to the policy reform, and these are now being addressed in several sector adjustment loans. In Argentina, some goods liberated from protective barriers in the first phase of reform were being reprotected by the use of official reference prices, ostensibly to guard against unfair trade practices. The current program therefore calls for instituting GATT-consistent customs valuation and substituting an antidumping system for the reference prices. Other programs, including those of Indonesia and Kenya, also include establishment or improvement of such systems.

Another advanced reform issue, that of the nature of tariff classifications, is being addressed in Morocco. Even after some reduction in the protective effects of nontariff barriers and tariffs was achieved, a complex and finely differentiated classification code was used to provide nontransparent protection to certain firms. This code is being rede-fined. Finally, some of the more advanced reformers—notably Indonesia, Mexico, and Morocco—are introducing measures aimed specifically at attracting foreign direct investment. For these countries, such investment can be an important source of new technology, entrepreneurial skills, and market contacts through which to expand exports and efficient import substitutes (chapter 8). A few less-advanced reformers (Kenya and Nigeria) also have such measures. In these countries, care should be taken to ensure that potential investors understand that current protection to domestic markets will be dismantled, so that investment (foreign or domestic) will not take place in inappropriate sectors where protection is currently high.

Many programs include measures to grant exporters access to duty-free imported inputs to insulate them from the effects of import tariffs. These schemes take the form of duty drawbacks, waivers, temporary admission regimes, or export processing zones. Kenya's program includes steps to establish or improve three different schemes. Many such schemes, however, concentrate only on rebating tariffs paid on imported inputs and do not insulate exporters from nontariff barriers that make the inputs difficult to get. Different types of exporters benefit from different schemes, yet few programs recognize this and differentiate their programs accordingly (see chapter 6).

Finally, some of the programs in Sub-Saharan Africa (Malawi, Nigeria, and Togo), rather than reducing tariffs, are taking steps to harmonize production taxes and tariffs, so that a product is taxed at the same level whether its origin is foreign or domestic. If carried to completion, this will essentially convert a trade tax into a less distortionary consumption tax, presumably at a fairly low rate if the whole package is approximately revenue-neutral. This approach is especially appropriate in cases where trade tax reductions would expand the budget deficit (chapter 7).

Summary and Conclusion

Implementation of the reforms by the recipients of the World Bank's trade adjustment loans has varied considerably across countries and by type of reform. Progress has been made in correcting misaligned exchange rates and in reducing impediments to exports, including restrictions on imports needed by exporters. Some countries have begun import reform by substituting tariffs for quantitative restrictions. Reduction of actual protection by lowering both quantitative restrictions and tariff levels has been slow, however, although the several exceptions include Chile, Korea, Mexico, and Turkey. In these countries, the bias against tradables and exportables is estimated to have declined as a result of these measures. For most countries, however, the data required to assess changes in the bias need to be assembled.

The World Bank has supported trade policy reforms through ninety-four adjustment loans to forty-two countries during 1979–88. Overall, there has been considerable reform of trade regimes, including some import liberalization. Given the strong emphasis on trade policy in adjustment lending, however, more intensive reforms might have been expected during this period. Four sets of factors, in addition to external conditions, have constrained stronger and more sustained reforms in various countries: macroeconomic performance and conflicts in design, weak supply response in low-income countries, resistance by vested interests to reform and inadequate conviction concerning its benefits, and weak implementation capacity. The supply response to trade policy reforms depends on reforms to strengthen institutions and to increase internal competition, but improvement in these areas has been inadequate.

Notes

1. Several studies have examined trade liberalization episodes of the past three decades. Studies by or for the World Bank include Sebastian Edwards, "Openness, Outward Orientation, Trade Liberalization, and Economic Performance in Developing Countries," Policy, Planning, and Research Working Paper no. 191, Country Economics Department, World Bank (Washington, D.C., 1989); Demetris Papageorgiou, Michael Michaely, and Armeane M. Choksi, *Liberalizing Foreign Trade*, vol. 7, *Lessons of Experience in the Developing World* (Cambridge, Mass.: Basil Blackwell, forthcoming); Vinod Thomas and others, *Restructuring Economies in Distress: Policy Reform and The World Bank* (New York: Oxford University Press, 1991); and World Bank, *World Development Report 1987* (New York: Oxford University Press, 1987).

2. The findings are based on Nadav Halevi, "Trade Liberalization in Adjustment Lending," World Bank background paper for this report (Washington, D.C., 1989); see also Sam Laird and Julio Nogués, "Trade Policies and the Debt Crisis," Policy, Planning, and Research Working Paper no. 99, International Economics Department, World Bank (Washington, D.C., 1988).

3. Export restrictions have included prohibitions based on economic or safety grounds, restrictive licensing, export quotas, export taxes, and regulations limiting an exporter's right to retain foreign exchange.

4. Quantitative restrictions have included import prohibitions, quotas, and restrictive licensing of various sorts. Other restrictions include foreign exchange licensing and control, advance import deposit requirements, and restricted import channels (as in the case of a state trading monopoly).

5. In addition to customs duties, common customs charges include customs surcharges, surtaxes, stamp taxes, and taxes on foreign exchange.

6. Loan recommendation reports; country memoranda; country briefs; audit reports; mission reports; background work for World Bank, *Adjustment*

Lending: An Evaluation of Ten Years of Experience, Policy and Research Series no. 1 (Washington, D.C., 1989); IMF reports; and a draft paper by John Whalley from a Ford Foundation project on "Trade Policy and the Developing World."

7. One should emphasize that tariff rates and the coverage of nontariff barriers are not comparable. Comparability would require estimating price differences resulting from the imposition of quantitative restrictions. Such data are not generally available. However, the tariff equivalents of quantitative import restrictions appear to be much higher than existing tariff rates.

8. Refik Erzan and others, *The Profile of Protection in Developing Countries,* UNCTAD Discussion Paper no. 21 (New York: United Nations Conference on Trade and Development, 1988).

9. GATT, *The Tokyo Round of Multilateral Trade Negotiations—II, Supplementary Report* (Geneva, 1980). J. M. Finger and Sam Laird estimate the average tariff for eleven industrial countries weighted by import values at 4.6 percent for 1983 ("Protection in Developed and Developing Countries—An Overview," *Journal of World Trade Law* 2, no. 6 [1987]). Reliable estimates are unavailable for agricultural products.

10. Finger and Laird, "Protection."

11. Sam Laird and Alexander Yeats, "Trends in Nontariff Barriers of Developed Countries, 1966–86," Policy, Planning, and Research Working Paper no. 137, International Economics Department, World Bank (Washington, D.C., 1988). Including "secondary trade restrictive intent" raises the figure to 27.2 percent, and estimates for imports "affected," rather than covered, are even higher—48 percent.

12. Refik Erzan, "Would General Trade Liberalization in Developing Countries Expand South-South Trade?," Policy, Planning, and Research Working Paper no. 319, International Economics Department, World Bank (Washington, D.C., 1989).

13. See, for example, Bela Balassa, "Outward Orientation," DRD Discussion Paper no. 148, Development Research Department, World Bank (Washington, D.C., 1985); W. M. Corden, *Protection and Liberalization: A Review of Analytical Issues* (Washington, D.C.: IMF, 1987); and Michael Michaely, "Guidelines for Country Economists for the Review and Evaluation of Trade Policies." CPD Discussion Paper no. 1986-7, Country Policy Department, World Bank (Washington, D.C., 1986).

14. In some cases, particularly in Sub-Saharan Africa, additional incentives were introduced for import substitution—for example, higher duties on imported inputs that competed with domestic production. (Increasing the duties on imported inputs reduces the protection provided to the finished goods that use them, although the net effect may or may not be to increase overall protection; see chapter 7.)

15. World Bank, "Competition Policies for Industrializing Countries," Industry Development Division, Industry and Energy Department, Sector Policy and Research (Washington, D.C., 1989).

16. Guinea undertook a large devaluation and then abolished import licensing. Tariffs were reduced to a uniform base rate of 10 percent, with surcharges of 20 to 40 percent on luxury imports. Subsequently some ad hoc

exemptions and controls were instituted, but overall, Guinea's trade regime has become substantially more open than before.

17. When quantitative restrictions on imports are binding before and after the depreciation, the exchange rate depreciation increases the price of exportables relative to importables.

18. Dani Rodrik concludes that the sustainability of policies is more important than their liberalization ("Liberalization, Sustainability, and the Design of Structural Adjustment Programs," Trade Policy Division, Country Economics Department, World Bank [Washington, D.C., 1988]).

19. Based on country studies carried out at the World Bank. See also, J. N. Bhagwati, *Foreign Trade Regimes and Economic Development* (New York: National Bureau of Economic Research, 1978); A. O. Krueger, *Liberalization Attempts and Consequences* (Cambridge, Mass.: Ballinger, 1978); I. M. D. Little, Tibor Scitovsky, and M. F. Scott, *Industry and Trade in Some Developing Countries: A Comparative Study* (New York: Oxford University Press, 1970).

3

Trade Policy Reforms and Performance

Evidence can be found of a strong positive association between economic performance and outward orientation. But because economic performance is the result of a variety of factors, identifying the precise policy links between them is difficult.[1] With this caveat, this chapter first examines evidence on the effects of outward orientation on performance and then turns more specifically to the connection between policy reform and performance.

The evidence from the 1980s corroborates the positive association between trade policy reform and output growth noted in previous work. Higher export and import growth rates were recorded in countries that achieved higher income growth during 1980–87.[2] Recipients of trade adjustment loans have experienced a stronger expansion in manufacturing and merchandise exports and a significantly higher output growth rate than others (table 3-1). A part of this recovery may be expected, because performance was poorer among trade adjustment loan recipients at the outset of the lending than among nonrecipients. The receipt of adjustment loans and improved performance, in turn, have been associated with stronger trade policy reforms—for example, with greater depreciation of the real exchange rate and larger increases in import-GDP ratios. These observations suggest a broad linkage between policy change and performance and justify, as a means of understanding the policy-performance connection, the more detailed look at the adjustment loan countries presented in this chapter.

Trade Policy and Growth in the Long Term

Studies have documented a strong and positive association between growth in exports and growth in output (see figure 3-1). The literature on the export-output link also provides some basis for postulating a growth contribution from exports—including their positive technological externalities stemming from exposure to larger external markets and greater competition (see chapter 6). A growing number of empirical studies of individual countries and of large samples also brings out the contribution of export growth to output performance. A study based on the experience of eleven economies during 1960–73 (Argentina, Brazil, Chile, Colombia, India, Israel, Mexico, Singapore, Korea, Taiwan, and Yugoslavia) concluded that a high rate of export growth has positive effects on output growth.[3]

Two limits to the observed export-output linkage ought to be noted. First, exports are a part of the total output, and therefore it is hard to talk about causality between the two. In any event, existing regression results do not permit the establishment of causality from export growth to output growth.[4] Where technical causality tests have been done, the results are mixed. However, although causality from exports to output has been confirmed for only a small number of countries, a lack of causality from exports to output has not been confirmed either. In most cases, a two-way causality seems to exist. Second, only a few studies are able to control for the trade policy bias of countries. Thus, even where the contribution of exports and outward orientation is established, this by itself provides only indirect evidence in favor of export-oriented policies.[5]

Impact of Trade Policy Reform

Evidence supports the view that outward-oriented approaches lead to better performance than do inward-looking strategies. The importance for export development of a favorable and relatively stable real exchange rate is also recognized. Less agreement exists on precisely which policy reforms underlie a greater outward orientation. Some authors conclude that government promotion of exports coupled with fiscal stability, rather than trade liberalization, explains the East Asian successes (see chapter 6 also).[6] Other studies show that the movement to a more liberal trade regime increases exports and output (see below).

Trade policy reform was found to boost performance in an analysis of ten countries (Brazil, Chile, Colombia, Egypt, Ghana, India, Israel, the Philippines, Korea, and Turkey).[7] The study showed that real devaluations generally resulted in important reductions in the premium on import licenses, lowered antiexport bias, and raised exports. The higher exports were associated with higher output and with no significant transitional costs of liberalization. Another analysis, based on effective rates of protection and domestic resource costs, found that trade policy reform generated static efficiency gains and that a lowering of the bias against exports improved export performance.[8] No evidence was found linking such reductions in trade bias to technological

Table 3-1. Exports and Output for Selected Country Groupings, 1980–88
(unweighted averages, in percent)

Category and country grouping	Average annual growth rate									Percentage change in growth rate	
	1980	1981	1982	1983	1984	1985	1986	1987	1988ᵃ	1984–86/ 1980–82	1985–87/ 1981–83
Volume of merchandise exports											
87 developing countries	5.4	2.4	2.6	0.1	6.6	5.2	3.7	6.0	4.4	49.0	19.2
10 intensive trade loan recipients	12.1	7.5	7.8	–4.9	11.5	3.5	9.2	7.5	3.5	–11.7**	94.2
26 trade loan recipients	9.1	4.8	2.2	–2.9	7.3	3.6	8.3	7.8	5.1	19.3***	380.5**
40 trade loan recipients	7.6	4.7	–0.4	–1.2	6.8	5.0	6.8	5.7	4.1	56.3***	464.5***
47 nonrecipients	3.5	0.3	5.1	1.2	6.5	5.4	1.0	6.3	4.8	44.9	92.4
*Volume of manufactures exports*ᵇ											
87 developing countries	18.4	9.7	1.2	11.2	9.8	10.6	7.2	5.5	10.7	–5.8	5.4
10 intensive trade loan recipients	26.8	20.2	–3.8	15.6	11.9	9.5	10.2	13.7	17.2	–26.9*	4.5**

26 trade loan recipients	18.7	7.3	0.9	6.7	9.0	11.5	5.0	12.2	12.2	−5.2*	92.6**
40 trade loan recipients	25.6	6.5	0.6	10.3	7.4	14.1	11.6	9.9	13.7	1.2**	104.6**
47 nonrecipients	11.9	12.6	1.7	12.1	11.8	7.4	3.5	1.7	7.9	−13.4	−52.2
GDP[c] at constant prices											
87 developing countries	3.6	3.4	1.8	1.2	2.5	3.1	3.2	2.3	3.3	−1.1	32.9
10 intensive trade loan recipients	0.2	2.4	1.1	0.2	2.1	2.7	3.8	4.2	4.1	128.8**	188.7**
26 trade loan recipients	3.4	2.2	0.7	0.6	2.7	3.3	4.2	3.7	3.8	60.2**	214.1**
40 trade loan recipients	2.7	2.8	0.3	0.4	2.2	3.5	3.9	3.2	3.6	63.7**	198.2**
47 nonrecipients	4.4	3.9	3.1	1.9	2.8	2.7	2.6	1.6	3.0	−29.8	−23.6

Note: A single asterisk indicates that the difference in means between the loan recipients and nonrecipients is significant at the 5 percent level. A double asterisk indicates that the difference in means between the loan recipients and nonrecipients is significant at the 1 percent level. See box 1-3 and table 1-2 in chapter 1 for the composition of the country groupings.

a. Preliminary estimates.

b. The definition of manufactures is taken from the Foreign Trade Statistics database, Economic Projections and Analysis Department, World Bank; it includes line items 5, 6 (excluding 68), 7, and 8 in the Standard International Trade Classification.

c. A similar relationship results from using other measures of output that exclude exports.

Source: World Bank data.

Figure 3-1. *Output and Export Growth for Eighty-eight Developing Countries, 1965-88*

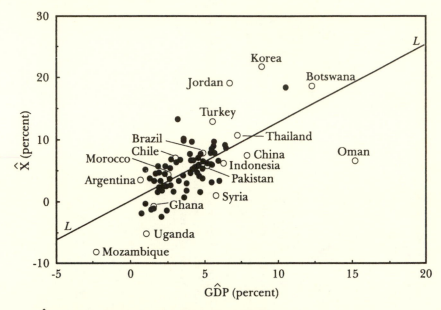

GD̂P = Average growth rate of GDP during 1965-88.
X̂ = Average growth rate of exports of goods and nonfactor services during 1965-88.
LL = Fitted line based on least-squares regression.
Source: Based on World Bank data.

superiority or to higher savings ratios. Chenery and others found that a policy shift from import substitution toward neutrality can account for an increase of as much as one percentage point in productivity growth, holding capital inflow and other indirect effects the same.[9]

Effects of Distortionary Interventions

Measuring interventions in a meaningful way is difficult—implying that the results of any single study should not be taken as definitive—but results are suggestive. Romer used government spending as a share of GDP as a proxy for the effects of intervention in the economy.[10] He estimated a production function using as inputs labor, human capital, the investment rate, and proxies for the effect of increased openness on technological change. After accounting for these factors, he found that the annual growth of GDP was reduced by about one percentage point for every increase of ten percentage points in the share of government spending in GDP. Balassa classified Sub-Saharan African countries as

Table 3-2. *Regression Results for Trade Flow Distortions and Output Growth*

Period	Constant	Invest-ment ratio	Labor force growth	Technology gap	Trade intervention	Number of countries	R^2
1960–82	−1.924	0.260	1.461	−0.037	−2.697	28	0.702
	(−1.111)	(6.533)	(3.573)	(−1.611)	(−3.766)		
1982	−7.935	0.323	1.992	−0.020	−3.137	30	0.503
	(−2.575)	(4.506)	(2.966)	(−0.575)	(−2.491)		

Note: Numbers in parentheses are *t*-statistics.

Source: Data are from World Bank, *World Development Report 1984* (New York: Oxford University Press, 1984), and IMF, *International Financial Statistics* (Washington, D.C., various issues).

relatively market-oriented or interventionist, based on interventions in capital, labor, and foreign exchange markets.[11] Using either a twofold classification or a threefold one (by including an intermediate category), his study found that private market economies on average gained shares in their total and agricultural export markets, while the interventionist economies lost shares. Scully classified eighty-six countries according to the degree to which public intervention directly determined resource allocation, regulated market activity, and redistributed income.[12] Higher levels of intervention were associated with less openness of the economy and, in turn, with lower rates of growth.

A background study for this book used an index of trade flow distortions based on actual sectoral trade flows between countries and the flows that would be predicted from each country's comparative advantage.[13] The index, which was taken to measure the degree to which policy interventions affected the composition of trade, was constructed from the difference between the predicted and actual flows. After taking into account the investment ratio, labor force growth, and educational attainment, the study found that countries with higher distortionary interventions tended to grow more slowly than others. One set of results is given in table 3-2.

Effect of Export and Import Restrictions

Another background study on long-term growth considers the effects of trade restrictions.[14] It controls for growth of capital, labor, and imported intermediate inputs and considers the effects of export and import restrictions on growth. The inclusion of imported intermediate inputs (in addition to the usually considered capital and labor) takes into account the constraint on their use that results from bind-

Table 3-3. Regression Results for Trade Restrictiveness and Per Capita Output Growth

Period	Constant	Per capita growth rate of capital	Per capita growth rate of imported intermediate inputs	Restrictions on exports and imports for exporters[a]	Restrictions on general imports[a]	Real exchange rate variability	Number of observations	R^2
1979–83	0.02 (1.96)	0.16 (3.35)	0.02 (0.68)	−0.01 (−2.09)	−0.005 (−0.61)	−0.05 (−1.55)	36	0.46
1975–85	0.02 (4.62)	0.19 (6.89)	0.06 (1.83)	−0.02 (−5.02)	0.002 (0.56)	−0.03 (−2.09)	70	0.72

Note: Numbers in parentheses are *t*-statistics.
a. Dummy variable.
Source: Lopez, "Trade Policy, Growth, and Investment."

ing trade restrictions. (It turns out that imported inputs are a binding constraint in countries with high export restrictions and not in others.) This analysis also distinguishes among the effects of export restrictions, import restrictions, and macroeconomic stability as measured by real exchange rate variability.

The regression estimates are based on thirty-five trade adjustment loan recipients for which 1975–85 data were available. The level of trade restrictiveness (see chapter 2) relates to trade regimes at the outset of trade adjustment lending. Thus, the year for which the trade restrictiveness is measured varies from country to country, in most cases falling between 1979 and 1983. Two time periods are considered: 1975–85 (subdivided into 1975–80 and 1981–85) and 1979–83, which corresponds more closely to the period in which restrictiveness was measured. Trade restrictiveness is represented by separate dummy variables for export and import restrictions (equal to 1 for countries with high restrictiveness—according to judgments in World Bank reports—and to 0 for others).

Ordinary least-squares estimates for the dependent variables output growth and output growth per capita (table 3-3) show a very good fit and a high level of significance for most variables. In addition to the expected positive effect of per capita growth in capital, the effect of imported intermediate inputs is generally positive and significant. The degree of real exchange rate variability is generally significant and is negatively associated with growth, which seems to confirm previous findings that economic uncertainty hurts growth. Furthermore, restrictions on exports and on imports used by exporters—as reflected by the coefficient of the export restriction dummy variable—are negatively and significantly associated with per capita growth. Import restrictiveness (as distinct from restrictions on imports for exporters and growth of imported inputs) is not found to be a statistically significant independent explanatory variable of per capita growth.

The results suggest that a reduction in export restrictions has a clearer association with GDP growth than does a reduction in import restrictions. They are also consistent with the generally held view that the efficiency effects of export liberalization are likely to be felt faster than those of import liberalization. The results suggest that the (Lerner) symmetry between direct export restrictions (and taxes) and import restrictions (and tariffs) may not necessarily hold in some situations—for example, in periods of prolonged balance of payments imbalance. In general, however, import restrictions are expected to have a negative effect on growth and exports. The evidence from ten episodes of trade restrictions in the 1950s, 1960s, and 1970s is that more than half the burden of import protection, because of its effects on relative prices, translates into an implicit tax on exports.[15] Another study of thirty-two developing and five industrial economies found that both the level and dispersion of effective protection rates for importables were strongly and negatively correlated with growth rates, correcting for the effect of other factors (discussed in the following section).[16]

Trade Policy Reform and Economic Recovery in the 1980s

In this section we examine the links between changes in trade policy associated with adjustment lending and short- to medium-term recovery of GDP in the 1980s. As before, we examine the effect on growth of exchange rate depreciation as well as trade restrictions, but here we focus on changes in trade restrictions in the 1980s based on trade reform implementation data (discussed in chapter 2). Evidence is presented from regression estimates, cross-country comparisons, and selected country studies.

GDP Growth, Financing, and Reform

In the first half of the 1980s, import compression was the dominant force behind the negative relation between resource balance and GDP. Figure 3-2 indicates the strong positive link between import growth and output growth for trade adjustment loan recipients, which is likely to be a two-way relationship. In one direction of causality, when GDP grows rapidly, the demand for imports grows rapidly as well. In the other direction, imports can affect output in at least two ways. First, increased competition from imports hurts inefficient production and should lead over time to more efficient domestic production (see section entitled "Constraints to a Stronger Supply Response" below for possible biases in estimation). Second, imported inputs of raw materials, intermediates, and capital goods affect production. When domestic savings are not easily converted into foreign exchange for imports, a relaxation of the foreign exchange constraint and of import controls can contribute to higher output in the short term.

Adjustment lending has supported import liberalization and has provided additional financing for imports. As indicated in table 3-4, the ratio of IBRD and IDA financial flows (measured by disbursements and transfers) to imports increased for the recipients of trade adjustment loans in the periods following the loans. The increase in this ratio for these countries was greater than the increase for countries that did not receive such loans. However, total (official and unofficial) financial flows relative to imports decreased more for the loan recipients than for the others. Thus, any improvement in the economic performance of the trade adjustment loan countries is not attributable entirely to the increased financing facilitated by the loans.

Figure 3-2. *Changes in Output and Import Growth for Trade Adjustment Loan Countries before and after Adjustment Lending*

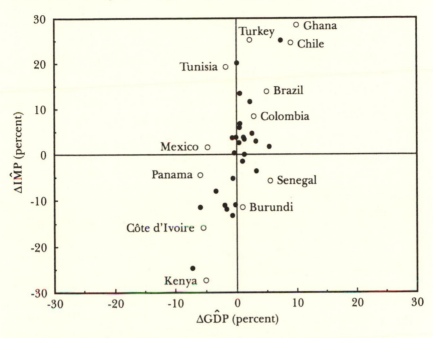

$\Delta G\hat{D}P$ = Percentage point improvement in the GDP growth rate for the three-year period after the first trade loan compared with the three-year period before.

$\Delta I\hat{M}P$ = Percentage point improvement in the import growth rate for the three-year period after the first trade loan compared with the three-year period before.

Source: Based on World Bank data.

Changes in trade policy, including real exchange rate adjustments, were expected to boost GDP by improving the efficiency of resource use. To assess this, we investigated whether changes in GDP growth associated with changes in financing and changes in other factors differ statistically between loan recipients and nonrecipients and between reformers and nonreformers. The dependent variable is the change in the average rate of GDP growth, comparing the rate after reform with the rate before. The independent variables are changes in financing (or, alternatively, in imports),[17] terms of trade, real exchange rate, and trade restrictions over the same periods. Changes in trade restrictions are represented by a dummy variable that assumes a value of 1 for trade policy–adjusting countries (according to chapter 2) and 0 for others. For a sample with reform implementation data, the effect of policy change is also assessed using a detailed classification of how much reform took place.[18] A positive and significant coef-

Table 3-4. *Change in the Ratio of Financial Flows to Total Imports for Trade Adjustment Loan Recipients and Nonrecipients*

Group and period	Disbursements			Transfers		
	Total	*IBRD*	*IDA*	*Total*	*IBRD*	*IDA*
Forty trade loan recipients						
Unweighted						
Preloan	0.282	0.018	0.008	0.184	0.014	0.008
Postloan	0.257	0.038	0.028	0.142	0.026	0.028
Difference	−0.025	0.020	0.020	−0.042	0.012	0.020
Weighted						
Preloan	0.368	0.019	0.002	0.227	0.014	0.002
Postloan	0.251	0.043	0.005	0.109	0.030	0.004
Difference	−0.117	0.024	0.003	−0.118	0.016	0.002
Forty-seven nonrecipients[a]						
Unweighted						
Preloan	0.243	0.012	0.015	0.162	0.009	0.015
Postloan	0.239	0.017	0.032	0.136	0.010	0.031
Difference	−0.004	0.005	0.017	−0.026	0.001	0.016
Weighted						
Preloan	0.259	0.014	0.005	0.147	0.011	0.005
Postloan	0.213	0.022	0.008	0.088	0.014	0.007
Difference	−0.046	0.008	0.003	−0.059	0.003	0.002

Note: Unweighted ratios were computed as $\Sigma(F_i/M_i)/N$, where F_i = average financial flows for the three-year period before or after the trade loan, M_i = average imports of goods and nonfactor services over the same periods, and N = the number of countries. Weighted ratios are computed as $(\Sigma F_i)/(\Sigma M_i)$.

a. For nonrecipients, the postloan period is 1984–86.

Source: World Bank data.

ficient of the dummy variable or of the index of reform is interpreted as an improvement in the mean change in growth rate for the reformers relative to nonreformers.

We first consider the forty trade adjustment loan countries relative to nonrecipients. Any effect on average GDP growth found in this comparison is the result of, among other things, the financing and policy changes supported by the loan. In a second comparison, exclusion of the four loan recipients identified in box 1-3 in chapter 1 as nonreformers or reform reversers (Guyana, Yugoslavia, Zambia, and Zimbabwe) and the inclusion of Bolivia and Haiti, which reformed their trade policy in the 1980s but did not receive loans, permits a contrast between the thirty-eight countries that actually instituted commercial policy reforms and the forty-nine nonreformers.

The independent variables considered explain about 20 to 60 percent of the variation in GDP growth (table 3-5). The coefficients of the

Table 3-5. Regression Results for Trade Loan Recipients and Trade Reformers and Change in Output Growth

Group	Constant	Change in financing	Change in terms of trade	Change in real exchange rate	Trade reform[a]	Number of observations	R^2	F-statistic
40 trade loan recipients compared with 47 nonrecipients[a]	0.33 (0.42)	0.0002 (0.32)	0.08 (2.55)	−0.05 (−2.54)	0.32 (0.29)	66	0.18	3.3
38 trade reformers compared with 49 nonreformers[a]	−0.29 (−0.40)	0.002 (0.33)	0.09 (2.85)	−0.04 (−2.43)	1.78 (1.67)	66	0.22	4.2
24 reformers[b]	−3.09 (−2.09)	0.02 (1.70)	0.09 (1.92)	−0.08 (−2.29)	3.38 (2.58)	24	0.60	7.0

Note: Changes refer to the average for the three years before the loan compared with the average for the three years after the loan. Numbers in parentheses are *t*-statistics.
a. Dummy variable for trade reform.
b. Selected on the basis of the index of the extent of policy change as measured by reform implementation data.
Source: World Bank data.

change in financing are always positive but are mildly significant only in the case of the sample with implementation data. The terms of trade change has the expected effects on GDP and is significant. A depreciation of the real exchange rate is associated with an increase in output growth. When the forty loan recipients are considered, the coefficient of the dummy is positive—that is, the recipients increased their growth rates on average between the two periods more than the others, given imports and terms of trade—but the increase is not statistically significant. When only the thirty-eight trade loan recipients that were also commercial policy reformers are considered, the coefficient of the dummy variable becomes more significant. As for the degree of reform implementation, the coefficient of trade reform is positive and statistically significant.

Performance Related to Trade Adjustment Lending

Changes in performance indicators for the twenty-six countries that received trade adjustment loans before 1986 are compared with the changes for the nonrecipients in table 3-6. The table is based on average changes in indicators for the three-year period after the first trade loan (excluding the year of the loan) compared with the three-year period before the trade loan.[19] The numbers in the table show how many trade loan recipient countries in each classification performed better on each indicator than their comparators after the start of trade adjustment lending. The plus and minus signs indicate an improvement (+) or worsening (−) of the average value of an indicator for the trade adjustment loan recipients in comparison with the average value of the same indicator for the nonrecipients.[20] For example, if the average export growth of recipients in a subgroup was 0.2 percentage points less than that of nonrecipients in the three-year period before trade adjustment lending started and 0.1 percentage points less in the three-year period after, the difference (0.1) is positive and the relative performance of the recipients improved.

Panel 1 shows that, on average, the change in performance on the trade indicators between 1981–83 and 1985–87 was better for the twenty-six pre-1986 trade loan recipients than for the forty-seven nonrecipients. Improvements in export and import indicators were greater than improvements in other indicators. The relative performance of the twenty-six trade loan recipients for the three-year period after the loan compared with the three-year period before the loan is presented in panel 2.[21] The last three rows in each panel show the total percentage of cases across all nine indicators in which trade adjustment loan countries (in three different classifications) did better than the others. The relative performance of trade adjustment loan countries is usually weaker when all forty recipients are considered than when the focus is on the twenty-six pre-1986 recipients or the ten intensive loan (three or more) recipients. A serious issue revealed by these comparisons is the relative worsening in the debt and investment indicators in several instances for the adjustment loan countries (a finding also reported in the 1988 World Bank report on adjustment lending).

Country Experience

Table 3-7 presents data on changes in commercial policy and the real exchange rate in eleven countries for which data are readily available.[22] Some of the data are not exactly comparable over time and across countries, and therefore the figures should be taken only as broad indicators. Reductions in import restrictions were substantial over the periods considered in Chile, Korea, Mexico, Morocco, the Philippines, and Turkey. Chile's dramatic reforms of 1974–79 were followed by a period of increased import barriers and then, in 1985–88, by important new reforms. Korea's reforms came in many waves from the 1960s onward, with significant improvements in the 1980s. All the countries in this table, except Korea, also experienced a large depreciation in the real exchange rate. (Korea had no major misalignment in its exchange rate to begin with.)

In most cases reforms also included a much broader range of policies. Any improvements in performance, therefore, should not be attributed to trade reform alone. GDP growth accelerated in the reform and postreform periods in Chile, Korea, Morocco, and Turkey. In Mexico (see box 3-1) and the Philippines, the growth rate recovered following reform. Total export growth also improved in most cases during the reform period and in all cases subsequently. In about half the cases, the growth rate of manufactures exports also picked up following reforms.

The association of a real exchange rate depreciation with a partial improvement (or recovery) in performance between the two periods is brought out by the experiences of several countries. Colombia, Kenya, Pakistan, and Thailand had little commercial policy reform between the two periods, but their real exchange rate adjustment was substantial. GDP growth in Colombia, Kenya, and Thailand recovered in the second period, while changes in export performance were mixed. In Argentina, which had increased protection coupled with a real devaluation during the second period, export growth deteriorated while GDP growth recovered.

Commercial policy liberalization alone seemed helpful in Korea in the 1980s, but Korea had reasonable macroeconomic stability and its currency was not overvalued. Chile's strong commercial policy reform

Table 3-6. *Performance Indicators for Trade Adjustment Loan Recipients before and after Trade Adjustment Lending: Twenty-six Pre-1986 Trade Loan Recipients Compared with Forty-seven Nonrecipients*

Indicator	Country classification					
	Low-income	Middle-income	Low- and middle-income	Sub-Saharan Africa	Highly indebted	Manufactures exporters
Number of trade loan recipients	9	17	26	11	10	7
Number of nonrecipients	20	27	47	18	4	8
Panel 1: 1985–87 compared with 1981–83						
GDP growth	9(+)**	12(+)**	21	10(+)**	3(−)**	5(+)
Investment/GDP	5(+)	14(+)	19	9(+)	6(−)	7(+)
Real exchange rate	8(+)*	15(+)**	23	9(+)*	8(+)	7(+)
Manufacturing exports growth	7(+)**	12(+)	19	10(+)**	1(−)**	4(−)
Import growth	8(+)**	12(+)**	20	8(+)**	4(−)	6(+)
Resource balance/GDP	4(−)	12(+)	16	5(+)	10(+)**	1(−)
Inflation	8(+)*	14(+)	22	10(+)**	7(−)	1(−)
External debt/exports	6(+)	17(+)*	23	8(+)	10(+)**	6(+)
Debt service/exports	5(+)	10(+)	15	4(−)	3(−)	7(+)
Share showing improvement[a]	0.74	0.77	0.76	0.74	0.58	0.70
10 intensive recipients	0.83	0.72	0.74	0.78	0.53	0.56
All 40 recipients	0.68	0.74	0.71	0.68	0.56	0.56

Panel 2: Three years after loan compared with three years before

GDP growth	5(+)	13(+)	18	6(+)	5(+)	4(+)
Investment/GDP	4(−)	11(+)	15	5(−)	8(+)	4(−)
Real exchange rate	7(+)	16(+)	23	10(+)*	9(+)	7(+)
Manufacturing exports growth	7(+)	14(+)	21	9(+)	5(−)	4(+)
Import growth	6(+)	14(+)*	20	6(+)	5(+)**	7(+)*
Resource balance/GDP	5(+)	11(+)	16	8(+)	8(+)	2(+)
Inflation	7(+)	13(+)	20	9(+)	6(+)	4(−)
External debt/exports	5(+)	14(+)	19	7(−)	9(+)	5(+)
Debt service/exports	5(−)	9(+)	14	3(−)	5(+)	4(+)
Share showing improvement[a]	0.63	0.75	0.71	0.64	0.67	0.65
10 intensive recipients	0.78	0.69	0.71	0.71	0.71	0.78
All 40 recipients	0.58	0.70	0.64	0.62	0.63	0.54

Note: The numbers in the table show for each performance indicator the number of trade adjustment loan recipients in each classification that improved in the period after the loan compared with the period before the loan relative to the change over the same periods for nonrecipients. The year of receipt of the first loan is excluded from the comparison in panel 2. The plus and minus signs indicate an improvement or a worsening, respectively, of the average value of an indicator for recipients compared with the change in the average value for nonrecipients.

A single asterisk indicates that the change in means for the recipients between the two periods relative to the change for nonrecipients is significant at a 10 percent confidence interval.

A double asterisk indicates that the change in means for the recipients between the two periods relative to the change for nonrecipients is significant at a 5 percent confidence interval.

a. The share of the product of the number of variables and the number of countries showing improvement in the total.

Table 3-7. Recent Evolution in Trade Policy and Performance for Selected Countries

Country and period[a]	Average tariff rate (percent) (1)	Coverage of QRs (percent) (2)	Index of real exchange rate (1980 = 100) (3)	Terms of trade (1980 = 100) (4)	Growth in manufactures exports[b] (percent) (5)	Growth in total exports (percent) (6)	Growth in GDP (percent) (7)
Argentina[c]							
1978–82	28.0	0.0	74.6	99.6	-1.8	10.7	-1.3
1983–87	35.0	42.0[d]	44.3	89.4	-2.0	1.2	1.6
1984–88	n.c.	n.c.	43.2	88.7	3.3	0.8	1.1
Chile							
1983–85	35.0	none	80.3	82.0	4.7	4.8	2.7
1986–87	20.0	none	56.0	74.9	3.8	9.2	5.6
1987–88	n.c.	n.c.	52.2	85.4	14.7	7.5	6.6
Colombia							
1983–85	61.0[e](1984)	65.7[d](1984)	103.4	97.3	-1.9	7.9	2.7
1986–87	52.0[e](1986)	50.2 (1986)	64.4	84.6	13.3	13.4	5.3
1987–88	n.c.	n.c.	59.6	69.6	9.5	4.7	4.5
Kenya							
1981–83	n.a.	71.3[f]	97.6	91.6	1.3	0.6	1.5
1984–86	28,35,55[g]	59.1	96.8	101.5	2.2	7.4	4.0
1985–87	n.c.	n.c.	88.6	94.1	5.5	6.8	5.0

Korea							
1980–82	28.3	27.7[h]	103.8	99.2	9.5	10.6	3.4
1983–85	22.3	16.7	99.8	100.8	7.5	9.2	8.3
1984–86	n.c.	n.c.	92.5	103.8	13.8	17.6	8.6
Mexico							
1983–85	24.4[i]	92.2[i](1984–85)	80.6	97.9	42.7	5.1	0.7
1986–87	20.5	37.0	58.0	69.5	27.0	6.9	−1.3
1987–88	n.c.	n.c.	62.1	68.9	15.5	9.8	0.9
Morocco							
1980–83	58.4[k](1983)	50.1[l](1983)	91.5	93.3	20.1	4.2	2.9
1984–86	41.5	41.0	74.8	93.8	4.3	3.0	4.1
1985–87	n.c.	n.c.	71.2	98.8	8.5	4.9	3.7
Pakistan							
1980–82	77.0	n.a.	105.6	97.3	6.8	8.6	8.0
1983–85	66.0	n.a.	99.3	92.1	9.4	9.2	6.6
1984–86	n.c.	n.c.	68.5	91.5	6.4	10.7	6.8
Philippines							
1980–83	36.5	37.0[m](1980)	100.1	92.4	9.9	5.4	3.3
1985–87	28.1	16.7 (1986)	81.3	94.8	1.8	4.4	0.8
1986–88	n.c.	n.c.	71.5	104.6	6.9	11.1	4.2
Thailand							
1983–85	32.3	n.a.	103.7	78.0	15.5	7.5	5.9
1986–87	33.8	n.a.	82.5	82.6	30.3	15.5	5.9
1987–88	n.c.	n.a.	78.7	88.3	28.8	20.1	9.7

(Table continues on the following page.)

Table 3-7. *(continued)*

Country and period[a]		Average tariff rate (percent) (1)	Coverage of QRs (percent) (2)	Index of real exchange rate (1980 = 100) (3)	Terms of trade (1980 = 100) (4)	Growth in manufactures exports[b] (percent) (5)	Growth in total exports (percent) (6)	Growth in GDP (percent) (7)
Turkey								
1984–85	n.c.	n.c.	28.4[n]	77.8	91.8	36.8	16.1	5.4
1986–87	n.c.	n.c.	18.8 (1987)	63.5	109.6	6.8	14.0	7.9
1987–88	n.c.	n.c.	n.c.	61.9	108.9	24.3	20.3	5.5

Note: QRs = quantitative restrictions; n.a. = not available; n.c. = not considered.

a. The latest period is lagged one year from the previous period in order to observe performance effects (columns 1 through 5). Thus policies in the last period are not considered, as indicated by n.c.

b. Manufactures include line items 5, 6 (excluding 68), 7, and 8 in the Standard International Trade Classification, based on World Bank data.

c. Argentina is not included among the twenty-four countries with implementation data (see chapter 2) because it did not receive its first loan until 1987. Argentina was also not considered a country with low initial trade restrictiveness because the classification was based on restrictions just prior to the lending.

d. Percentage of import value.

e. Including a 19.5 percent surcharge.

f. Globally allocated or restricted (that is, not automatically approved).

g. Capital, intermediate, and consumer goods respectively, 1984–85.

h. Percentage of import items not on the automatic approval list; about 40 percent of the items on the list, however, are subject to exemptions.

i. Weighted by 1986 production for all years; excludes 5 percent surcharge.

j. Subject to licensing as a percentage of the value of 1986 production.

k. Including surcharges.

l. Licensed and prohibited items as a percentage of the total number of items.

m. Restricted items as a percentage of the total number of items.

n. Licensed items as a percentage of the total number of import items.

Source: Amarendra Bhattacharya and J. F. Linn, *Trade and Industrial Policies in the Developing Countries of East Asia*, World Bank Discussion Paper no. 27 (Washington, D.C., 1988); internal reports of the World Bank; and World Bank, IMF, and UNCTAD data.

in the latter half of the 1970s had far-reaching effects (see box 3-2). Argentina's reversal of commercial policy reform (among other things) seems to have hurt export performance. In the remaining countries, contributions to improved performance came from both exchange rate and commercial policy reforms. Of course, there are also many examples of little policy change or of policy reversals, especially in the group of forty-seven countries that did not receive trade adjustment loans. Within the group of forty countries that did receive loans, policy reversals occurred in some cases (for example, Guyana, Yugoslavia, and Zambia), but partial reform was more common, as in the case of Côte d'Ivoire (see box 3-3).

Policy Implications

Trade policy reforms of the 1980s have relied on all three instruments to encourage export growth—policies to achieve real devaluation, direct reduction of the bias against exports (removal of export restrictions and of restrictions on imported inputs used in export production), and a lowering of the protection provided to import substitutes. In most instances, a real devaluation raises equiproportionately the prices of exportables and importables (except for those importables for which quantitative restrictions are binding). Unused resources or resources from nontradable sectors then flow to all tradable sectors. Since a real devaluation both encourages exports and discourages imports, it can induce a reduction in the trade deficit (or produce a surplus) quickly.[23] To sustain the devaluation in real terms, however, requires that less expansionary fiscal and monetary policies be followed domestically and that imports be liberalized.

Introducing direct export incentives (which have included nonsubsidy measures such as temporary admissions and duty drawbacks for exporters and, less commonly, direct subsidies) without reducing import protection or depreciating the real exchange rate can lead to increased export growth and generate a trade surplus (or reduce a deficit). (In practice, however, subsidies have often been ineffective and costly; see chapter 6.) Like devaluation, direct export incentives can imply a squeeze on nontradables. They also can require a high savings rate, that is, a reduction in current consumption. Lowering import protection combined with a devaluation releases resources from inefficient protected sectors to exportables, nontradables, and the remaining efficient import-substituting sectors. The effect on exports, however, is indirect and perhaps not as immediate as with direct export measures. With this approach, however, a given increase in exports is accompanied by a smaller decline in real wages and smaller distortions in consumption, together with greater efficiency increases than are possible under the previous strategy.

Box 3-1. *Trade Policy Reform and Performance in Mexico*

Mexico's quantitative restrictions covered 60 percent of imports in 1981 and increased to 100 percent in 1982 in response to a balance of payments crisis. By 1980, effective protection had reached 128 percent for capital goods and consumer durables, 43 percent for intermediates, 9 percent for nondurable consumer goods, and 18 percent for the agriculture sector. Export controls were also pervasive, covering 797 of 3,026 export positions in 1976. There was a mild liberalization between 1976 and 1980 and export controls were reduced to 578 positions, but they continued to cover 85 percent of nonoil exports. A cross-sectoral analysis found that total factor productivity growth for each sector between 1972 and 1982 was strongly and negatively correlated with the fraction of the sector covered by quantitative restrictions.

Starting with a devaluation in 1982 and some tentative steps to free more products from export controls and to grant exporters access to credit and duty-free imported inputs, Mexico began to adopt trade policy reforms. In 1983, exporters in the domestic tariff area were allowed temporary admissions of inputs required for the production of exports. In mid-1985, quantitative restrictions on imports were removed from products representing about 45 percent of tradable production. By April 1988, quantitative restrictions covered 23 percent of such production. Tariffs, after being raised slightly to cushion the decline in protection resulting from the reduction in quantitative restrictions, were gradually decreased from an average of 23.5 percent (in mid-1985) to 11 percent (in April 1988), with a consequent reduction in dispersion. Mexico applied to join the GATT, and formally did so in August 1988.

In 1983 and 1984, manufactures exports showed strong growth in response to the devaluation of 1982 and a domestic recession brought about by the

The relative emphasis that is given to each instrument of reform should reflect conditions in each country at the outset of reform. Korea had a reasonably appropriate exchange rate during its trade reforms of the 1980s, while most of the other trade adjustment loan countries had a substantially overvalued exchange rate. Impediments to exports and to imports needed for export production were also widespread in many countries. The majority of countries depreciated the exchange rate and reduced export restrictions significantly. Import liberalization was in general milder. The emphasis on exchange rate and direct export reform was justified, given the strong response of exports to direct incentives and the importance of insulating exporters from the effects of import duties as tariff reform is initiated (see chapter 7). Additional benefit from further action on export policy (but not import policy) is less likely the more the restrictions in the export re-

need to stabilize the economy. The devaluation was not sustained in real terms, however, and exports fell in 1985 as the real exchange rate appreciated. Between mid-1985 and the end of 1987, the exchange rate was essentially floated, and it depreciated significantly. This depreciation, together with the import reforms, encouraged exports, which grew strongly in 1986 and 1987. One study of the effect on private sector exports since 1980 of exchange rate movements and import liberalization concluded that for every 10 percent overvaluation of the real exchange rate relative to a hypothetical equilibrium, exports fell by about 11 percent (with a lag of four quarters) and for every 10 percent increase in quantitative restriction coverage, exports declined by about 6 percent (with a lag of two quarters).[1]

Although Mexico now has one of the least protective commercial policies among developing countries, sustained results will also depend on evolution of the real exchange rate and macroeconomic stability. The government has made a tremendous effort to stabilize the economy (including a very large reduction in expenditures and the fiscal deficit), and the program appears to be succeeding. Other ongoing reforms of the regulatory structure will also support the trade policy reforms.

1. A. Ten Kate, "Trade Liberalization in Mexico since July 1985: Some Estimates of Its Economic Impact," background study for "Mexico: Trade Policy Reform and Economic Adjustment," Trade, Finance, and Industry Operations Division, Latin America and the Caribbean Country Department II, World Bank (Washington, D.C., 1988).

gime are corrected, which implies that a shift in emphasis toward import policy reform would be appropriate in many countries.

Effects of Trade Policy Reform on Employment

Trade policy reform changes relative incentives: it improves the profitability of exportable production and reduces the incentives for import substitution and, in most cases, for the production of nontradables. Because labor intensity differs among these sectors, trade liberalization is not likely to be neutral with respect to employment. Studies using input/output tables for several countries have shown that in most cases production of exportable commodities is the most labor-intensive, followed by production of nontradables and then by production of import substitutes. For this reason, trade liberalization and exchange rate ad-

Box 3-2.   *Trade Liberalization and Manufacturing in Chile*

From 1940 to 1970, Chile pursued an import-substitution policy based on increasing intervention in commodity and factor markets. Interventions and protectionism increased during 1970–73, followed by rapid trade liberalization between September 1973 and June 1979. In September 1973 ad valorem tariff rates ranged from 0 percent to 750 percent, with half the tariffs above 80 percent. Import prohibitions affected 187 tariff positions as defined by the Brussels Tariff Nomenclature. For 2,872 tariff positions, there was a deposit requirement of 10,000 percent of the CIF import value, due ninety days before importing. By August 1975, the maximum tariff rate had been reduced to 105 percent and the average to 65 percent. Most redundant protection had been eliminated, and within the next four years a uniform tariff of 10 percent was achieved (except for certain motor vehicles). All other restrictions on imports and incentives to export were eliminated, reducing the level of protection and tariff dispersion (see table). Between 1979 and 1982, average protection was 10 percent. Although serious macroeconomic imbalances and external shocks led to a major recession during 1982–84, trade reforms were not significantly rolled back. By 1988, average protection was down to 15 percent after having risen briefly to 35 percent. Since 1977, Chile has had virtually no quantitative restrictions. Chile is now among the countries with the lowest and most uniform rates of protection in the world.

Effective Protection in Chile, 1967, 1974, and 1979
(simple averages, in percent)

Sector	Effective protection		
	1967	1974	1979
Consumer goods	138.8	189.7	13.2
Intermediate goods	172.9	139.6	14.0
Machinery and transport equipment	265.3	96.0	13.0
Equally weighted arithmetic mean	176.7	151.4	13.6
Standard deviation	279.0	60.4	1.7
Variability coefficient	1.57	0.40	0.12
Range	1,163.0	216.0	6.0

The share of foreign trade in GDP has fluctuated greatly in Chile during the century:

1929	1951–55	1965–70	1971–73	1980–82	1985–87
66.3 percent	21.7 percent	24.0 percent	20.3 percent	32.6 percent	47.6 percent

As a result of changing trade policies since the mid-1970s, the share of trade in GDP has increased by more than 50 percent over levels during the 1960s and early 1970s. Econometric estimates of total factor productivity (TFP) growth for the manufacturing sector indicate that average annual TFP growth was -0.61 percent during 1960–70 and 2.5 percent during 1977–81.[1] Economywide gains induced by the reforms are estimated to have contributed up to 2.3 percentage points of GDP a year during 1977–81, when growth was high despite relatively low investment and employment levels.[2] At the same time, adjustment to trade liberalization is estimated to have contributed about 5 percent to unemployment during the transition.[3]

Trade reforms have also resulted in changes in concentration and profitability, as shown by the following price-cost margins and concentration ratios derived from Chile's 1967 and 1979 manufacturing census:[4]

	Nominal protection	*Price-cost margin*	*Four-firm concentration ratio*	
			Ratio	*Number of establishments*
1967	74 percent	48 percent	49 percent	7,384
1979	12 percent	32 percent	62 percent	5,010

The change in economic regime (including trade liberalization) increased concentration but reduced profitability, suggesting both that economies of scale were realized as a result of trade liberalization and that oligopolistic interaction diminished. Comparisons of economies of scale for manufacturing between 1967 and 1979 indicate a greater exploitation of economies of scale in 1979 than in 1967. The evidence also suggests that the exploitation of economies of scale was greatest for sectors that experienced the largest reduction in effective protection between 1967 and 1979.[5] The reduction in profitability is also consistent with an increase in the elasticity of demand facing domestic firms. Further econometric evidence supports the "import-discipline" hypothesis that after the role of other factors is taken into account, sectors that had the highest import-penetration ratios between 1967 and 1979 also showed the largest decline in price-cost margins.

---

1. Barbara Mierau, "Trade Regimes and Productivity Performance: The Case of the Chilean Manufacturing Sector" (paper presented at the Conference on Current Issues in Productivity, Rutgers University, Graduate School of Management, Newark, New Jersey, December 9, 1987).

2. Timothy Condon, Vittorio Corbo, and Jaime de Melo, "Productivity Growth, External Shocks, and Capital Inflows in Chile during 1977–81: A General Equilibrium Analysis," *Journal of Policy Modelling* 7 (Fall 1987):379–405.

3. Sebastian Edwards and Alejandra Cox-Edwards, *Monetarism and Liberalization: The Chilean Experiment* (Cambridge, Mass.: Ballinger Publishing Co., 1987).

4. Price-cost margin = sales price minus variable cost as a percentage of variable costs. Data shown are from Jaime de Melo and Shujiro Urata, "The Influence of Increased Foreign Competition on Industrial Concentration and Profitability," *International Journal of Industrial Organization* 4 (September 1986):287–304.

5. James Tybout, Vittorio Corbo, and Jaime de Melo, "The Effects of Trade Reforms on Scale and Technical Efficiency: New Evidence from Chile," Trade Policy Division, Country Economics Department, World Bank (Washington, D.C., 1988).

Box 3-3. *Trade Policy in Côte d'Ivoire*

In the second half of the 1970s and in the early 1980s, Côte d'Ivoire introduced quantitative restrictions and arbitrary reference prices for calculating tariffs for a wide range of imports competitive with domestic manufactures. During the boom years in the second half of the 1970s, Côte d'Ivoire benefited from the surge in world coffee and cocoa prices. The increases in revenue, most of which were captured by the government, were used to promote investment and expand public spending and infrastructure. A sharp decline in world coffee and cocoa prices, unmatched by a cutback in government spending, led to severe macroeconomic imbalances that forced the government to adopt an austerity program in 1982, which was followed by trade reform in mid-1984. Both programs were supported by structural adjustment loans from the World Bank.

The trade reform was extended in 1986 and early 1987. The reform removed quantitative restrictions and reference prices, rationalized the tariff structure so as to give approximately the same effective protection to all manufacturing activities, and introduced temporary tariff surcharges, which declined over a five-year period, to allow firms previously protected by nontariff measures time to adjust. Côte d'Ivoire's nominal exchange rate is fixed in relation to the French franc at a rate that is the same for a number of franc-zone African countries. Since it was estimated to be considerably overvalued in real terms and could not be devalued, the reform simulated a partial devaluation by setting tariffs at higher levels than would otherwise have been selected and by introducing an export subsidy scheme for manufactured and some primary exports.

The use of tariffs and export subsidies proved a poor substitute for devaluation, which could have given the same incentives to import substitution and export production with much lower tariffs and lower or no export subsidies. First, the system was inflexible and unable to handle the further substantial reduction in the competitiveness of Ivoirien industry that resulted from the appreciation of the French franc against the U.S. dollar and many other currencies during 1985–88. In 1987 an attempt was made to partially offset this appreciation with tariff increases, but the way it was done undermined some of the previous rationalization of the tariff structure and reduced incentives for exports. Second, the reforms depended on a competent and honest customs administration, but a declining trend in administrative capacity, which was already pronounced in the 1970s, continued in the 1980s. This led to large-scale underinvoicing and increased smuggling and contributed to delays and corruption in managing the export subsidy scheme. Third, the concept of the export subsidy as a substitute for devaluation was never fully understood or accepted by the government. As a result of this and a continuing fiscal deficit, the first export subsidy payments were delayed until mid-1988, and payments were suspended in 1989. Even though the scheme allowed some large firms to maintain their exports in the face of the appreciating exchange rate, many smaller exporters were never paid, and transaction and other lobbying costs were reported to be substantial. Finally, the inability to curtail underinvoicing directly was given as a reason for the reintroduction of reference prices and some quantitative import restrictions by 1989.

Côte d'Ivoire's experience underlines the problems faced to one degree or another by most of the franc-zone countries. A prerequisite for realizing the potential advantages of the monetary arrangement with France is the imposition of a degree of fiscal discipline. In the case of Côte d'Ivoire, loss of fiscal discipline was triggered by the boom in 1975–77 in the prices of coffee and cocoa, which account for 50 percent of export earnings. Public expenditure as a share of GDP increased sharply in response to the boom and continued to increase long after the boom had ended, rising from about 15 percent in 1977 to about 26 percent in 1983.[1] The resulting fiscal deficit rose from about 3 percent of GDP in 1977 to a high of 13 percent in 1982. This was financed by foreign aid flows and increased public debt. At the same time, the French franc was depreciating and some neighboring trading partners were devaluing. The net result was an appreciation of Côte d'Ivoire's real exchange rate and a severe erosion of the competitiveness of the manufacturing sector. Appreciation of the French franc reinforced this effect.

This experience offers two major lessons. First, trying to maintain a fixed exchange rate while following expansionary macroeconomic policies will create external imbalances. Second, while in theory commercial policy can be used to substitute for a nominal devaluation, in practice any serious reform of commercial policy is difficult to carry out successfully, especially when tariff evasion is a problem.[2] In these countries, the only realistic solutions may be either abandonment of the fixed exchange rate or a one-time devaluation to restore competitiveness, followed by an improved mechanism to ensure non-expansionary fiscal policy in the future. Devaluation, of course, would carry its own costs, not the least of which may be the negative impact on the financial system, which in Côte d'Ivoire has substantial French franc–dominated liabilities. The alternative means of achieving a real devaluation—maintaining a lower inflation rate than the country's trading partners—would be a relatively long and risky process.

1. See Shantayanan Devarajan and Jaime de Melo, "Adjustment with a Fixed Exchange Rate: Cameroon, Côte d'Ivoire, and Senegal," *World Bank Economic Review* 1 (May 1987):447–87.

2. See S. A. O'Connell, "Uniform Trade Taxes, Devaluation, and the Real Exchange Rate," Policy, Planning, and Research Working Paper no. 185, Country Economics Department, World Bank (Washington, D.C., 1989).

Source: Background note by Ann Harrison and Gary Pursell, Trade Policy Division, Country Economics Department, World Bank.

justment packages may be expected to have a beneficial effect on employment in the long term.

Evidence is available that countries that have followed outward-oriented policies generally have a better record on employment creation and unemployment rates (in the non-resource-intensive sectors) in the long term than those that have adopted import-substitution strategies.[24] This is consistent with the evidence that export production is in general more labor-intensive than production in the rest of the economy. Although these findings indicate the expected positive long-term effects on employment of reform after the adjustment process is completed, they do not provide insights into the short-run adjustment process that takes place immediately after trade policy reform is introduced.

In the short term, the decreased incentives to import substitution and possibly to nontradable sectors that are associated with trade liberalization could lead to a decrease in employment in those sectors. This decrease may not be immediately offset by an expansion of employment in the export sector. Furthermore, delays in increasing labor absorption may occur in the export sector because of the time lag before new investments mature, slow adjustments in labor skills to new requirements, and restrictions on labor mobility.

Authors of individual country studies in the study by Papageorgiou, Michaely, and Choksi generally concluded that no association can be established in individual countries between trade liberalization and short-run unemployment in the manufacturing sector.[25] In the aggregate as well, no clear link has been shown between changes in unemployment and trade reform episodes. In eight of the eighteen cases shown in table 3-8, the rate of unemployment decreased, although in one case the progress in the last year of reform was reversed in the next year. In the remaining ten cases, the rate of unemployment increased following reform. Most reform episodes, however, took place simultaneously with other ongoing changes in the economy (macroeconomic adjustment, changes in external terms of trade), which makes it difficult to attribute changes in unemployment to trade reform itself. In general, where economic growth was robust, unemployment decreased with reform. Where aggregate unemployment increased, country analyses made for this study link the increase to factors that caused a downturn in growth, rather than to trade liberalization.

Although hard evidence is lacking, anecdotal evidence suggests that trade reform creates unemployment in the short term in some countries (see also boxes 3-2 and 3-3). Observers also allude to negative effects on income in the short term from commercial policy reform and devaluation. A study of four Latin American countries concluded that in the case of a real exchange rate devaluation, the real wages of un-

Table 3-8. *Unemployment during Selected Episodes of Trade Liberalization*

Liberalization episode[a]	Episode period	Percentage of labor force unemployed			
		1 year before episode	Average during episode	Last year of episode	1 year after episode
Argentina 1	1967–70	5.6	5.1	4.9	n.a.
Chile 2	1974–81	4.8	13.6	23.7	22.5
Colombia 1	1964–66	7.9	8.7	10.1	12.2
Colombia 2	1968–82	8.8	10.0	9.4	9.4
Israel 1	1952–55	9.1	8.8	7.4	7.8
Israel 2	1962–68	3.6	5.4	6.1	4.5
Israel 3	1969–77	6.1	3.4	3.9	n.a.
Korea 1	1965–67	9.9	7.0	6.3	5.2
Korea 2	1978–79	4.1	3.5	3.8	5.3
New Zealand 3	1982–84	3.7	4.8	4.9	n.a.
Peru	1979–80	7.1	6.9	6.8	7.0
Philippines 1	1960–65	6.3	8.0	8.2	9.4
Philippines 2	1970–74	6.9	6.5	4.7	5.0
Singapore	1968–73	8.1	6.2	4.8	4.7
Spain 2	1970–74	1.1	2.1	2.9	3.9
Spain 3	1977–80	5.3	9.1	11.5	14.4
Turkey 2	1980–84	9.4	11.7	12.7	n.a.
Yugoslavia	1965–67	5.6	6.6	7.1	8.0

n.a. = Not available.
a. For countries with more than one episode, number denotes the order in the series.
Source: Papageorgiou, Michaely, and Choksi, *Liberalizing Foreign Trade.*

skilled workers absorbed most of the required adjustment while the wages of skilled labor (mostly in the formal sector) decreased by substantially less.[26] Real wages in large manufacturing firms appeared to be much more downwardly rigid than the real wages of nonprofessional self-employed workers (usually in the informal sector). The burden of the short-run wage adjustment therefore fell on the poorer segments of the labor force, although the effect may have been an increase in employment.

A recent OECD study examined the effect of external trade policy reform on income distribution.[27] The empirical side of the study relied on the experience with reform in Costa Rica, Malawi, Malaysia, Morocco, Peru, and Taiwan. By and large, the study found that the development of labor-intensive export industries that results from reform has, in line with theory, a favorable effect on employment generation. Exceptions include export crops originating on large plantations. Inward-oriented growth strategies and protectionism can increase inequality, while outward-oriented strategies—particularly those involving export diversification—can reduce it.

Constraints to a Stronger Supply Response

To estimate the supply response to trade policy reform accurately is not easy. For one thing, there can be a negative bias in the estimates of changes in the growth rates of reformers. When GDP is valued in constant prereform prices, tradables, which are expected to expand the most, are undervalued because the prices at which their output is valued are artificially low. Thus GDP growth between pre- and postreform periods can be underestimated for reformers. Another problem is that other factors that affect this response are never constant during reforms.

The evidence of thirty reform episodes in the study by Papageorgiou, Michaely, and Choksi, most of which took place before 1980, shows that the average growth rate of GDP increased from 4.45 percent for the three-year period before the reform to 5.45 percent one year after and declined slightly to 5.35 percent during the three-year period after. The increase was greater for the episodes involving the strongest reforms. (The judgment on the strength of reform is subjective.) According to tables 3-1 and 3-6, trade policy loan recipients improved GDP growth relative to their own preloan growth rates, as well as relative to the nonrecipients as a group or to specific comparable countries. But table 3-6 also shows that almost half the recipients did not improve in terms of relative growth rates. There is considerable variation across countries in the supply response. In many countries, it has been weaker than expected.

Several constraints to an adequate supply response can be identified.[28] Some of these relate to the credibility of the reforms. Reforms that are not expected to last will not inspire entrepreneurs to make the investments needed to expand production in newly profitable sectors. To be credible, trade policy reforms must be consistent with fiscal and monetary policy (see chapter 5). Credibility is also enhanced if the reform program is launched with strong steps and clear public commitment by the government (see chapter 4).

Domestic regulatory policies can also inhibit the supply response (see chapter 7). Price controls or laws governing wages keep firms from seeing the true social value of inputs and outputs and responding accordingly. An adequate supply response requires that labor as well as capital move from some sectors to others, and laws that make it hard to hire or fire workers or declare bankruptcy interfere with this process. Sometimes, regulations governing the transport sector increase the costs of shipping goods to and from the border and thereby discourage investment in the tradables sector. Foreign direct investment can play an important role in some countries, so laws that discourage it may reduce the supply response (see chapters 6 and 8).

Public sector policies in a number of countries are not supportive of rapid adjustment to a changed incentive structure (see chapter 7). In centrally planned economies, the central allocation mechanism is insufficiently flexible in reallocating resources (see box 2-2 in chapter 2). Parastatal monopolies or market domination, especially in agricultural markets, sometimes prevent the effects of devaluation from being passed on to export producers. In a number of countries, a poorly functioning or corrupt customs service imposes additional burdens on international trade. The cost and delays caused by requirements for excessive and nonstandardized documentation for imports and exports can be of equal or greater importance.

Insufficient attention to the institutional needs of exporters has often been a problem (see chapter 6). In particular, as long as tariffs or other restrictions are placed on imported inputs used by exporters, some mechanism must be introduced to allow exporters to import them free of duty. Inadequate infrastructure sometimes constrains a response to changed incentives (see chapter 7). This is true not only of physical infrastructure (highways, ports, railways), but also of educational infrastructure. This constraint is particularly severe in Sub-Saharan Africa.

Protectionism in international markets in recent years may have discouraged exports in some cases (see chapter 8). Although developed countries have low tariffs and generally represent promising markets for developing countries' manufactured exports (see chapter 6), in a few important products (for example, textiles and clothing) trade restrictions have prevented some countries from realizing their full potential for expanding supply.

Finally, a realistic assessment of the constraints to supply response should recognize that cultural patterns generated by past policies may not change overnight. Decades of policies inimical to the private sector, especially to merchants and traders, have left some countries with only a small number of experienced entrepreneurs. This problem is particularly manifest in several countries in Sub-Saharan Africa. As policies and incentives change, this nucleus of experienced entrepreneurs will grow, but this expansion involves a learning process and will take time. Meanwhile, the few entrepreneurs who have withstood the negative policies should be expected to realize a high financial return on their scarce talents. This will attract more participants to the private sector.

Summary and Conclusion

This chapter corroborates the positive association between exports and output growth found in previous studies. Tracing the influence of individual measures in the mix of policies behind superior export and GDP growth is more complex, however, because of the presence of a variety of potential causes. Both the longer-term experience and the adjustment episodes of the 1980s show a positive contribution to performance from trade policy and other structural reforms. Real exchange rate depreciation and reductions in antiexport bias are linked to improved performance in output and exports. In the context of adjustment lending, additional financing has been an important contributor to relative improvements, as have policy reforms. Trade adjustment loans are associated with a mild improvement in performance. This improvement is stronger when the focus is on recipients of early and intensive (three or more) loans. The improvement in performance is still stronger and statistically more significant when the comparison is between those judged to be trade policy reformers and those judged to be nonreformers, rather than simply between loan recipients and nonrecipients.

The evidence indicates gains from the combination of exchange rate depreciation and commercial policy reform. Generally, the positive effects on exports and growth resulting from a real devaluation with export reform would be expected to be more immediate than those from a real devaluation with import liberalization. At the same time, experience suggests that longer-term and sustained development of exports and output depends not only on export policies but also on import liberalization. While import liberalization is often expected to cause short-term unemployment, a nineteen-country study found no clear empirical evidence linking the two on aggregate.[29] There is evidence in another study, however, of an association between decreases in the real wages of low-income laborers and a real devaluation.[30]

Notes

1. Even when factors other than trade reform—such as external shocks, size of the bureaucracy, status of property rights—are incorporated in the analysis, the observed association between trade policy and economic outcome may still at least partly reflect some other, ignored considerations.

2. World Bank, *Adjustment Lending: An Evaluation of Ten Years of Experience,* Policy and Research Series no. 1 (Washington, D.C., 1989).

3. Output growth was higher not only because of the higher growth of exports (as a part of output), but also because of higher growth of other components of output as well. See Bela Balassa, "Development Strategies and Economic Performance," in Bela Balassa and associates, *Development Strategies in Semi-Industrial Economies* (Baltimore: Johns Hopkins University Press, 1982). On the robustness of the export-GDP association in low-income countries, see, for example, R. M. Kavoussi, "Export Expansion and Economic

Growth: Further Empirical Evidence," *Journal of Development Economics* 14 (1984):241–50; and Rati Ram, "Exports and Economic Growth: Some Additional Evidence," *Economic Development and Cultural Change* 32 (January 1985):415–25. The results are not as conclusive with respect to low-income countries.

4. Nor do they indicate whether causality runs in the opposite direction, as suggested, for instance, by Ronald Findlay, "Growth and Development in Trade Models," in Ronald Jones and Peter Kenen, eds., *Handbook of International Economics,* vol. 1 (Amsterdam: North-Holland, 1984). On causality tests, see W. S. Jung and P. J. Marshall, "Exports, Growth and Causality in Developing Countries," *Journal of Development Economics* 18 (1985):1–12. There is, of course, considerable controversy concerning causality tests.

5. For the 1973–78 period, Balassa shows that outward orientation is positively correlated with economic growth ("Exports, Policy Choices and Economic Growth in Developing Countries after the 1973 Oil Shock," *Journal of Development Economics* [May-June 1985]). These results are not subject to the two-way causality problem because they compare the effects on economic growth of export orientation, import substitution, and additional net external financing.

6. See, for example, J. D. Sachs, "Trade and Exchange Rate Policies in Growth-Oriented Adjustment Programs," Department of Economics, Harvard University (Cambridge, Mass., 1987).

7. J. N. Bhagwati, *Anatomy and Consequences of Exchange Control Regimes* (Cambridge, Mass.: Ballinger Publishing Co. for National Bureau of Economic Research, 1978).

8. A. O. Krueger, *Foreign Trade Regimes and Economic Development: Liberalization Attempts and Consequences* (Cambridge, Mass.: Ballinger Publishing Co. for National Bureau of Economic Research, 1978).

9. Hollis Chenery, Sherman Robinson, and Moshe Syrquin, *Industrialization and Growth: A Comparative Study* (New York: Oxford University Press, 1986).

10. P. M. Romer, "What Determines the Rate of Growth and Technological Change?" Policy, Planning, and Research Working Paper no. 279, Country Economics Department, World Bank (Washington, D.C., 1989).

11. Bela Balassa, "Incentive Policies and Agricultural Performance in Sub-Saharan Africa," Policy, Planning, and Research Working Paper no. 77, Development Economics Department, World Bank (Washington, D.C., 1988).

12. G. W. Scully, "The Political Economy of Free Trade and Protectionism" (paper prepared for the Liberty Fund conference on the Political Economy of Neo-mercantilism and Free Trade, Big Sky, Montana, June 9–11, 1988).

13. The index is from E. Leamer, "Measures of Openness," in Robert E. Baldwin, ed., *Trade Policy Issues and Empirical Analysis* (Chicago: University of Chicago Press for National Bureau of Economic Research, 1988). The policy analysis is presented in Sebastian Edwards, "Openness, Outward Orientation, Trade Liberalization, and Economic Performance in Developing Countries," Policy, Planning, and Research Working Paper no. 191, Country Economics Department, World Bank (Washington, D.C., 1989).

14. Ramon Lopez, "Trade Policy, Growth and Investment," Trade Policy Division, Country Economics Department, World Bank (Washington, D.C., 1989).

15. See World Bank, *World Development Report 1987* (New York: Oxford University Press, 1987), p. 80. Exact estimates of the implicit tax on exports from a 10 percent tax on imports ranged from 4.3 percent to 9.5 percent. See Kenneth W. Clements and L. A. Sjaastad, *How Protection Taxes Exporters,* Thames Essays no. 39 (London: Trade Policy Research Center, 1984); and David Greenaway and C. R. Milner, "'True Protection' Concepts and Their Role in Evaluating Trade Policies in LDCs," *Journal of Development Studies* 23 (January 1987):200–19.

16. Bernhard Heitger, "Import Protection and Export Performance— Their Impact on Economic Growth," *Weltwirtschaftliches Archiv* 123, no. 2 (1987):249–61.

17. Total imports rather than intermediate imported inputs are used because complete data are not available on the latter for the 1980s.

18. Nadav Halevi, "Trade Liberalization in Adjustment Lending" (World Bank background paper for this report [Washington, D.C., 1989]) provides a three-way classification of how much reform was proposed and a five-way classification of how much of the proposal seemed to have been carried out. The product of these two classifications gives an illustrative index of policy implementation.

19. See also Riccardo Faini and others, "Macro Performance under Adjustment Lending," Policy, Planning, and Research Working Paper no. 190, Country Economics Department, World Bank (Washington, D.C., 1988); Bela Balassa, "A Quantitative Appraisal of Adjustment Lending," Policy, Planning and Research Working Paper no. 79, Development Economics Department, World Bank (Washington, D.C., 1989). For the limitations of such comparisons, see Mohsin S. Khan, "The Macroeconomic Effects of Fund-Supported Adjustment Programs: An Empirical Assessment," IMF Working Paper (Washington, D.C.: IMF, 1988).

20. For most indicators, a positive change is an improvement. For four indicators—resource balance/GDP, inflation, external debt/exports, and debt service/exports—a positive change is a worsening (shown in the table by a minus sign). For the real exchange rate, a greater real depreciation between periods for recipients than that for comparators is an improvement.

21. The period varies for each country, depending on the date of its loan.

22. While in chapter 2 we used qualitative information to assess changes during 1980–87, here we restrict the analysis to specific subperiods for which quantitative estimates of policy changes are available. Thus the evidence in this subsection is not comprehensive and does not give precisely the same picture as the fuller discussion in chapter 2.

23. For evidence of the close relation between the real exchange rate and the trade balance, see A. C. Harberger, "Applications of Real Exchange Rate Analysis," *Contemporary Policy Issues* 7 (April 1989):1–25.

24. Krueger, *Foreign Trade Regimes.*

25. Demetris Papageorgiou, Michael Michaely, and Armeane Choksi, *Liberalizing Foreign Trade,* vol. 7, *Lessons of Experience in the Developing World* (Cambridge, Mass.: Basil Blackwell, forthcoming).

26. See R. E. Lopez and L. A. Riveros, "Wage Responsiveness and Labor Market Disequilibrium: Exploring the Components of Open Unemployment." Policy, Planning, and Research Working Paper no. 85, Country Economics Department, World Bank (Washington, D.C., 1988).

27. François Bourguignon and Christian Morrison, *External Trade and Income Distribution* (Paris: OECD, 1989).

28. These are closely related to the factors that contribute to the "enabling environment" for private sector development. See World Bank, *Developing the Private Sector: A Challenge for the World Bank Group* (Washington, D.C., 1989).

29. Papageorgiou, Michaely, and Choksi, *Liberalizing Foreign Trade.*

30. Lopez and Riveros, "Wage Responsiveness."

4

The Political Economy of Trade Policy Reform

At least since the time of Adam Smith, reformers have been trying to persuade governments to liberalize trade, but with only mixed success. Lake describes such an incident. "In May of 1930 more than a thousand members of the American Economic Association issued a petition urging Congress to vote down the tariff bill then pending in the conference committee and the president to veto the measure should it come to him for signature. One month later President Hoover signed the Smoot-Hawley tariff act into law."[1] Although trade is much freer among industrial countries today than it was fifty years ago, restrictions remain significant and have been increasing (see chapter 8). Despite pervasive distortions and an urgent need for reform in many developing countries, the resistance to trade reform has been considerable, and comprehensive reforms and unqualified successes have been few. A better understanding of what makes trade policy reform difficult should help reformers promote changes in this area more effectively.

Obstacles to Reform

None of the obstacles discussed in this chapter is new to trade policy analysts and reformers; yet most reformers rarely acknowledge the difficulty of implementing this kind of reform.[2] The traditional paradigm treats policy-making as if it were conducted by a single decisionmaker who controls certain instruments in order to maximize a social welfare function consisting of a few target variables such as growth in per capita income and its distribution among broad groups. The policymaker is presumed to have available a variety of policy instruments, adequate information about the external environment and the status of the target variables, and a correct model of the relationship between the instruments and the targets. From this point of view, opposition to reform must be the result of ideological aversion or simple misinformation and must be overcome by political will. Consequently, reformers are steered toward a narrow set of options based on attempts to convince a small group of policymakers of the technical soundness of a specific reform package.

In actuality, decision-making is the result of a complex political-economic process in which participants are guided by a variety of motives. Misinformation about the external environment, self-interest, ideological aversion to certain policies, and an inadequate understanding of the relationship between policies and outcomes may distort the thinking of most or all of the participants. Trade reform would be difficult, however, even if none of these conditions prevailed.

Asymmetries between Winners and Losers

The main difficulty of trade reform is the asymmetry in the incentives for political action between those who benefit from reform and those who suffer. The potential gains from reform are large in the aggregate, but are often spread over many (sometimes unidentifiable) beneficiaries. Thus, the potential gains to each one are often relatively small, while the costs of organizing such a large group to exert political pressure are high. Potential losses from trade reform tend to be concentrated on smaller, more cohesive groups, making the incentives for political action by each individual higher and the costs of organizing them lower. This is easiest to see in a proposal to remove or reduce protection for producers of an import substitute. The potentially large benefits of such an action are diffused over the myriad consumers of the product. The benefit to any one consumer may be so small that it is not worth that consumer's while to attempt to influence the political decision. The loss to each producer, however, may be substantial, sometimes representing the difference between wealth and bankruptcy. Producers, therefore, will have a strong incentive to try to block liberalization.

Peru provides a good example of this asymmetry at work. As the process of tariff reductions reached its peak in 1980, criticism mounted in the press. By a ratio of 2 to 1, articles by opponents of trade reform, mainly organized groups and representatives of the largest firms in Peru, outnumbered articles by supporters of reform, written mainly by government officials.[3] A recognition of this asymmetry can help to mobilize support for reform. For example, in Chile reformers actively bolstered the political voice of those who stood to gain and increased their ranks. The traditionally protectionist manufacturers' association was transformed by an influx of diversified exporters, who were willing to exert political pressure to keep the trade regime outward-oriented. Thus, when Chile's tariff was raised from 10 percent to 35 percent in the early 1980s, the association was among the critical voices arguing (with eventual success) that it should be reduced. When producers are organized into large umbrella organizations, many of the benefits from trade reform will accrue within the group, thereby deflecting it from opposition. This is the case with industrial producers in Germany, which is the least protectionist (with regard to manufacturing) of the nations of the European Communities (EC).[4]

In most developing countries, particularly in Sub-Saharan Africa, trade reform has a prorural bias; protection has turned the internal terms of trade against agriculture, and reform would reduce this bias. But the poverty and isolation of the farmers who would benefit from reform make it difficult for their interests to be organized.[5] Large numbers of cocoa and other farmers in Ghana have benefited from devaluation and the marketing board's loss of control over cocoa prices, but this has not been transformed into greater political support for the government. (Yet, resentment over higher food prices among a smaller number of more easily organized urban dwellers—especially students, who live in proximity to each other and have time to spare—makes itself keenly felt, as evidenced in Ghana and Nigeria). Large landowners, who might serve as spokesmen for agricultural interests, often have conflicting interests because they tend disproportionately to be recipients of subsidized inputs.[6]

Another factor that makes it difficult to organize many small potential winners into a reform coalition is that free riding is more pervasive in large, amorphous groups than in smaller, well-defined ones. Individual consumers and exporters may recognize that they will benefit from trade reform and may wish the reformers well, but they also know that their support alone is unlikely to make much difference. They will benefit from the reformers' success even if they have not contributed to it.

Another source of asymmetry is that the costs may be felt immediately whereas the benefits may not come for some time. This is especially true if benefits from reform depend on the response of investments that will take years to carry out and still more years to begin to bear visible fruit. The bus rider whose transportation costs double or the urban bread consumer whose food outlays skyrocket because of the effect of devaluation on imported petroleum or wheat may discount heavily the possibility of one day earning high wages in an export firm.

Winners, moreover, may not be identifiable at the early stages of reform. In Colombia, for example, one of the principal beneficiaries of the trade and exchange rate reforms in the late 1960s and early 1970s has been exporters of cut flowers and all those related to the industry. Yet none of these beneficiaries could have supported the reforms when the reform process began in 1968 because the activity, which had exports worth US$120 million in 1982, virtually did not exist then. No one had predicted exports of flowers. Entrepreneurs may take advantage of reforms in ways that are entirely unpredictable.

The intellectual climate in many countries creates another asymmetry. Pessimism about the effects of trade reform on exports suggests that there can be no winners from it. And concern about rising protectionism in industrial countries reinforces this view. Such pessimism also receives support from the "illusion of inefficiency." When a trade regime is protectionist and the currency is highly overvalued, almost all producers or potential producers will conclude that they are hopelessly noncompetitive in the international market. At the exchange rate prevailing under a highly distorted trade regime, virtually every tradable activity requires either protection or export subsidies to survive. Little wonder trade liberalization in such an environment has scant popular support.

A still more subtle problem is that exporters often do not see the benefits that will accrue to them from liberalization of imports policy. When they do, they often see only a part of those benefits: obtaining inputs at international prices. They are less likely to make the macroeconomic connection between the liberalization and the implied devaluation of the sustainable equilibrium real exchange rate, which would shift the relation between the price of their output and their other costs.[7] This lack of understanding means that exporters may cease to be a part of the reform coalition once they have obtained some simple reforms (a reasonably efficient duty drawback or bonded warehouse scheme, for example). This was the case in Colombia in the 1970s. The exporters association pushed for increased credit and insurance subsidies, and the powerful Federation of Coffee Growers supported subsidized inputs and opposed overt taxation of coffee exports.[8] Neither attempted to obtain a more depreciated real exchange rate or lower protection of manufacturing.

Government as the Subject of Reform

The difficulties discussed so far are those created by the interplay of extragovernmental interests and policy-making. The government, however, is not a passive player pushed around by other interest groups. Government and government officials may be directly affected by trade reform. State-owned enterprises are often among those most threatened by competition from imports. In Chile in 1976, for example, when trade liberalization was fairly advanced, tariffs remained exceptionally high on imports of steel products that were also produced by the state-owned steel plant. Trade reform in Argentina has seldom dared attack the high-cost steel produced by the plant owned by the armed forces. Bangladesh sugar imports were tightly regulated to preserve the high-cost production of sugar in government-owned mills, even when the government had to subsidize the distribution of sugar. In Peru, the first reversals of the 1980 attempt at trade reform involved reprotecting the outputs of state-owned enterprises.[9]

Trade reform is also threatening to the officials who administer trade restrictions. Even in the least corrupt system, trade reform means less importance and smaller budgets for trade regulators, if not outright elimination of their powers. In most cases, reform also means less opportunity for officials to make discretionary decisions, which can be traded for money and favors. The officials involved, of course, have good access to decisionmakers (and sometimes are themselves the decisionmakers), and most can be expected to oppose reform. In Indonesia, for example, corruption in the customs administration was so extensive that the government was forced to transfer the entire staff to other kinds of work and contract with a foreign firm to provide customs services.[10] Colombia provides another vivid but not atypical example. A proposal was made to raise tariffs on (noncompeting) automobile kits for assembly, with the aim of reducing effective protection on the final good and raising revenue. The proposal was defeated after vigorous opposition by the government body holding shares in the automobile assembly firm and the head of a trade regulatory body who had ties to the firm.[11]

Theory and experience have identified the kinds of institutions that are more or less likely to favor reforms. In part these differences are explained by the same kinds of asymmetry that explain the behavior of private interests. A government agency that regulates or promotes a specific sector tends to identify with that sector. Its budget and prestige rise and fall with the standing of its clients. Like its clients, such an agency will oppose trade reforms with general benefits but with costs specific to existing firms in its sector. This is especially the case if the agency also has a role in administering existing trade policy, as is usual with respect to quantitative restrictions. Thus, ministries of industry or commerce have often opposed reform. Rubio, Rodriguez, and Blum, referring to the situation in Mexico before 1988, note that "the Bank of Mexico—concerned with inflationary pressures and foreign exchange scarcity—exerts pressure to liberalize foreign trade, while the Ministry of Commerce—responsible for industry, . . . makes every effort to avoid hurting its constituents."[12] (This is no longer the case with the Ministry of Commerce; see below.) In Sri Lanka in 1984–85, the Ministry of Industry was able to derail tariff reforms affecting state enterprises. In the United States in 1979, when protectionists wanted to make it easier to prove dumping, they succeeded in shifting this decision-making function from the Department of the Treasury to the Department of Commerce.

The special-interest agency par excellence is, of course, the legislature, whose members represent specific, local interests. The post–World War II liberalization of trade policy in the United States would have been impossible without the shift in the locus of tariff-making from the Congress to the president permitted by the 1934 Reciprocal Trade Act. By the same token, increased congressional involvement in U.S. trade policy in recent years has been associated with increasing protectionism. So strong is this difference of perspective that politicians often change opinions as they change branches of government. Lake has remarked that "between 1890, when he chaired the House Ways and Means Committee [the tariff-writing committee] and 1897, when he accepted the presidency, [William H.] McKinley was transformed from an ardent protectionist . . . into the nation's strongest advocate of export expansion and reciprocity."[13] In most developing countries, trade policy is in the domain of the executive, but the legislature may become a focus of opposition to reform.

General-interest agencies, by contrast, have little to lose from the discomfort of the firms and sectors harmed by trade reform and may expect to benefit from the aggregate improvement reform may bring. Thus ministries of finance and economy and central banks are generally more sympathetic to trade reform than are ministries of commerce and industry. Because of cross-cutting pressures, ministries of agriculture often do not support trade reform even when agriculture as a whole is likely to benefit. Its constituents may see visible costs such as higher prices for fertilizers and imported machinery (whose prices are raised along with those of other inputs), while the effect on output prices is likely to be more diffuse. Ministries of planning or development are pulled in different directions. Although they are general-interest agencies and may not be closely identified with the losing sectors, they may be the repository of the regime's defenders of illiberal policies.

In some regimes (the Philippines under Marcos and Nicaragua under Somoza were typical cases), trade policy is subordinated to considerations of income distribution (such as handouts to the personal estate, family, and friends of the chief of state). In other countries, illiberal trade regimes are an important source of rents that can be distributed to buy political support for the regime.

Finally, most governments seek to prevent changes in the existing income distribution, whatever it may be. One explanation given for the prevalence of entrenched import-substituting trade policies in Latin America is an unwillingness to see the loss of the local manufacturing that had been stimulated by the massive decline in the terms of trade for agriculture during the Great Depression and by the unavailability of imports during World War II. Trade policy protected these sectors even though the workers and owners of manufacturing firms had incomes far above the national averages. The English Corn Laws were the result of pressure from agricultural interests for protection from the renewal of grain imports from the Continent, which had been interrupted by the Napoleonic Wars.[14] In the United States, voluntary export restraints were negotiated for automobiles and steel, even when auto and steel workers were among the highest-paid industrial workers.

Interests, Institutions, and Ideology

Reformers find they must deal simultaneously with a mutually reinforcing set of interests, institutions, and ideology. With enough time, any one of these factors will create the other two. Protection originally imposed to satisfy the political demand of some interest group will be justified by an assertion of the special importance of that group's activity. Powerful vested interests can develop around activities promoted initially for noneconomic reasons. For example, quantitative control of imports came to India as a measure designed to free foreign exchange for the war effort. The Iron and Steel Controller, the Textile Commissioner, and the Directorate of Technical Development set up at that time still exist, and the last "is the most important controller of imports and exports for large-scale industry."[15] Specialized institutions are also required to administer, adjust, and expand protection. These institutions will themselves create a justification for their existence and a need for the protection they administer.

Reformers must bear in mind that an existing structure of trade policy is the result of a political equilibrium. Favor to one group and harm to another is unlikely to be wholly accidental. Protection of manufacturing has been adopted in many parts of Latin America as a way of undermining the political power of landowning oligarchies. In such a political economy, protectionism may be advanced by modernizing elites regardless of the economic costs it imposes. In Africa, trade liberalization may be resisted, at least in the short run, because nonindigenous traders or minority ethnic groups are seen as its chief beneficiaries. Freer trade may also be associated with a return to a "colonial" economic structure (although colonial governments did not allow their colonies to trade freely) and, in the popular mercantilist view, importing is thought to benefit foreigners. In Korea, for example, opposition to liberalization results from an alliance among small industrialists and farm interests likely to be materially harmed by freer imports and "traditionalist intellectual circles which tend to view market liberalization and the resulting heightened interdependence with the rest of the world as a loss of national independence and cultural identity."[16]

Implications for Reformers

Long periods of economic stability make trade reform difficult. Decisionmakers see little need for change. If illiberal policies have existed for long periods, substantial investment will have taken place based on those policies. Trade reform that would impose capital losses will be vigorously opposed. Vested interests will have developed good contacts with policymakers and will probably have a well-articulated justification for the privileges they enjoy. Good macroeconomic performance in India and Colombia, for example, has enabled these countries to avoid crises, notwithstanding their highly restrictive trade policies. So far, neither country has instituted major trade policy reform. Each has strong institutions that administer the policies and a tight-knit structure of import-substituting firms and trade associations that support the status quo. Even a large decline in per capita income, as in Zambia, may not favor dramatic reform if the regime's political structures and client-patron relationships remain intact.[17]

Successful reform, therefore, often occurs when there is a sharply demarcated change in regime. A transition from a civilian to a military government (Pakistan in 1959, Chile in 1974), or vice versa (Argentina in 1976, Spain in 1977), is propitious for an attempt at trade reform, as is an overwhelming electoral victory of one party over another (Jamaica in 1980, Sri Lanka in 1977). The lowest tariff levels in the United States between the Civil War and the aftermath of World War II—the Underwood tariff of 1913—were the work of the self-consciously reformist Wilson administration, which was willing to punish the trusts through greater import competition. The reciprocal Trade Agreements Act, which set the stage for future tariff reforms, was enacted by the newly elected Roosevelt administration in response to the failure of the Smoot-Hawley tariff of 1930 and its association with the intensification of the Depression.

Crisis and Change

Reforms can sometimes be easier to implement in a time of external crisis. A crisis undermines the justification for the existing policy and can shred the coalition that supported it. Even severe import and foreign exchange licensing could not prevent a foreign exchange crisis in Nigeria in 1986, for example, and the failure of these instruments destroyed support for them. When imports virtually ceased, even previous beneficiaries of the licensing system became losers, and a part of the antireform coalition was shattered. A sharp acceleration of inflation, as in Mexico in 1986, can also create the sense of crisis that makes dramatic change possible (although high inflation makes reforms more difficult to execute successfully; see chapter 5). In a crisis, the deteriorating situation under existing policies may seem more risky to policymakers than reform.[18] Crises also tend to make trade reforms more successful by depressing incomes, thereby ensuring that there will be no flood of imports when restrictions are relaxed. By creating excess capacity in tradable sectors, crises also encourage greater orientation toward external markets.

Chances of lasting reform will be strengthened if illiberal trade policies (or the total cutoff of outside funds) have compressed the trade balance to the requisite degree before trade policy reform (in the sense of realigning the relative prices of tradable goods) begins. In this way, trade reform is less likely to receive the misdirected blame for the distress caused by the macroeconomic policies needed to reduce the excess aggregate demand in most crises. In Zambia, in contrast, reform of the foreign exchange allocation mechanism coincided with the shrinking availability of foreign exchange, thereby causing the public (and some international nongovernmental organizations!) to view reform as the *cause* of the shortage. Not surprisingly, the attempt at reform was abandoned.

Crises discredit former policies and are typically dealt with by the general-interest agencies that are the most sympathetic to trade reform, thereby strengthening their position vis-à-vis other agencies. In Mexico, for example, the Salinas administration has used general-interest agencies such as the central bank and the finance ministry as think tanks and as a source of staff for other agencies. These general-interest agencies also typically have closer links to external supporters of reform.

Even in circumstances of crisis and change, however, premature or indecisive trade reform can be worse than no reform at all. To take one example, a significant reduction in import restrictions without substantial real devaluation, even if the resultant increase in imports can be financed, can be politically devastating. The surge in imports and howls of complaint from import substituters can easily become a symbol of the "failure" of the reform program, and there will be no happy exporters to defend it. In the mid-1970s, the Lopez Michelsen administration in Colombia, elected by an extraordinarily large popular majority, announced a liberalization that would make Colombia the "South Korea of South America." In fact, the liberalization was quite weak. Moreover, because of the boom in coffee prices, the real exchange rate was allowed to become highly overvalued. The result was a decline in nontraditional exports, a flood of smuggled imports, and stagnation of the manufacturing sector. The succeeding Betancur government pointed to this failure of "liberalization" as an excuse to impose some of the most illiberal trade policies of the past two decades.

Similarly, reformist governments in Peru attempted trade liberalization between 1978 and 1980, but government opinion became divided, the real exchange rate appreciated after 1980, and policy reversals soon began. The García regime that followed adopted much more restrictive policies.

The Role of Ideas

New regimes are not wedded (or are less wedded) to the policies of the regimes they replace, but this does not guarantee that trade reforms will be adopted even if the change in regime occurs in an atmosphere of crisis. Reformers still have to seize the moment, and their ability to do so depends in part on being intellectually prepared. Trade reforms were successful in Indonesia in 1984 and Chile in 1974 in large part because reformers had ready a critique of the old order and specific proposals for change. In Indonesia, reformers had begun a program of studies well before the crisis of 1983. Thus they were armed with estimates of existing levels and patterns of effective protection that could not be justified by any reasonable criteria, horror stories of inefficiency, instances of negative value added, and other arguments that were very persuasive. In Morocco in 1983 and Mexico in 1985, reform-oriented policymakers had detailed information on the protective structure (including the tariff equivalents of quantitative restrictions) because of studies prepared by small research teams that had been funded by the World Bank. (As noted in chapter 2, this kind of information is rarely available.) The power of ideas should not be underestimated.[19] Reformers must also be prepared to rebut the intellectual justification for the existing trade regime. Their arguments may differ significantly, depending on whether protection is being justified ideologically (to maintain state control of the commanding heights of the economy) or is being explained pragmatically (to deal with a structural deficit in the balance of payments).

If reformers are well prepared, trade reform measures usually contribute to the resolution of other problems. If the fiscal deficit needs to be reduced, substituting tariffs for quantitative restrictions and taxing the domestic production of highly protected import substitutes can be shown to address the problem while moving relative prices in the right direction. If the terms of trade deteriorate, devaluation and a lowering of high protection rates will promote exports and encourage the efficiency needed to offset lower real income. If inflation accelerates, it may be argued (as it was in Mexico) that lower protection will increase competition and help break the cost-push spiral. If the terms of trade improve, devaluation and a lowering of protection will ward off the effects of Dutch disease (see box 6-4 in chapter 6) on exports. These arguments are not meant to suggest that trade liberalization is a panacea for all economic ills. Any program has to make economic sense on its own terms and will typically involve actions in a variety of areas. Some steps toward trade reform, however, can usually be woven into the response to almost any crisis.

Once the reform process is under way, reformers need to maintain an applied research team to respond to complaints, answer attacks on the program, and reach out to inform and politically reinforce nascent beneficiaries.[20] The importance of such a team was demonstrated in Indonesia and Chile and, in a negative way, by its absence in Peru.[21] Although the government of Bangladesh has never been fully committed to trade reform, a group of reformers in the Trade and Industry Policy Reform Program in the Planning Commission has made slow but steady progress by continuing to put forward liberalization measures.

Commitment, Pace, and Sequencing

Once the decision has been made to initiate reform, bold, highly visible, and publicly justified measures seem most likely to ensure success. A public commitment by the head of the government can be crucial to success, as in the case of Pérez of Venezuela, Babangida of Nigeria, and Salinas of Mexico; the lack of such commitment by Belaúnde in Peru and Kaunda in Zambia clearly contributed to failure. Executive leadership can galvanize support for reform among beneficiaries to offset the opposition of special interests. In the United States before President Cleveland's advocacy of lower protection in 1887 (as part of an export-promoting strategy), tariff reform was not on the national agenda, so his Secretary of State actively organized farm interests to support the initiative. Similarly, The Emergency Committee for American Trade, an organization of large corporations, was formed at the request of President Johnson to support liberalization under the Kennedy Round of multilateral trade negotiations. A decisive commitment also has the effect of discouraging lobbying efforts to resist and undo the reform program by reducing the perceived probability of their success.

Strong deeds need to accompany strong words. Timid first steps cannot be hidden from those negatively affected, but they stand little chance of attracting support from potential winners. As in Korea, the program should be transparent and announced in sufficient detail and far enough in advance to allow parties to make the necessary adjustments. Combining steps toward import liberalization in many sectors with staged devaluations of the real exchange rate seems the best policy for attracting the support of exporters and some import substituters to counterbalance the opposition of those whose protection is being removed. However, a large devaluation is a strong signal to exporters, whose response will prove that the reform program is working and negate pessimism about exports. Strong commitment and bold first steps also send a signal that the impetus toward reform is likely to be sustained and may thereby encourage a faster supply response. A study involving many countries found strong evidence that trade reform programs are more likely to be sustained if they are started with a strong, rather than a tentative, move.[22]

The optimal pace of reform, which has been much debated from the standpoint of economic efficiency, is also important from the political standpoint. The outer bounds of the rate of reform are clear: administrative constraints prevent everything from being done at once, even if that were desirable economically, while a long-drawn-out execution of any one phase allows opponents time to organize and reestablish links with officials carrying out the reforms. Nelson recommends "Fabian strategy and blitzkrieg tactics."[23]

Implementation

Reforms are more likely to be executed when there is a shift in the nature and locus of decision-making on trade matters. In Nigeria, for example, foreign exchange allocation was shifted from the bureaucracy to an auction supervised by the central bank. In Venezuela, the foreign exchange allocating agency was abolished. At the beginning of trade reform in Peru, the subsecretariat of commerce was shifted from the Ministry of Industry to the Ministry of Finance. In Mexico, although the formal powers of the trade-regulating bureaucracy were not disturbed, its higher offices were filled with staff transferred from agencies friendly to reform. In Colombia, in contrast, attempts to liberalize import licensing have been unsuccessful, in part because the agency that administers import licenses has been in charge of the liberalization.

Reforms that take place according to simple rules that are easily understood and explained, such as periodic removal of a preannounced number of quantitative restrictions or phased reductions in maximum tariffs, have many advantages.[24] An inflexible program that leaves little room for discretion reduces the incentive of special interests to organize opposition to the reforms. Conducting detailed studies of what to do during the implementation stage (as opposed to during the precrisis stage) can be counterproductive if this gives opponents of reform time to organize. Reforms whose execution depends on detailed, industry-specific knowledge shift the locus of decision-making back to the institutions that administered the unreformed system, increasing the chances that reform will be subverted. This is apparently what happened during the later stages of reform in Indonesia. Simplicity also permits reformers to oversee the execution of trade reform. Movement toward uniform tariffs and toward total elimination of quantitative restrictions is easy to monitor. If tariffs are to be set according to complicated rules and decisions have to be made about which quantitative restrictions are to remain, it is difficult to prevent the process from being captured by protectionist forces or even to know whether that is occurring. Another form of simplification, the elimination of exceptions from the unreformed tariff, was politically helpful in Chile, where it channeled the interests of previously favored parties (including some parts of the government) toward a reduction in the general level of tariffs. These considerations suggest that uniform tariffs have political advantages that are independent of whether they are strictly optimal economically.

Reformers have sometimes found it necessary partially to compensate the politically powerful who stand to lose from trade reform.[25] Elaborate antidumping procedures have been set up in Mexico and Chile, for example. Extremely protracted liberalization is another form of accommodation of losers, but it has the disadvantage that it postpones the benefits as well. An example is import liberalization in Korea, which has been a stated policy since 1967. Integration agreements, such as the "Europe 1992" plan, often establish or increase funding to compensate some regions that are expected to be adversely affected. Depreciation of the real exchange rate also mitigates the losses of importers who lose protection as a result of lowered tariff or nontariff barriers.

Paradoxically, compensation of losers may be particularly necessary from a political point of view if the losers are not among the poorest and most vulnerable groups of society, but instead are powerful and well connected. Baldwin makes the point that "President Eisenhower had to impose oil import quotas to minimize the opposition of congressional members from oil- and coal-producing states to the extension of the Trade Agreements of 1955."[26] Similarly, part of the political bargain that secured passage of the 1974 Trade Act in the United States (to implement the Kennedy Round tariff reductions) was the renewal of steel import quotas. Compensatory measures to increase factor mobility (for example, worker retraining or severance payments) can also increase the benefits of reform. These types of programs support the political sustainability of the reforms, since they shift voters from adversely affected groups to groups that gain from the reforms. In the United States, another part of the political bargain leading to acceptance of the Kennedy Round tariff reductions was liberalization of the provision of the Trade Adjustment Assistance Act that provided training for displaced workers. Still, the issue must be approached pragmatically. The feasible compensations that can be offered are dwarfed by the economic adjustments that even favored social groups undergo during crises, and compensation runs the risk of creating new distortions and difficulties in administering the reform program.

Once trade reform is well under way, international agreements may be used by reformers to fend off pressures to backtrack. Mexico and Chile have used the GATT in this way. In the United States, GATT agreements have often provided an effective way for the president to resist protectionist sentiment emanating from Congress.[27] Unfortunately, GATT agreements are less useful to policymakers in withstanding pressures for protection through quantitative restrictions (especially voluntary export restraints) than through tariff rates. This explains in large part why protectionist pressures in industrial countries have been expressed in the rising use of nontariff barriers. Agreements on trade reforms with multilateral institutions could conceivably play the same role in stabilizing reforms, but only if there were fairly broad support for the agreement to begin with. Reforms that are tainted by the suspicion of having been exacted under duress are probably less likely to last than those that have no external support at all.

Summary and Conclusion

Reformers need to take into account the fact that politics plays a major role in the formation of policy. As individuals, beneficiaries of trade policy reform usually perceive lower net benefits from attempts to influence decision-making than do losers. Reform of illiberal trade regimes also threatens vested interests within government. Such vested interests can be found within protected state-owned enterprises, among trade regulators who derive prestige and profit from the status quo, or among those at the highest levels of government who may wish to use rents generated from illiberal trade regimes for personal ends or to cultivate political support.

Reforms are often delayed until a crisis or change in regime occurs. Premature and half-hearted reforms may be counterproductive. While awaiting the proper moment, reformers should prepare their intellectual arguments and be ready to advance trade reform under whatever circumstances may emerge. Although the preferred paths to reform will depend on the situation in the country involved, in general reforms are more likely to be believable and sustainable if launched boldly with strong initial measures and with explicit public explanation. Implementation of reforms should be entrusted to agencies that have a relatively small protectionist constituency and should proceed by simple and transparent stages that are not contingent on additional detailed studies. Partial and transitional compensation of losers (such as retraining of workers) may be necessary to sustain the reforms and to facilitate reallocation of resources.

Notes

1. David Lake, *Power, Protection, and Free Trade* (Ithaca, N.Y.: Cornell University Press, 1988), p. 1.

2. But the difficulty is not unique to trade reform. Most of the factors that make trade policy reform difficult make reform of tax or financial policy difficult as well.

3. Julio Nogués, "The Timing and Sequencing of Trade Liberalization: Peru," World Bank International Economics Department (Washington, D.C., 1987).

4. F. D. Weiss, "Domestic Dimensions of the Uruguay Round: The Case of West Germany in the European Communities," in H. R. Nau, ed., *Domestic Politics and the Uruguay Round* (New York: Columbia University Press, 1989).

5. Mancur Olson, *The Logic of Collective Action,* 2d ed. (Cambridge, Mass.: Harvard University Press, 1971).

6. A. O. Krueger, "Some Preliminary Findings from the World Bank's Project on the Political Economy of Agricultural Pricing," in International Association of Agricultural Economists, *XX International Conference of Agricultural Economists: Invited Papers* (Buenos Aires, 1989).

7. Even major exporting sectors, such as agriculture or aircraft in the United States, which have professional staffs to represent them, often argue for freer trade only in terms of creating income abroad that can be spent on U.S. exports or as a way of obtaining the reduction of trade barriers abroad.

8. J. Garcia-Garcia, "Impediments to Trade Liberalization in Colombia," in M. Wolf and L. Sjaastad, eds., *Impediments to Trade Liberalization in Latin America* (London: Gower Press, for the Trade Policy Research Center, forthcoming).

9. Nogués, "Timing and Sequencing of Trade Liberalization."

10. R. R. Barichello, "Indonesian Trade Reforms in the Mid-1980s: Policies, Processes, and Political Economy" (paper prepared for Harvard Institute International Development Conference on Systems Reform in Developing Countries, Marrakesh, Morocco, October 26–29, 1988).

11. Garcia-Garcia, "Impediments to Trade Liberalization."

12. L. Rubio, C. Rodriguez, and R. Blum, "The Making of Mexico's Trade Policy and the Uruguay Round," in Nau, *Domestic Politics,* p. 184.

13. Lake, *Power, Protection, and Free Trade,* p. 137.

14. And they were repealed not because (or not only because) of the persuasiveness of economists, but because of the lobbying efforts of the Anti-Corn Law League, a cotton industry interest group. See G. M. Anderson and R. D. Tollison, "Ideology, Interest Groups, and the Repeal of the Corn Laws," in C. K. Rowley, R. D. Tollison, and G. Tullock, eds., *The Political Economy of Rent Seeking* (Boston: Kluwer Academic Publishers, 1988).

15. A. V. Desai, "The Politics of India's Trade Policy," in Nau, *Domestic Politics,* p. 93.

16. Kim Kihwan and Chung Hua Soo, "Korea's Domestic Trade Policies and the Uruguay Round," in Nau, *Domestic Politics,* p.148.

17. T. M. Callaghy, "Toward State Capability and Embedded Liberalism in the Third World: Lessons for Adjustment," in J. M. Nelson and John Waterbury, eds., *Fragile Coalitions: The Politics of Economic Adjustment* (New Brunswick, N.J.: Transaction Books, 1989).

18. M. S. Grindle, *The New Political Economy: Positive Economics and Negative Politics* (Cambridge, Mass.: Harvard Institute for International Development, 1989).

19. To a critic who complained to Thomas Carlyle that his books were "only ideas," Carlyle retorted: "There was once a man called Rousseau who wrote a book containing nothing but ideas. The second edition was bound in the skins of those who laughed at the first." (Quoted in J. N. Bhagwati, *Protectionism* [Cambridge, Mass.: MIT Press, 1988]).

20. G. Tullock, "How to Do Well While Doing Good," in D. C. Colander, ed., *Neoclassical Political Economy* (Cambridge, Mass.: Ballinger Publishing Co., 1984).

21. These teams can generate data on changes in levels of trade restrictions and the response to these changes. Evaluations of the relationships among reform, response, and the politics of the reform process currently suffer from the lack of such data.

22. Michael Michaely, Armeane Choksi, and Demetris Papageorgiou, "The Design of Trade Liberalization," *Finance and Development* 26 (March 1989):2–5.

23. J. M. Nelson, "The Politics of Long-Haul Economic Reform," in Nelson and Waterbury, *Fragile Coalitions,* p.14.

24. Even reforms relying on fairly complex rules, such as conversion of quantitative restrictions into tariff equivalents, are feasible if executed outside the normal bureaucracy (Israel) and not captured by protectionist forces.

25. Of course, any important change in economic policy will probably be accompanied by partial compensation of the losers. For example, after the U.S. Civil War, western farmers were compensated for the increase in protection to northern manufacturers by the distribution of public lands and by rapidly growing markets. "Vote yourself a farm, vote yourself a tariff" had been a Republican slogan in the election of 1860. The free-trading South, then under Reconstruction government, did not have to be compensated.

26. R. E. Baldwin, "The Political Economy of Trade Policy," *Journal of Economic Perspectives* 3 (Fall 1989):119–35.

27. P. S. Nievola, *Process Protectionism: Blame Avoidance Politics in U.S. Trade Policy* (Washington, D.C.: American Political Science Association, 1988).

5
Macroeconomic Environment and Trade Policy

The modern economic history of developing countries is replete with attempts to liberalize trade. Many of the efforts undertaken over the past three decades have not been sustained, however. In a large number of cases, the failures have been the result not of the trade reforms themselves but of inconsistent macroeconomic policies.[1]

Countries often embark on trade liberalization in the wake of an economic crisis associated with unsustainable fiscal and balance of payments deficits and inflation. To restore macroeconomic balance, they seek to reduce the fiscal deficit through a reduction in government expenditure and to lower restrictions on trade. In that situation, the sequencing of stabilization and trade policy reform measures becomes a key issue. Should they be undertaken simultaneously, or is there a specific pattern of sequencing that is more advisable? The answer depends on the extent of the initial macroeconomic disequilibrium, because policy trade-offs differ under different initial conditions.

Stabilization in the 1980s

The sharp reduction in the availability of external financing for developing countries in the early 1980s required either an equally sharp reduction in the fiscal deficit or an increase in domestic borrowing or money creation, which leads to inflation. Trade policy reform was thus often initiated in an environment of mild to high inflation, large fiscal deficits, and serious balance of payments difficulties. These problems were not independent; the fiscal deficits were monetized and thus became a driving force behind the inflation and balance of payments problems. Of the forty countries receiving World Bank trade adjustment loans between 1979 and 1987, four started with very high inflation rates (exceeding 100 percent a year), five with high rates (40 to

100 percent), and six with moderate rates (20 to 39 percent). The rest had relatively low rates of inflation.

A subset of twenty-four of the forty trade adjustment loan countries for which sufficient implementation data were available (see box 1-3 and table 1-2 in chapter 1) was examined to investigate the interaction between macroeconomic adjustment and the intensity of trade reform.[2] Table 5-1 presents average data on inflation and fiscal deficits for those countries, grouped according to the intensity of their exchange rate and commercial policy reforms during 1980–87 (see table 2-2 in chapter 2). Along those two dimensions of reform, a combination of high intensity in both or of high in one and moderate in the other is categorized as "substantial" reform, while a combination of moderate and moderate or high and low is deemed "moderate" reform. All other combinations, including policy reversals, are classified as "mild" reform.

Although aggregation hides details specific to each country, the systematic differences that emerge are informative. Initial situations differ. The average fiscal disequilibrium in the years preceding trade reform was large in all groups; it was slightly lower in the substantial and moderate reform groups. (Among the substantial reformers, Chile and Korea had initial deficits that were lower than the group average.) The substantial and moderate trade reformers managed to reduce both their fiscal deficit and their inflation rate by much more than did the mild reformers. This suggests that stabilization and trade reform can be carried out simultaneously and successfully. The difference in relative success in stabilization is further highlighted when the substantial trade reformer group excluding Mexico (second row of each panel) is compared with the rest. This group had the greatest success in reducing the fiscal deficit and inflation, followed by the moderate group. The mild trade reformers also had very little success in stabilization.

Stabilization and the Effectiveness of Trade Policy Reform

Stabilization affects not only the need for restrictions on trade related to the balance of payments but also the behavior of two key variables critical to trade reform: the real exchange rate and the real interest rate. Movements of those variables during stabilization depend on the initial degree of macroeconomic disequilibrium, as manifested in the rate of inflation. In addition, cuts in public investment induced by stabilization, especially if they fall on infrastructure investment, influence the effectiveness of trade reform in generating a supply response. Thus

Table 5-1. Macroeconomic Indicators before and after Reform in Twenty-four Trade Adjustment Loan Countries
(unweighted average for each group, in percent)

Indicator and country group	3 years before reform	2 years before reform	1 year before reform	Year of reform	1 year after reform	2 years after reform	3 years after reform
Inflation rate							
Substantial reform	31.5	34.3	30.6	55.5	25.9	22.9	22.6
Excluding Mexico[a]	30.6	33.0	26.6	48.9	20.3	17.4	17.0
Moderate reform	12.4	11.8	12.3	9.3	8.9	8.1	7.6
Mild reform	15.5	15.7	15.3	17.4	14.8	16.9	19.3
Fiscal balance/GDP							
Substantial reform	−4.8	−6.4	−7.8	−7.2	−6.1	−4.4	−4.6
Excluding Mexico[a]	−5.1	−6.4	−6.5	−7.1	−5.9	−3.6	−2.6
Moderate reform	−7.2	−7.8	−6.0	−5.8	−5.4	−5.1	−4.7
Mild reform	−8.0	−6.8	−8.6	−8.9	−8.4	−8.0	−13.8
Resource balance/GDP							
Substantial reform	−5.2	−3.4	−2.5	−1.5	0.4	−0.7	−1.1
Excluding Mexico[a]	−5.6	−3.5	−3.6	−3.1	−0.7	−1.5	−1.9
Moderate reform	−8.8	−8.6	−7.1	−6.4	−7.1	−6.0	−4.4
Mild reform	−6.2	−9.9	−7.5	−7.8	−6.4	−6.4	−3.2

Note: The countries in each group are as follows: substantial—Chile, Colombia, Ghana, Jamaica, Korea, Mauritius, Mexico, and Turkey; moderate—Bangladesh, Madagascar, Morocco, Pakistan, Panama, the Philippines, and Thailand; and mild—Côte d'Ivoire, Guyana, Kenya, Malawi, Senegal, Togo, Yugoslavia, Zambia, and Zimbabwe.

a. For Mexico, changes in operational deficit (that is, excluding the very large interest payments) are a more meaningful measure of fiscal effort because changes in interest payments on old debt are generated by factors outside the government's control.

Source: The classification in table 2-2, chapter 2, which is based on World Bank and IMF data.

the crucial questions are how can stabilization help or hinder trade policy reform and under what conditions.

Fiscal Deficits and Trade Restrictions

Large fiscal deficits are at the heart of major inflation and balance of payments crises in developing countries.[3] An expansionary monetary policy, which is often the consequence of money financing of deficits, also contributes to the problems. Overvalued real exchange rates, arising from expansionary fiscal and monetary policies that are inconsistent with the nominal exchange rate policy, have frequently led to generalized increases in restrictions on imports and capital movements intended to reduce the loss of international reserves. Thus, protection motivated by balance of payments considerations is likely to expand in countries with a growing fiscal deficit, rising inflation, and a worsening external balance. Restrictions motivated by balance of payments problems are conceptually distinct from trade restrictions imposed mainly for resource allocation and income distribution purposes—that is, generally to affect the pattern of production and consumption. Only in low-inflation countries does the protective structure respond primarily to the resource-allocation motive.[4]

The imposition of trade and foreign exchange controls closely follows the emergence of macroeconomic crises. Table 5-2 shows this relationship for selected countries in Latin America and Africa in the two years preceding a stabilization program and devaluation. These are the years in which the crises were developing and coming to a head. The table reveals a clear rise in trade and foreign exchange restrictions in the years of falling reserves and growing balance of payments problems. Analysis of the forty trade adjustment loan countries also shows that the use of quantitative restrictions in the prereform period was greater in countries with severe balance of payments difficulties.

In the absence of any reduction in the fiscal deficit or depreciation of the exchange rate, the removal of trade controls would worsen the current account deficit. However, as long as the fiscal deficit and money supply growth are sufficiently reduced before or simultaneously with liberalization, the excess demand for imports can be lowered and the current account deficit kept in check. Table 5-1 shows that the substantial trade reformers succeeded in reducing their fiscal deficit and current account deficit, notwithstanding substantial liberalization. Stabilization is essential if the reduction of trade restrictions is not to aggravate the current account deficit.

Table 5-2. *Trade and Foreign Exchange Restrictions in the Two Years Preceding Fiscal and Exchange Rate Crises in Selected Countries*

Country and crisis year	Payments restrictions on transactions	Tariffs, duties, and cost-related measures
Bolivia		
1979	Increased restrictions on a number of current payments in 1978.	Since 1977 most imports were subject to a 5–25 percent advance deposit; this was increased to 500 percent for 600 items in 1978.
1982	All sales of foreign exchange subject to authorization. Prohibition of imports of some industrial goods.	Advance deposit requirement of 5–25 percent lowered in 1981.
Chile		
1982	Payments highly liberalized. No restrictions imposed.	Flat (10 percent) import tariff not altered prior to devaluation.
Ecuador		
1982	Multiple exchange rates and two-list import structure. Restrictions successively increased after 1981.	Coverage and rates of advance deposits increased and import tariffs raised in early 1981.
Mexico		
1976	Import licenses required for almost all items, and public imports severely restricted.	Nonessential imports subject to a 10 percent surcharge. Replaced by increasing average import duty from 15 percent to 20 percent.
1982	Import licensing and quotas; the first were greatly increased in 1981.	Continued increase in import duties throughout 1981.
Malawi		
1981		Customs duties increased on a wide range of items, and the rate of surtax was raised from 15 percent to 20 percent. All imports subject to a 20 percent advance deposit.
Mauritius		
1981	Importers unable to obtain domestic or foreign credit for imports of "low-priority items" (goods with tariffs in excess of 20 percent).	A 10 percent across-the-board surcharge imposed on all duties payable on imports.

Country and crisis year	Payments restrictions on transactions	Tariffs, duties, and cost-related measures
	Licenses required for imports of noncapital goods. Foreign exchange licenses introduced as an additional requirement for importers with approved import licenses.	
Senegal 1980	Special license required for imports of textiles. Import licensing imposed on imports of electrical equipment.	Import taxes raised for most foodstuffs and some manufactured products.
Zambia 1983	All import applications had to be approved by the Bank of Zambia. All imports had to be financed by letters of credit with a minimum term of 90 days. Foreign exchange allowances suspended for tourist travel.	

Source: Sebastian Edwards, "Exchange Controls, Devaluations, and Real Exchange Rates," *Economic Development and Cultural Change* 37 (April 1989):457–94; and IMF, *International Financial Statistics* (Washington, D.C., various issues).

Real Exchange Rates

A nominal devaluation can lead to a real depreciation only if domestic prices do not rise by the same magnitude as the devaluation. As long as the fiscal deficit and consequent monetary expansion are sufficiently reduced, the devaluation will not be inflationary and real depreciation will occur. Empirical evidence strongly suggests that when accompanied by appropriate macroeconomic policies, nominal devaluations produce a real and sustained depreciation in the level of the exchange rate. Countries experiencing increased inflation following a devaluation, and thus rapid erosion of the real depreciation, are those that accompanied the exchange rate adjustment with expansive monetary and fiscal policies.[5] The experience of the substantial reformers supports this empirically.

Generally a cost-push increase in the domestic prices of imports is expected to follow a devaluation. However, when there are binding quantitative restrictions, the larger the prereform share of imports subject to such controls, the smaller the impact on the domestic price level. Devaluation will only reduce the scarcity premia obtained by the importers; it will not raise their domestic prices. There is substantial evidence of this phenomenon in Sub-Saharan Africa (Ghana in 1984, Guinea in 1986, Mozambique in 1987, and Uganda in 1983).

Even in the absence of pervasive import controls, reform-induced reductions in tariffs would mitigate the one-time increase in prices, although the presence of wage indexation would aggravate it. Generally, the inflationary potential of a one-time rise in the price level resulting from a devaluation will be limited if sufficient fiscal restraints are in place. In addition, when depreciation is accompanied by import liberalization, which is often the case under trade policy loans, it dampens inflationary pressures by enhancing competition and import availability (as in Tanzania and Uganda, for example).

An important source of tension between stabilization and liberalization programs is that successful trade liberalization must be supported by a real depreciation, while disinflation can result in an appreciation of the real exchange rate (see box 5-1 on the real exchange rate).[6] Nevertheless, as long as the necessary depreciation of the real exchange rate can be ensured and maintained, trade liberalization can be undertaken during disinflation.[7]

In countries with moderate inflation, institution of a crawling peg system consistent with reductions in the fiscal deficit can minimize the tension. For example, through some variant of a crawling peg, Chile, Colombia, and Morocco maintained a steadily depreciating real exchange rate during trade reform, while Kenya and Mauritius maintained a constant real exchange rate after an initial real depreciation. These countries maintained depreciating real exchange rates even under substantial disinflation. Table 5-3 shows that ten countries reduced their inflation rate to half their previous rate or less within three years and still managed a real depreciation.[8]

In countries where, because of a prolonged period of overvaluation and trade and exchange controls, a large proportion of current transactions take place through a parallel foreign exchange market, the official exchange rate is a poor indicator of the opportunity cost of foreign exchange.[9] The extent of overvaluation is manifest in the parallel market premium on foreign exchange. Since exporters are required to surrender their foreign exchange receipts at the official rate, the premium is an indicator of the size of the tax on exports. This tax has been quite high at different periods in Ghana, Jamaica, Sierra Leone, Somalia, Tanzania, Uganda, Zambia, and Zaire.

Elimination of overvaluation through devaluation when there is an entrenched parallel foreign exchange market presents greater problems. It requires deft economic management because the parallel market is sensitive to expectations of current and future policy. Periodic devaluations of the official rate may fail to lower the parallel market premium unless sufficient reductions in the fiscal deficit are expected to be initiated and sustained. Ghana (1983–86) and Zaire (1983–85) succeeded in reducing overvaluation through periodic depreciation of the official rate largely because of sustainable and credible reductions in their budget deficits. In contrast, Zambia's program failed precisely because the fiscal situation was out of control.

In countries with very high inflation and strong inflationary expectations, disinflation policies often involve reducing the fiscal deficit and introducing instruments to control expectations and anchor domestic prices.[10] The exchange rate is frequently used as a stabilization instrument. In such situations, either the rate is fixed or the rate of crawl of the nominal exchange rate is less than is needed to compensate for the rate of inflation. Argentina and Uruguay in the late 1970s provide examples of massive real appreciation resulting from disinflation guided by exchange rates. Such appreciation inhibited the reallocation of resources sought by liberalization.[11] Experience suggests that it is best to postpone trade policy reform if the stabilization strategy is likely to lead to a period of real appreciation.

Because of the difficulty of achieving the real depreciation usually required for a successful trade policy reform, the strategy of pursuing stabilization and trade policy reform simultaneously has generally been unsuccessful when the exchange rate is used as an anti-inflationary instrument. One possible exception is Mexico, which continued to implement trade liberalization measures after beginning a stabilization program in 1988 that included using the exchange rate as a nominal anchor for domestic prices. So far, at least, it appears that inflation has been substantially reduced and the reform program has remained on track.

Mexico differed from other countries that have tried this in at least three ways. First, and most important, Mexico's stabilization program addressed the underlying causes of inflation—the fiscal deficit and consequent monetary expansion—rather than relying on the exchange rate as the major stabilization instrument. Second, before Mexico froze the exchange rate in 1988, the real rate had been substantially depreciated from its level in mid-1985 when import liberalization began. Thus, even though the real rate has appreciated since early 1988, its level by the end of 1989 was still about 33 percent more depreciated than the level of mid-1985. Third, the government had already taken strong trade reform measures before the stabiliza-

Box 5-1.   *Real Exchange Rate Realignment and Adjustment*

The behavior of the real exchange rate (RER) is one of the most important determinants of a country's ability to adjust. What is important, however, is not the absolute level of the current RER but its relationship to its long-term sustainable equilibrium level. When the current RER deviates from its long-term sustainable equilibrium, the country faces a situation of real exchange rate misalignment. If the current RER is appreciated (depreciated) relative to its long-term equilibrium level, the country has an overvalued (undervalued) RER. Historically, situations of overvaluation have generally been translated into balance of payments difficulties, macroeconomic disequilibrium, heightened uncertainty, reduced investment, and stagnation.

The Equilibrium Real Exchange Rate

To determine whether the RER in a particular country is overvalued, it is necessary to evaluate the evolution of the equilibrium real exchange rate (ERER). The ERER is the price of tradables relative to nontradables that, for given long-term equilibrium (or sustainable) values of other relevant variables such as trade taxes, international prices, capital and aid flows, and technology, leads to the simultaneous attainment of internal and external equilibriums and is compatible with long-term economic growth. Internal equilibrium means that the nontradable goods market clears in the current period and is expected to be in equilibrium in the future. External equilibrium means that the current account balance in the present period and the balances expected in the future satisfy the intertemporal budget constraint that the discounted value of the current account balance be equal to zero. In other words, external equilibrium means that the current account balances (present and future) are compatible with long-term sustainable capital flows. This definition of the ERER considers only real variables; monetary variables are normally the determinants of the actual RER.

Four implications follow from this definition of the ERER. First, when there are changes in any of the other variables that affect the internal and external equilibriums (for example, the terms of trade), there will also be changes in the ERER. For example, the RER required to attain equilibrium when the world price of the country's main export is low will not be the same as that required when the price is high. The ERER is itself a function of several variables, including import tariffs, export taxes, real interest rates, and capital controls. Second, there is not one ERER, but a path of ERERs through time. Third, the path of ERERs is affected not only by the current values of the fundamental determinants, but also by their expected future values. Fourth, in analyzing the interaction between fundamentals and ERERs, it is important to distinguish between permanent and temporary changes in the fundamentals.

To determine whether a country's RER is in equilibrium, it is not enough to compare its current value with historical levels. Not only is the actual RER important, but also its long-term sustainable equilibrium level. Thus the historical (and expected) behavior of the fundamental determinants of the ERER should be scrutinized. It is common to find situations where changes in fundamentals have affected the sustainable ERER to such an extent that even when the current RER is greatly depreciated relative to the past, overvaluation and disequilibrium prevail. This was, for example, the case in Chile during the early 1980s.

The Chilean Experience

Between 1965 and 1970 there was a steady real depreciation in Chile, which broadly corresponded to a mild trade liberalization (see graph below). A crawling peg nominal exchange rate helped to achieve and maintain this depreciating real exchange rate. During 1970–73, expansive macroeconomic

Real Exchange Rate Index, 1965-88
(1980 = 100)

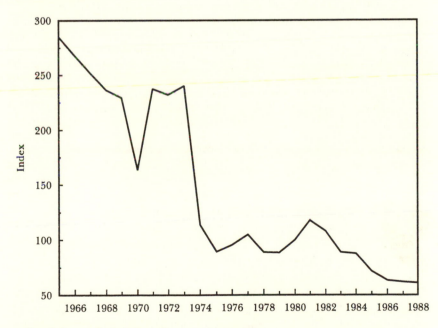

Note: An increase in the index indicates a real appreciation.
Source: World Bank estimate.

(Box continues on the following page.)

Box 5-1 *(continued)*

policies and the imposition of massive exchange controls resulted in forces that caused the real exchange rate to appreciate. The terms of trade fluctuated without exhibiting a trend. During this period, Chile's RER became severely overvalued.

Between the periods 1965–73 and 1974–84 there was a structural break in RER behavior in Chile. During 1974–84, despite broad fluctuations, the RER was at all times significantly more depreciated than at any time during the previous ten years. Two events that greatly affected the behavior of RER fundamentals are behind the real depreciation between 1965–73 and 1974–79. First, there was a dramatic liberalization of international trade. Second, there was a steep, and apparently permanent, deterioration of Chile's terms of trade as a result of a decline in the price of its main export, copper. These two changes in fundamentals required a real depreciation to maintain external equilibrium.

Between 1979 and 1982 the (much discussed) real appreciation of the Chilean peso took place. This appreciation can be attributed to two interconnected factors: (a) between 1979 and 1981 capital controls were greatly relaxed, which allowed a massive inflow of foreign funds and caused the ERER to appreciate; and (b) the fixing of the nominal exchange rate in June 1979, as a way of bringing down inflation, also contributed to the observed real appreciation. This loss in competitiveness after mid-1979 was, according to most observers, one of the main reasons for the collapse of the Chilean economy in 1982–83. Although the RER appreciated during 1979–82, it was greatly depreciated relative to its 1965–73 level. This illustrates how changes in fundamentals can change the ERER. An RER that would have been excessively depreciated in the 1970s, before the tariff liberalization and structural worsening of the terms of trade, was fatally appreciated in the early 1980s.

tion program began, so that even the appreciating exchange rate did not call into question the credibility of the program.

In countries with very high and chronic inflation a broader "heterodox" approach is adopted. In this approach, many prices—product prices, wages, the exchange rate, and the nominal interest rate—are frozen, controlled, or at least subject to predetermined scales. It was tried in 1985–86 in Brazil, Argentina, and Israel with varying degrees of success.[12] The fact that relative prices are frozen or are moved arbitrarily makes for an inhospitable environment for initiating trade reform.

Real Interest Rates

In economies with very high inflation, stabilization programs often raise the real interest rate, at least temporarily.[13] Real interest rates climbed to a monthly rate of 6 percent in Argentina in the aftermath of the Austral plan and surpassed an annual rate of 38 percent in Chile in 1981 and 34 percent in Uruguay in 1982. The increase in real interest rates appears to be unavoidable, even if temporary. When a high expected rate of inflation results in a high nominal interest rate, but the actual rate of inflation is lower than expected, the ex post measured real interest rate rises. Also, as the stabilization program lowers inflation, the level of real money balances can be too low relative to demand, leading to a high nominal interest rate. Although under such situations interest rates may fall following adjustment, the consequent uncertainty in their levels is likely to inhibit private investment.[14]

The foregoing discussion suggests that countries with low rates of inflation can pursue trade policy reform fairly independently of stabilization, because a depreciating real exchange rate is relatively easy to sustain when fiscal restraint is maintained. In the case of moderate to high inflation rates, a well-managed crawling peg can also ensure a depreciating real exchange rate during disinflation. In addition, as long as macroeconomic pressures are being controlled, restrictions motivated by balance of payments problems can be dismantled simultaneously. Under conditions of very high and variable inflation, however, it may be advisable to postpone liberalization until some macroeconomic stability has been achieved. High relative price variability, as well as the potential for real appreciation arising from stabilization using the exchange rate as a price anchor, is likely to provide confusing signals to both producers and investors, thereby making trade reform difficult to manage.[15]

Public Investment

Even under relatively low rates of inflation, the supply response to changes in relative prices may be weak under conditions of reductions in public investment induced by stabilization. In the 1980s, reductions in the fiscal deficit came primarily from cuts in public expenditure rather than from increases in revenue, and the largest percentage of reductions came in capital spending.[16] Public investment fell sharply in several trade reform countries, in particular, Côte d'Ivoire, Mexico, Morocco, and the Philippines. Evidence also suggests that spending on infrastructure declined more sharply than did other categories of capital expenditures. Only Chile, Colombia, Korea, and Turkey, three of

Table 5-3.   *Real Exchange Rates under Episodes of Disinflation in Selected Countries*

Country[a] Year	Inflation rate (percent)	RER index[b]	Country Year	Inflation rate (percent)	RER index[b]
Disinflation with real appreciation			*Disinflation with real depreciation*		
Pre-1980s			Pre-1980s		
Argentina			Bangladesh		
1976	443.2	100.0	1974	54.7	100.0
1979	159.5	232.0	1977	8.6	47.7
Chile			Somalia		
1974	504.7	100.0	1980	58.8	100.0
1977	91.9	122.1	1982	22.6	62.5
1980	35.1	147.9	Turkey		
Costa Rica			1980	110.2	100.0
1982	90.1	100.0	1983	32.9	68.5
1985	15.1	105.8	Uruguay		
Ghana			1973	97.0	100.0
1977	116.5	100.0	1976	50.6	83.9
1980	50.1	126.9	Zaire		
Uruguay			1979	108.6	100.0
1968	125.3	100.0	1982	36.2	74.9
1970	17.0	123.9	1980s		
Zaire			Philippines		
1968	53.3	100.0	1984	50.8	100.0
1971	5.8	117.4	1987	3.8	78.6
1980s			Zaire		
Burundi			1982	77.1	100.0
1979	36.6	100.0	1985	23.8	36.1
1982	5.8	128.9	Ghana		
Chile			1983	122.9	100.0
1980	35.1	100.0	1986	24.6	16.2
1982	9.9	106.7	Madagascar		
Jamaica			1982	31.8	100.0
1978	34.9	100.0	1985	10.6	82.0
1981	12.7	111.0	Mauritius		
Uruguay			1980	42.0	100.0
1979	66.8	100.0	1983	5.6	82.0
1982	19.0	147.9	Nigeria		
			1984	39.6	100.0
			1986	5.4	47.9

a. This includes countries with an initial inflation rate of 35 percent and above that cut inflation in half within three years.

b. An increase in the RER index indicates an appreciation.

Source: IMF, *International Financial Statistics* (Washington, D.C., various issues).

which are among the significant trade reformers, managed to sustain or raise the rate of public investment as a share of GDP.

The mode of public expenditure adjustment has important implications for trade policy reform. A sustained supply response to reform is critically dependent on new investment, especially private investment, but private investment in export sectors can be inhibited if the supporting infrastructure is inadequate (see chapter 6). There is systematic evidence for Malawi, Mexico, and Turkey to confirm that investment in infrastructure has a positive effect on the profitability of the private sector. Thus, reducing public investment in infrastructure which is complementary to private investment would undermine the supply response. In contrast, public investment in manufacturing or other non-infrastructure is likely to compete with and crowd out private sector investment.

What is important with respect to public investment is not only its level but also its composition (infrastructure versus noninfrastructure) and quality (effectiveness in raising total output). Trade reform can sometimes help to determine which among various infrastructure investment projects are the most urgent (see chapter 7). For example, the increase in cotton production in Tanzania following reform helped to highlight areas in which transportation was a critical bottleneck for cotton exports. So long as supporting public investment in infrastructure remains inadequate in terms of either its level or its focus on sectors and areas, the supply response to reform will be poor.

Revenue Effects of Trade Policy Reform

Liberalization measures will improve efficiency, but they can either improve or worsen the fiscal situation both indirectly and directly, thereby helping or hindering stabilization efforts. The indirect effect can arise either from the impact of liberalization on the financial system (especially if a government tries to keep loss-making banks afloat—see box 5-2) or from its effect on the profitability of public sector manufacturing enterprises.

The direct effect, which is discussed here, stems from the revenue implications of liberalization in countries in which trade tax revenues constitute a large proportion of total government revenue. According to *World Development Report 1988,* revenues from explicit trade taxes such as tariffs, import surcharges, and export duties accounted for 38 percent of total tax revenue in low-income and 19 percent in middle-income developing countries in 1985. For individual countries, dependence on trade taxes ranges from 4 percent in Brazil to 58 percent in The Gambia. Fiscal dependence on trade taxes is greatest in Sub-

Box 5-2. *Trade Policy Reform and Financial Sector Reform*

Trade policy reform involves changes in the profitability of firms. Exporters typically benefit from devaluation. Some producers of import substitutes whose markets were previously heavily protected lose as quotas are replaced by less-than-equivalent tariffs (importers that had access to the quasi rents generated by quotas also lose), whereas others gain because the benefits of devaluation more than compensate for the loss of protection. Sustained real devaluation also involves a fall in the foreign exchange price of nontradables and thus in the price of nontraded relative to traded goods.

The resulting resource shifts can have a significant impact on the financial system. Banks and borrowers with debts denominated in foreign exchange experience a rise in debt burdens and debt service relative to asset values and earning streams (except, possibly, for exporters). Some countries, such as Brazil and Chile, have instituted measures to shift part of the loss from private firms to the government. If the capital account is open (or porous), real interest rates may rise to offset an anticipated real devaluation, and so all debt service, whether domestic or foreign-funded, increases (as in Indonesia and Malaysia, for example). Because of the confluence of trade reforms and macroeconomic adjustment, interest rates may be high as a result of moderate inflation, restrictive monetary policies implemented for balance of payments purposes, or heavy domestic government borrowing intended to finance the public sector's own higher external debt service (as in Brazil and Turkey, for example).

The banking system is typically also heavily exposed to highly protected firms in the import-competing sectors, some of which may be heavily indebted. The impact of trade policy reforms can thus be to weaken the balance sheets of important borrowers and financial intermediaries; this is the "asset-value" stock impact of rearranging the flows of goods and payments. Lenders, however, do not capture much of the gains that accrue to firms that benefit from the reforms. This is true, first, because import-competing firms typically account for a larger share of the modern economy and are more capital-intensive than exporting firms, and, second, because the distribution of returns is asymmetric between banks and borrowers. The upside potential for banks is quite limited (the profit margin on the interest on the loan), whereas the downside potential is large (default of the entire loan amount). The reverse is true for borrowers because of their limited liability.

Anything causing greater dispersion of returns to borrowers is likely to weaken bank portfolios. As in Turkey, borrowers tend to become polarized. The stronger have less need of bank finance because they are able to strengthen their balance sheets by retentions. The weaker come to rely more on loans and pose a greater risk to the banking system. The group into which a firm falls is generally determined by its initial level of indebtedness and the location of its market. Sometimes an ownership dimension is important;

thus, while Brazil's private corporate sector retrenched sharply in the mid-1980s, benefited from measures to shift exchange losses to the government, and strengthened its balance sheets, the public enterprises, which were initially more highly leveraged, fell more and more deeply in debt.

The impact of this portfolio deterioration depends largely on the extent to which the financial institutions, and their regulators, are willing and able to maintain financial soundness. With good prudential regulation and supervision, losses are recognized rapidly and written off; this may lead to some difficulties, but in a reasonably well-diversified financial system and given reasonably good economic performance after reform, the impact should be manageable. Malaysia has managed to contain the ill effects on its banking system, but even there unregulated financial institutions ran into difficulties. Usually, however, prudential regulation is weak, loans to loss-making firms are rolled over, and the portfolio quality of the financial system suffers an accelerating decline as distress borrowing crowds out borrowing by the potentially profitable firms that the trade policy reform sought to encourage. The financial system then becomes an impediment to the smooth reallocation of resources. At the same time, the fiscal cost implicit in the government's (usually unstated) commitment to bail out the system mounts rapidly. For developing countries, estimates of this cost have ranged from 5 percent to 30 percent of GDP.

A special case of systemic reform (which may include trade policy reform as a component) is the liberalization of centrally planned economies. This poses special problems for the financial system, as shown by the recent experiences of East European countries and China. Sometimes enormous changes in relative prices and the profitability of different firms are superimposed on a regulatory structure ill adapted to a market economy. It is difficult to predict the impact on bank portfolios, but it appears that substantial parts of the portfolios would be nonperforming following a major reform.

Trade policy reforms are probably a less important source of financial sector problems than adjustment to adverse terms of trade or capital account shocks. Nevertheless, the consequences for asset values and the financial sector should be factored into the initial evaluation of the trade policy reform. Some components might be built in at an early stage to anticipate the problem—for example, an effective auditing and loan classification system might be included with the initial reform operations. The alternative, as in Turkey, is to wait until the problem becomes widespread and very costly.

Source: Financial Policy and Systems Division, Country Economics Department, World Bank.

Saharan Africa, followed in order by Asia, the Middle East and North Africa, and Latin America and the Caribbean. Import taxes dominate trade tax revenue in most cases. Explicit export duties are relatively unimportant except in a few countries, but revenue from implicit export taxes can often be more significant than formal export duties.

The high dependence on trade taxes in developing countries makes their fiscal balance vulnerable to changes in trade tax revenue induced by liberalization. The key policy issues are how best to anticipate the effect of trade reform measures on fiscal balance and how to develop alternative, more efficient revenue measures. Although tariff reduction has the potential to lower import tax revenue, devaluation generally has a positive valuation effect on the revenue bases of import taxes, except where the government is a net buyer of foreign exchange. The positive effect of devaluation has in several cases been an important factor in mitigating the revenue effects of tariff liberalization. Elimination or reduction of exemptions from import duties, which relate mainly to imported inputs, is also unambiguously revenue enhancing. So is replacement of a ban by a nonprohibitive tariff, or a quota by an equivalent tariff. The total effect on revenue thus depends on the combination of measures contained in the trade reform program.

Import Tax Revenue

Since the revenue effect of liberalization will be most visible under episodes of substantial reform, we focus first on the fifteen trade adjustment loan countries that can be categorized as substantial and moderate reformers (see note on table 5-1) during 1980–87. In seven of these countries, reform consisted predominantly of reductions in duty exemptions and a switching of protection from nonprice to price measures (a reduction in the share of imports subject to nontariff restrictions); this group is referred to as the "quota reformers." In the remaining eight countries, tariff reduction was a more dominant aspect of trade reform; this group is called the "tariff reformers." As expected, import tax revenue as a share of GDP rose after reform for the quota reformers and fell for the tariff reformers (table 5-4). Because of differences in initial conditions, however, not all quota liberalizers experienced the same extent of change in revenue. The size of the favorable impact on revenue differed according to the preform shares of duty exemptions, import bans, and quota imports not subject to tariffs.[17]

Not all tariff liberalizers faced declines in revenue, nor should such declines be considered inevitable. A lowering of very high duties can reduce customs evasion and thereby raise revenue by increasing the share of official transactions in total imports. The positive valuation ef-

Table 5-4. *Import Tax Revenue of Fifteen Substantial Reformers by Type of Reform, before and after Reform*
(percentage of GDP)

Group[a]	3 years before	2 years before	1 year before	Year of reform	1 year after	2 years after	3 years after
Eight tariff reformers[b]	2.8	2.8	2.7	2.5	2.2	2.2	2.3
Seven quota reformers[c]	2.7	2.7	2.6	2.7	3.2	3.3	3.4

a. The assignment of countries to these two groups is based on information on programs and implementation in Nadav Halevi, "Trade Liberalization in Adjustment Lending," Trade Policy Division, Country Economics Department, World Bank (Washington, D.C., 1989).

b. Chile, Korea, Mexico, Morocco, Panama, the Philippines, Thailand, and Turkey.

c. Bangladesh, Colombia, Ghana, Jamaica, Madagascar, Mauritius, and Pakistan.

Source: World Bank data.

fect of a nominal depreciation that accompanies reform has been useful in mitigating or avoiding revenue declines. Reductions in very high tariff rates (concertina cuts) can increase revenue under some conditions, while proportionate reductions in all tariffs (radial tariff reform) are likely to be revenue-reducing (chapter 7). If import demand is price elastic at the prereform tariff-inclusive price (which is the case if tariff rates exceed the maximum-revenue tariff), tariff liberalization can increase revenue. A fall in tariff rates would then lead to a more-than-proportionate rise in imports and thus to an increase in revenue. The larger the share of imports with such high tariffs, the greater this positive impact.

This response of imports to tariff reductions, however, cannot always be relied upon. First, pervasive import quotas or foreign exchange rationing could prevent tariff reductions from leading to a rise in imports and thus in revenue. Concertina reductions in tariffs in the presence of quotas have been accompanied by lower import tax revenue in Kenya (1983–85), Tanzania (1981–83), and Thailand (1980–83). Other countries in Sub-Saharan Africa that have high tariffs and widespread quantitative controls could experience the same effect. Second, the negative income effect of stabilization policies on imports often leads to a substantial loss in revenue, as was clearly the case in Mexico (1982–84) and the Philippines (1980–83). Third, given aggregate demand, depreciation to a more realistic exchange rate will tend to lower imports. But if realistic exchange rates and low tariffs are accompanied by a rise in exports, imports may also rise as a result of the income effect and relaxation of the foreign exchange constraint, if it was binding. In Chile (1985–88) and Korea (1985–88), reductions in tariffs were not accompanied by decreases in import-tax revenue even though initial tariffs were low. This was largely because of an autonomous rise in imports. Thus, before initiating tariff reductions during stabilization, it may be necessary to consider the changes in a country's overall level of imports that may arise from changes in trade policy, export growth, and aggregate demand policies.

Export Tax Revenue

Removal or reduction of explicit export taxes has proved problematic in only a few cases: Tanzania (1981–83), Uruguay (1984–86), and Argentina (1987–88). In Argentina, the failure to implement a new land tax measure, which was expected to compensate for the decline in revenue, was followed by the reimposition of export duties.

The effect of reform measures on implicit export tax revenues has been of greater concern. Implicit tax receipts in the form of public export marketing board surpluses (generated by setting the producer prices of export commodities below border prices) have on occasion exceeded revenue from explicit export taxes.[18] Generally, trade policy reform has had a positive revenue effect in this respect, even when the producer prices of export commodities were increased substantially, as in Ghana and Tanzania. The valuation effect of exchange rate depreciation and the volume response to higher producer prices have usually raised the surplus. However, where marketing boards were abolished for efficiency reasons, as in Nigeria and Senegal, government receipts were hurt.

Effect on the Fiscal Deficit

In some instances, the adverse revenue effects of reforms were offset by changes in domestic tax measures that increased revenue. Many such measures were introduced in the trade adjustment loan countries and included improved tax administration and collection (Ghana, Pakistan, and Thailand), increased rates and coverage of sales and excise taxes (Malawi, Mauritius, Mexico, and the Philippines), and introduction of a value added tax, or VAT (Jamaica, Morocco, and Turkey). On occasion, the measures were explicitly intended to offset the anticipated decline in trade tax revenue, although this did not always happen owing to the poor timing of the tax measures.

Mexico and Morocco provide an interesting contrast in this respect. Both countries had about the same level of revenue dependence on trade taxes, both substantially reduced expenditures, and both initiated radial tariff reform measures and suffered declines in explicit trade tax revenue.[19] In Mexico, this loss was cushioned by increases in receipts resulting from increases in sales taxes (value added taxes as well as direct sales taxes) made possible largely because the VAT system had been put in place three years before the 1983 trade reform. By the time a more substantial import liberalization was initiated in 1985, trade tax revenue constituted only a minuscule proportion of total tax revenue. Morocco failed to generate the offsetting increases in revenue that were anticipated from initial increases in rates of sales taxes and subsequent introduction of a VAT system. Transitional difficulties in implementing the VAT led to lower-than-expected receipts from indirect taxes in the first two years (1986–87), although receipts rose substantially later.[20] In addition, direct taxes failed to generate sufficient revenue because of new tax exemptions introduced in sectors that were growing. The collapse of world phosphate prices finally triggered a partial reversal of Morocco's tariff reform.

The experiences of Ghana and Zambia provide a contrast with respect to another measure: correction of overvaluation leading to exchange rate unification (see section above on real exchange rates). If the government is a net buyer of foreign exchange (as is the case in Ghana and Zambia), devaluation worsens the fiscal balance. This adverse effect has been quite significant in many countries where overvaluation was large.[21] In Ghana, but not in Zambia, this was offset by revenue from other sources. Through vastly improved administration, collection, and enforcement practices, Ghana doubled the share of tax revenue in GDP between 1983 and 1985. Reductions in distortions led to an increase in official transactions (relative to unofficial transactions) and hence contributed to increased revenues. Achieving additional increases in revenue from changes in the tax structure took time, however, and so Ghana proceeded slowly—and perhaps for that reason, successfully—with exchange rate unification. In contrast, Zambia implemented few new tax measures. A decline in nontrade tax receipts and a rise in expenditure increased the fiscal deficit in the first two years of the Zambian reform, leading to a reversal in 1987.

Reforms involving mainly a switch from quantitative restrictions to tariffs can be undertaken under most circumstances. Tariff reductions in revenue-constrained situations should preferably be accompanied by such a switch in import measures, together with a reduction in the coverage of exemptions and bans. In determining the appropriate mix of liberalization measures, the potential revenue impact of the package should be assessed ahead of time. If liberalization consists mainly of tariff reductions—which is often the case in later stages of trade reform— the declines in tariff revenue would need to be compensated for by increases in other government revenue, especially if expenditures have already been reduced substantially and cannot be squeezed much further. Such offsetting increases could be generated by raising the prices of public sector services or output or by raising domestic indirect taxes.

The resulting shift away from reliance on import taxes and toward increased dependence on domestic indirect taxes or value added taxes would improve the efficiency of revenue generation.[22] However, institutional constraints can make implementation of the value added tax difficult or that of a retail-level sales tax infeasible. Nevertheless, the scope for extending the coverage and increasing the rates of factory-level sales and excise taxes should be tapped.[23] In any case, the timing of compensatory revenue measures is of critical importance.

Complications of the Debt Burden

Complications arising because of heavy debt overhang also need to be considered in the design of trade reform measures. For example, the excessive debt-servicing obligations of highly indebted countries have undermined their capacity to invest, and investment is critical to a sustained response to trade reform. In the 1980s, this and other related problems have been particularly acute not only in countries with very high rates of inflation, but also in countries with relatively low inflation.

One problem arises from the fact that substantial real devaluations are required to generate a trade surplus in the face of reduced capital inflows. The need for this large real depreciation under a disinflation program, given the difficulties discussed above, demands competent macroeconomic management, which is even more necessary because large devaluations put pressure on the fiscal deficit by increasing the domestic-currency cost of servicing foreign debt.[24]

Furthermore, even if the necessary trade surplus is achieved, a fiscal problem remains because exports are generated mainly in the private sector. The resulting surplus has to be taxed to generate revenue for public sector debt-servicing. With limited tax handles, particularly in the low-income countries of Sub-Saharan Africa, there may be a temptation to raise revenue by increasing trade taxes. Even if increases are not sought, there is likely to be considerable resistance to a reduction in trade tax rate. In several highly indebted middle-income countries, the need for revenue to service debt has led to taxes on financial intermediation. Such an outcome has adversely affected investment and resource reallocation—both targets of liberalization. All these problems suggest the importance of careful management of trade reform, not its postponement, because the need for increased efficiency of the external sector is most pressing under a debt crisis.

Credibility, Investment, and Sustainability

Trade policy reform works only to the extent that resources move to sectors that have become more productive under the reform. The process of moving resources involves costs that entrepreneurs will be willing to incur only if the new set of relative prices is expected to continue. Only then will new private investment be forthcoming. Expectations about the reform's unsustainability can be self-fulfilling: if lack of credibility leads to a low investment response from the private sector, reform becomes difficult to sustain. The lack of credibility in Argentina was pervasive soon after reforms were initiated in 1976. An aborted price freeze in 1977 and the government's failure to implement preannounced tariff reductions on time undermined the credibility of tariff reform. Firms anticipating a change avoided reallocation and used foreign funds to finance their losses.

When fiscal and exchange rate policies are inconsistent and the real exchange rate appreciates, firms will perceive a high probability that exports will fail to develop and, consequently, that the reform may be reversed. In this case, firms will refrain from investing in sectors that have become more profitable under the reform because the reform-induced change in relative profitability is not expected to be sustained. The real exchange rate acts as a signal, conveying information to the private sector on the likelihood of a sustained liberalization. A steep real appreciation, by undermining the current account, generates expectation of a reimposition of trade controls. This was most evident in Uruguay between 1979 and 1981 when, because of appreciation, firms preferred to wait instead of reallocating resources. If stabilization policies require a real appreciation, as is often the case under very high and chronic inflation, there is a case for postponing trade reform on the grounds that it might otherwise lack credibility.

Similarly, wildly fluctuating real exchange rates, resulting from half-hearted attempts at real depreciation or unsuccessful efforts toward exchange rate unification, imply uncertain profitability for many sectors. Variability in other relative prices, such as interest rates, sends the same signals of impermanence. Since investment typically involves adjustment costs and irreversibilities, the greatest adverse impact of increased relative-price variability falls on private investment.[25] Trade policy reform should preferably be initiated after high relative-price variability has been reduced sufficiently to make changes in relative prices induced by reform both meaningful and credible.

Failure to reduce the fiscal deficit also generates public skepticism about the ability of government to sustain trade reform, particularly because trade taxes are often invoked as the easiest and quickest means of increasing revenue.[26] Attempts by the private sector to anticipate the reversal of tariff reform can also destabilize the liberalization process.[27] It is therefore necessary, after initiating reform, to minimize any appearance of conflict between stabilization and trade policy reform. This could be done by pursuing policies that are likely to reduce relative-price variability, depreciate the real exchange rate, reduce the fiscal deficit, and produce steady or rising investment ratios.

Summary and Conclusion

The concern of this chapter was the potential conflict between macroeconomic stabilization and trade policy reform. Although they have generally been mutually supportive, they have also undermined each other in certain situations. Stabilization efforts affect the real exchange rate and the real interest rate, depending on the initial inflation and the policies used to reduce it. In countries that are highly dependent on trade taxes, some trade liberalization measures have worsened the fiscal deficit through their effect on government revenue. Although a shift from quantitative restrictions to tariffs has raised revenue, tariff reductions have sometimes lowered it.

In most situations, it is desirable to carry out trade reforms simultaneously with stabilization. Under mild to high inflation, stabilization efforts are supportive of trade policy reform. Quantitative restrictions on trade induced by balance of payments considerations can be reduced as the fiscal deficit and monetary financing of the deficit are reduced. Other restrictions can also be lowered as long as a devaluation or a crawling peg can maintain an appropriately depreciating real exchange rate.

The supply response to reform depends on the credibility of macroeconomic policy and supportive public investment. Under very high and variable inflation, policy credibility is easily undermined. Fluctuations in relative prices and interest rates provide confusing signals. Furthermore, if stabilization programs use the nominal exchange rate as an anchor for prices, the resulting real appreciation conflicts with the objectives of reform. Under such circumstances, it is preferable to postpone trade policy reform until the fiscal deficit and inflation are under control. Trade reforms that increase revenue support stabilization efforts by reducing the fiscal deficit. So when the deficit is a serious problem, tariff reductions should be combined with the elimination of import bans and exemptions and the replacement of quantitative restrictions by tariffs. Alternatively, tariff liberalization should be undertaken when other, more efficient revenue-raising measures or policies to reduce expenditure can be introduced to compensate for the loss in tariff revenue or after the fiscal crisis is over.

Notes

1. A World Bank research project concludes that there are "extremely strong links between trade liberalization and the accompanying macroeconomic policies. The latter appear to be special in determining the survivability of the trade liberalization" (Michael Michaely, Armeane Choksi, and Demetris Papageorgiou, "The Phasing of a Trade Liberalization Policy: Preliminary Evidence," CPD Discussion Paper no. 1986–42, Country Policy Department, World Bank [Washington, D.C., 1986], p. 14).

2. Fifteen of the twenty-four economies started with low inflation. Five countries had moderate inflation. Two of them (Mexico and Ghana) experienced very high inflation, while another two (Turkey and Yugoslavia) had high inflation. Three of these four are also among the substantial reformers.

3. Although there is no one-to-one analytical link between fiscal deficit and inflation, large budget deficits do, sooner or later, tend to create high inflation. For an analysis, see Stanley Fischer, "The Economics of the Government Budget Constraint," Policy, Planning, and Research Working Paper no. 224, Development Economics Department, World Bank (Washington, D.C., 1989); for evidence, see A. O. Krueger, *Foreign Trade Regimes and Economic Development: Liberalization Attempts and Consequences* (Cambridge, Mass.: Ballinger Publishing Co. for National Bureau of Economic Research, 1978); and World Bank, *World Development Report 1988* (New York: Oxford University Press, 1988).

4. The level of protection under sustainable macroeconomic equilibrium can be interpreted as resulting from political economy considerations—from competition among different pressure groups to obtain protection and other rents. This equilibrium is, however, inefficient.

5. See R. Cooper, *Exchange Rate Devaluation in Developing Countries,* Princeton Essays in International Finance 86 (Princeton, N.J.: Princeton University Press, 1971); Michael Connolly and Dean Taylor, "Adjustment to Devaluation with Money and Nontraded Goods," *Journal of International Economics* 46 (August 1979): 281–94 and "Exchange Rate Changes and Neutralization," *Economica* 46 (August 1976); and Sebastian Edwards, *Exchange Rate Misalignment in Developing Countries* (Baltimore, Md.: Johns Hopkins University Press, 1988).

6. Insufficient adjustments in the administered exchange rate during disinflation can result in appreciation. If the nominal exchange rate is explicitly used to anchor domestic prices to world prices for purposes of disinflation, real appreciation is unavoidable. Also, under a floating exchange rate system, restrictive monetary policy can appreciate the real exchange rate by raising domestic interest rates above foreign rates.

7. See A. O. Krueger, "Interactions between Inflation and Trade Objectives in Stabilization Programs," in William Cline and Sidney Weintraub, eds., *Economic Stabilization in Developing Countries* (Washington, D.C.: Brookings Institution, 1981).

8. A comparison of the results of eleven stepwise devaluations and seven crawling peg devaluations in Latin America during 1964–82 confirms this in

Sebastian Edwards, *Real Exchange Rates, Devaluation, and Adjustment: Exchange Rate Policy in Developing Countries* (Cambridge, Mass.: MIT Press, 1989).

9. If a large proportion of current (and illegal) capital transactions is carried out through a parallel foreign exchange market in which there is a high premium, as is true in many countries of Sub-Saharan Africa, the official exchange rate system becomes a surrogate for a tax, subsidy, and income transfer mechanism, rather than an indicator of foreign exchange cost. Under these conditions, the parallel market rate provides a better measure of the relative price of tradables. See Brian Pinto and Sweder van Wijnbergen, "Exchange Rate Regimes in Africa," Country Policy Department, World Bank (Washington, D.C., 1987).

10. See Vittorio Corbo and Jaime de Melo, "Lessons from Southern Cone Policy Reforms," *World Bank Research Observer* 2 (July 1987): 111–42; and Miguel Kiguel and Nissan Liviatan, "Inflationary Rigidities and Orthodox Stabilization Policies: Lessons from Latin America," *World Bank Economic Review* 2 (September 1988): 273–98.

11. In economies with very high inflation, generalized wage indexation also means that whenever inconsistent macroeconomic policies are translated into a real exchange rate overvaluation, they will also generate a rate of growth of real wages that will exceed productivity gains.

12. See Rudiger Dornbusch and M. H. Simonsen, *Inflation Stabilization with Incomes Policy Support* (New York: Group of Thirty, 1987); Mario Blejer and Nissan Liviatan, "Fighting Hyperinflation: Stabilization in Argentina and Israel, 1985–86," *IMF Staff Papers* 34 (September 1987): 409–38; and C. L. Martone, "Fiscal Policy and Stabilization in Brazil," Policy, Planning, and Research Working Paper no. 50, background paper for *World Development Report 1988*, World Bank (Washington, D.C., 1989).

13. A number of studies have found that during major episodes of disinflation, the ex post real interest rate becomes very high. See Rudiger Dornbusch, "Lessons from the German Inflation Experience of the 1920s," in Rudiger Dornbusch and Stanley Fischer, eds., *Macroeconomics and Finance* (Cambridge, Mass.: MIT Press, 1987); Vittorio Corbo, Jaime de Melo, and James Tybout, "What Went Wrong with Recent Reforms in Southern Cone Countries?" *Economic Development and Cultural Change* 24, no. 3 (1986); Sebastian Edwards and Alejandra Cox-Edwards, *Monetarism and Liberalization: The Chilean Experiment* (Cambridge, Mass.: Ballinger Publishing Co., 1987); and Joseph Ramos, *Neoconservative Economics in the Southern Cone of Latin America (1973–83)* (Baltimore: Johns Hopkins University Press, 1986).

14. Interest rates can also rise when governments try to replace receipts from the inflation tax and foreign borrowing with those from domestic borrowing, as in the case of Turkey. See Ritu Anand and others, "Turkey: External Debt, Fiscal Policy, and Sustainable Growth," Country Operations Division (Turkey), Europe, Middle East, and North Africa Department, World Bank (Washington, D.C., 1989).

15. See Stanley Fischer, *Real Balances, the Exchange Rate, and Indexation: Real Variables in Disinflation*, NBER Working Paper no. 1497 (Cambridge, Mass.: National Bureau of Economic Research, 1984).

16. See Ajay Chhibber and J. K. Shirazi, "Public Finance in Adjustment Programs," Policy, Planning, and Research Working Paper no. 128, Country Economics Department, World Bank (Washington, D.C., 1988); W. R. Easterly, "Fiscal Adjustment and Deficit Financing during the Debt Crisis," Policy, Planning, and Research Working Paper no. 138, Country Economics Department, World Bank (Washington, D.C., 1989); and Norman Hicks, "Expenditure Reductions in High-Debt Countries," *Finance and Development* 26 (March 1989): 35–37.

17. For example, reductions in duty exemptions had a larger revenue-enhancing effect in Mauritius than in Jamaica, Kenya, and Senegal, in part because the prereform share of exempted imports was much larger in Mauritius. Similarly, the reduction in reliance on quantitative restrictions had a greater revenue-enhancing effect in Kenya (1980–82) than in Jamaica or Senegal, because the initial share of import bans was much greater and the prereform proportion of quota imports not subject to tariffs was much larger.

18. For example, in Côte d'Ivoire, such revenue from cocoa and coffee averaged 6.2 percent of GDP during 1976–85—considerably higher than the average of 2.5 percent accruing from explicit export duties. See Christian Schiller, "The Fiscal Role of Price Stabilization Funds: The Case of Côte d'Ivoire," IMF Working Paper (Washington, D.C.: IMF, 1988), table 3, p. 9.

19. Both countries obtained about a quarter of their tax revenue from trade taxes. Elimination of explicit export duties on forty-seven items and tariff reductions on forty-six items in 1983 led to a drop in Mexico's trade tax revenue of 4.5 percent of GDP (1982–84); Morocco suffered a fall of 2.5 percent of GDP (1983–86).

20. For example, VAT revenue fell because tax credits were not fully offset by reductions in exemptions or by increases in tax rates, credits on existing inventories were granted in order to extend the VAT to the wholesale level, and the time period over which tax credits could be claimed was shortened.

21. Jamaica, Sierra Leone, Somalia, Uganda, and Zaire have experienced such effects because their trade reform programs often included efforts to reduce or eliminate overvaluation. In countries where the government is a net seller of foreign exchange (such as Nigeria and Mexico), such exchange rate reform has been fiscally advantageous.

22. Various studies show that the efficiency cost or economic cost of domestic taxes on the sale of final goods only (retail sales tax and value added tax) is lower than the cost on all sales (turnover taxes) and that the economic cost of taxes on all sales is lower than the cost of taxes on international transactions. There is also evidence to suggest that collection costs are lowest for trade taxes.

23. For possibilities in Sub-Saharan Africa, refer to Zmarak Shalizi and Lyn Squire, "Consumption Taxes in Sub-Saharan Africa: Building on Existing Instruments," CPD Discussion Paper no. 1986–34, Country Policy Department, World Bank (Washington, D.C., 1986).

24. See Dani Rodrik, *The Welfare Economics of Debt Service*, NBER Working Paper no. 2655 (Cambridge, Mass.: National Bureau of Economic Research, 1988). On fiscal implications see also Easterly, "Fiscal Adjustment."

25. Instability in foreign exchange availability and monetary conditions has been found to inhibit investment and growth. See G. K. Helleiner, "Outward Orientation, Import Instability and African Economic Growth," in Sanjaya Lall and Frances Stewart, eds., *Theory and Reality in Development* (New York: St. Martin's Press, 1986); and Roger Kormendi and Philip Meguire, "Macroeconomic Determinants of Growth: Cross-Country Evidence," *Journal of Monetary Economics* 16 (September 1985): 141–63. For an analytical model showing this effect, see Dani Rodrik, "Liberalization, Sustainability and Design of Structural Adjustment Programs," Trade Policy Division, Country Economics Department, World Bank (Washington, D.C., 1988).

26. Although its dependence on trade taxes was negligible, Chile raised its uniform tariff rate when faced with declining nontrade tax revenue. See Vittorio Corbo, "Public Finance, Trade, and Development," Policy, Planning, and Research Working Paper no. 218, Country Economics Department, World Bank (Washington, D.C., 1989).

27. When credibility is lacking, trade reform can lead to welfare losses via (excessive) foreign borrowing to finance an increase in imports or capital flight. See Guillermo Calvo, "Fractured Liberalism: Argentina under Martinez de Hoz," *Economic Development and Cultural Change* 34, no. 3 (1986): 511–33.

6

Policies for Export Development

Many countries urgently need to expand international trade to allow their economies to grow and develop. Rising export earnings make adjustment less painful, lighten debt burdens, and support higher growth rates by increasing import capacity. Growth of exports and imports also increases access to the benefits of international trade, including new ideas, modern technology, competition, economies of scale, and the creation of domestic industries around new markets.

Increasing exports through policy reforms in developing countries has proved no simple task, however. Achieving a satisfactory response has required attacking the task vigorously over a period of several years from different angles and at several levels, paying specific attention to supply. Both broad economywide and narrower policy and institutional measures are needed.

Development of both manufactured and primary exports requires supportive macroeconomic policies. An appropriate and stable real exchange rate is needed, which calls for sound fiscal and monetary policies. Both overvaluation and wide, unpredictable fluctuations of the real exchange rate are inimical to exports, the latter because they contribute to uncertainty in the business climate.[1] There have been substantial reforms of exchange rate policies in the 1980s, but lessons in managing exchange rates for better export performance have seldom been fully applied.[2] A reduction of import protection is also fundamental to the long-term growth of exports. The importance of a stable macroeconomic environment and low import protection is discussed in detail in chapters 5 and 7.

High protection levels for manufacturing industries, as well as measures that keep export prices artificially low, such as export restrictions and implicit or explicit export taxes, have depressed primary exports in a number of countries. Manufactured exports, however, which in most countries have the best prospects for long-term growth, are seldom burdened by export taxes. Substantial growth in manufactured ex-

Table 6-1. Exports of Merchandise and Nonfactor Services from Developing Countries, 1974–87

Export category	Value, 1987 (billions of U.S. dollars)	Percentage share of merchandise and nonfactor services			Average annual growth (percent)					
		1974	1980	1987	Volume		Unit value index		Value/MUV[a]	
					1974–80	1981–87	1974–80	1981–87	1974–80	1981–87
Merchandise exports	380.7	86.6	84.9	82.4	6.2	4.3	10.0	−2.3	6.2	−1.0
Fuel	66.2	23.1	29.6	14.3	2.7	0.5	21.3	−5.8	13.0	−8.3
Manufactures	185.0	18.3	27.2	40.0	13.4	9.4	10.2	−1.1	14.0	4.7
Food and beverages	57.6	19.8	15.6	12.5	4.6	3.4	8.1	−4.0	2.3	−3.7
Nonfood agriculture	21.2	7.7	5.6	4.6	−0.3	1.7	12.1	−1.9	1.9	−3.5
Metals and minerals	25.0	9.8	6.7	5.4	5.6	2.5	4.8	−3.2	1.0	−3.8
Nonfactor services	81.6	13.4	15.1	17.6	—	—	—	—	8.2	1.3
Travel and tourism	29.0	4.6	5.0	6.3	—	—	—	—	7.7	2.3
Transport and shipment	22.1	4.0	5.0	4.8	—	—	—	—	10.5	−1.3
Memorandum item										
OECD manufactured exports	1,299.2	—	—	—	4.6	3.7	10.3	2.8	4.7	3.0

—Not applicable.

Note: The figures in this table were derived by aggregating data for the developing countries listed in table 1-2 in chapter 1. Value and share figures for merchandise and nonfactor services do not add up to the totals shown. Commodity group figures for merchandise exports do not equal the reported totals because comparable country data were not always available. One billion equals 1,000 million.

a. MUV = index of unit value of manufactured exports from industrial countries (see also note 4 at the end of this chapter).

Source: Merchandise exports, World Bank data; nonfactor services, IMF, *Balance of Payments Statistics* (Washington, D.C., various issues).

ports depends on a variety of institutional reforms (in addition to macroeconomic and trade policies). These reforms are the main focus of this chapter. In general, improvements in policy exert a powerful effect on entrepreneurs only when the reforms are visible, sustained, and expected to continue.

Export Performance in the 1980s

Table 6-1 shows the superior growth rate of manufactured exports from developing countries compared with other exports.[3] During 1974–87 developing countries' manufactured exports grew at high annual rates averaging over 11 percent in volume and over 9 percent in purchasing power as measured against the manufactured exports of industrial countries.[4] The growth rates were somewhat lower after 1980 than before, reflecting the expanded absolute size of these exports as well as less favorable conditions in the world economy. By 1987, manufactured exports constituted 40 percent of the value of developing countries' merchandise and nonfactor service exports, up from 18 percent in 1974. In a wide range of manufactured products, exports from some developing countries to OECD countries have been so competitive in price and so acceptable in quality that their swift growth seems to have been limited mainly by constraints on learning processes and on the ability to increase export supply. By 1987, the share of developing economies in world manufactured exports had reached 12 percent. This growth has taken place despite the increasing use of nontariff barriers by developed countries (see chapter 8).

Exports of primary products grew in volume at slow to moderate rates in 1974–87 but suffered large price declines during 1980–87. Their combined purchasing power relative to the manufactured exports of industrial countries rose sharply until 1980 as oil prices soared, but then fell to well below their 1974 level.

Exports of nonfactor services are a significant component of overall export expansion. Tourism is an important source of export receipts in a number of countries (Egypt and Jamaica, for example). Exports of nonfactor services increased in purchasing power during 1974–87 at faster rates than total merchandise exports and are now about one-fifth as large as merchandise exports. Growth rates of both types of exports have fallen since 1980, however. Even more significant in their impact on export receipts for some countries (Pakistan and Yemen, for example) have been trends in factor service receipts—particularly workers' remittances (which are not presented in the table).

Export performance has been poor in many countries, good in some, and spectacular in a few, such as Turkey and the four East Asian economies of Korea, Taiwan, Hong Kong, and Singapore. These East Asian economies have maintained policy regimes strongly favorable to manu-factured exports for well over twenty years. Hong Kong and Singapore now have per capita incomes too high for them to be considered devel-oping economies, and Taiwan and Korea account for about two-fifths of the combined manufactured exports of developing economies and rank first and second in total exports. Of the countries that received trade adjustment loans, about one-third increased their share in total exports to industrial countries from developing countries (table 6-2).

The exports of the poorer developing countries continue to be par-ticularly meager, and their growth rates are often weak. In low-income countries, exports per person in 1987 averaged US$46 excluding China and India, or US$34 including them, compared with US$2,476 in high-income countries and US$356 in middle-income ones. Official development assistance received in 1987 exceeded merchandise ex-ports in at least fifteen countries with populations over 5 million and nearly matched them in others.

Exports in a majority of developing countries have suffered serious setbacks in the 1980s. More than half the developing countries had ab-solutely lower merchandise exports in 1987 than in 1977 in terms of purchasing power measured against the manufactured exports of in-dustrial countries. The purchasing power of exports in terms of manu-factured products fell during this decade by more than half in seventeen countries and by one-quarter to one-half in eighteen others. Moreover, many of the countries that did manage an increase gained little—not enough to offset their own population growth or the rising cost of servicing their debts.

Manufactured exports have continued to rise in several developing market economies in which they were already important by 1980. Tur-key has achieved striking increases in these exports as a result of deval-uation and reforms implemented in the early 1980s. Recent policy changes have led to strong responses in Mexico and, on a smaller scale, in Indonesia. Several countries that already had promising policies be-fore the 1980s, including Malaysia, Mauritius, Portugal, and Thailand, have improved them further, with impressive results. Exchange rate and other reforms are beginning to achieve substantial responses in India and Morocco and have led to favorable responses in Bangladesh, Sri Lanka, and Tunisia. Other countries that are heavily dependent on manufactured exports and are striving to make them grow faster in-clude Brazil, Costa Rica, Cyprus, Dominican Republic, Haiti, Hungary, Jordan, Malta, Pakistan, the Philippines, Poland, Uruguay, Yugoslavia, and Zimbabwe. These exports are also important for other economies such as Argentina, Colombia, Egypt, El Salvador, Guatemala, and Ja-maica. The largest and most striking increase in manufactured exports

Table 6-2. Shares of Exports to Industrial Countries of Seventy-five Nonoil-Exporting Developing Countries, 1978–88

Country group	Number of countries	Export share (percent)		Percentage growth in share from 1978 to 1988[a]
		1981	1988	
Nonoil-exporting developing countries	75	100.0	100.0	0.0
Trade adjustment loan recipients	37[b]	55.9	59.5	0.9
With rising share	12	30.4	42.4	4.7
Korea		9.8	18.5	7.7
Pakistan		0.8	1.2	0.1
Turkey		1.7	2.9	8.2
Yugoslavia		3.2	3.6	2.4
With declining share	25	25.1	16.9	−5.0
Argentina		4.1	1.3	−6.9
Côte d'Ivoire		1.6	0.7	−7.5
Philippines		4.1	2.9	−3.5
Zambia		1.4	0.7	−12.3
Nonrecipients of trade loans	37[c]	44.1	40.5	−1.1
With rising share	9	12.3	17.5	7.2
China		8.4	11.8	8.9
Gambia, The		0.02	0.04	1.9
Portugal		2.7	4.2	6.4
Sri Lanka		0.3	0.4	2.0
With declining share	28	31.8	23.0	−4.5
Bolivia		0.3	0.1	−13.8
Peru		1.9	0.9	−7.5
Poland		2.7	2.3	−6.7
Sudan		0.3	0.1	−10.4

Note: This table presents the exports of the seventy-five nonoil-exporting developing countries in the sample of eighty-seven countries considered in this report as a percentage of exports from all developing countries (*IMF* definition) to industrial countries.

a. This is the coefficient of a least-squares regression of the natural logarithm of the countries' share over time. It thus shows by what percentage (of itself) the share rose or fell each year on average between 1978 and 1988.

b. The forty trade adjustment loan countries excluding oil exporters (Indonesia, Mexico, and Nigeria).

c. The forty-seven nonrecipients of adjustment loans, excluding the ten oil exporters.

Source: IMF, *Direction of Trade Statistics* (Washington, D.C., various issues).

has come in China. Its manufactured exports grew from about US$3.7 billion in 1977 to about US$28 billion in 1987.

Practical Ways to Develop Manufactured Exports

Manufactured exports tend to get started in developing countries with relatively low labor costs. Over time, conditions important for the continued growth of exports are a reasonably educated work force, law and order, a well-developed infrastructure, and an efficient and reliable administration. Low-cost skilled manpower, experienced entrepreneurs, and a stable framework of property rights are also highly desirable. As the East Asian countries have shown, once the economy is oriented toward export production and the appropriate skills are learned, the export mix can be upgraded as wages rise.

Business Realities

Local firms responding to orders from foreign buyers account for the largest share of manufactured exports from developing countries. Their products usually have to meet exacting and frequently changing specifications with regard to materials and technical requirements. For consumer goods, finish, styling, packaging, labels, and the like are also important. The delivered product must be ready to go straight to the final customer or the retailer's display rack, and the order must be delivered by a given date. Thus everything needed to make the product must be available locally at modest cost, or the country will be disqualified as a source of supply.

Most foreign buyers prefer to give orders to firms that already have considerable export experience and require little instruction and assistance. This is one reason success is cumulative. Nonetheless, some risk-taking buyers, in exchange for very low prices, will work closely with inexperienced suppliers to teach them what is required and how to improve their management, technology, work flow, and much else. Such assistance from foreign buyers enables local firms to acquire valuable information and technology at little cost. But these buyers, too, prefer firms that have considerable industrial experience and capacity and are located in countries that provide a favorable policy environment rather than artificial incentives. Because of this contact with knowledgeable foreign buyers, local firms seem to learn much more from manufactured exports made to order for industrial countries than from exports of natural-resource products and standard local products made possible by subsidies, a recession, preferences from neighbors, or barter trade deals.

Requirements for Success

A central pillar of export success is macroeconomic stability, together with an adequate (that is, favorable) exchange rate. These features have been the hallmark of the rapid growth in manufactured exports from East Asia—from Hong Kong, Indonesia (in recent years), Japan, Korea, Malaysia, Singapore, Taiwan, and Thailand.

Another central pillar is an efficient system for providing exporters with rapid, reliable access to the inputs they need at prices that are no higher than tax-free international prices. To ensure that this is the case, imports of inputs required (whether directly or indirectly) for the production of exports need to be systematically freed from delays, quantitative restrictions and other nontariff barriers, customs tariffs, other import taxes, and indirect taxes—even if domestic substitutes for these imported inputs are available. Exporters also benefit if consumables (such as fuel oil) and spare parts are readily available at close to international prices. Most of the world's manufactured exports from market economies come from places where exports enjoy a virtual free-trade environment with regard to the taxation and availability of inputs. In most developing countries, however, the need for improved access to inputs is still considerable.

One way in which successful exporting countries have provided exporters with easy, duty-free access to imported inputs has been by following a policy of zero tariffs on imported inputs across the board. Hong Kong and Singapore are virtual free ports, and their export results have been spectacular.

Only a few countries have managed to develop strong manufactured export sectors while simultaneously maintaining high protection for domestic industries that compete with imports. The reason is twofold. First, high protection discourages exports indirectly by overvaluing the exchange rate and attracting domestic productive resources to industries that compete with imports. Second, heavily protected economies are typically characterized by administrative rationing of foreign exchange and import licenses, so it is administratively difficult to provide access to inputs at international prices. Duty waiver or temporary admission schemes are difficult to manage when high protection causes domestic prices for imports to diverge greatly from international prices, because the incentives for cheating, abuses, and diversion of inputs are multiplied.

Economies that have achieved strong export growth with protectionist policies—notably Korea and Taiwan—did so through a complex combination of policies and circumstances not easily replicated in other countries (see box 6-1). The unique circumstances included authoritarian regimes that were able to suppress rent-seeking behavior

Box 6-1. *An East Asian Model: Korea*

Korea's experience in the 1960s and 1970s is similar to that of Taiwan during the same period and to Japan's earlier experience. In all three cases, governments maintained quantitative restrictions in the import regimes while encouraging strong export growth. In Korea the shares of exports in GDP and in value added in manufacturing increased from 3.5 percent and 19.3 percent, respectively, in 1965 to 23.9 percent and 85.4 percent in 1981. Korea succeeded by following principles of sound macroeconomic management while coordinating export, import, and other policies in order to provide broadly neutral incentives for manufactured goods.

Macroeconomic Management

Korea consistently managed the real exchange rate to keep exports profitable and to minimize excess demand for imports. This was achieved by periodic nominal devaluations and aggregate demand policies that never allowed inflation to get out of hand. In only two of the years from 1970 to 1986 did the real exchange rate deviate significantly (by more than 14 percent) from the base year of 1980.[1] This degree of stability (which existed in earlier periods as well) is rare in the developing world. In a sense, macroeconomic policy was subordinated to the commitment to export because it was clear that expansionary fiscal and monetary policies and the consequent overvaluation of the exchange rate were fundamentally inconsistent with that goal.

Trade and Investment Policies

The government created special regimes for both direct and indirect exporters that enabled them to obtain inputs rapidly and at world or near-world prices. Thus exporters were insulated from the negative effect of import protection. A facility covered the working capital requirements of exporters at rates lower than normal bank lending rates for rationed domestic credit and much lower than informal curb market rates. Both the input and credit facilities were automatically available to all exporters without discrimination.

New investments in manufacturing needed government approval and support and relied on finance from the government banks. In most cases these decisions reflected consultation with private entrepreneurs, but in others the government was a leading promoter and, in a few cases, the entrepreneur as well. With some exceptions, the predominant criterion for these decisions was whether the investment could be profitable when exporting a major share of its output and while benefiting from no more than the standard export incentives. No advance assurance of special emergency assistance was generally

1. According to an internal World Bank report. Primary data are from the IMF. Real exchange rate estimates were based on deflation by the wholesale price index.

given, and, in fact, the bankruptcy rate among exporting firms was relatively high.

Various policies ensured that firms did not withdraw from exports to the protected domestic market. Above all, the government managed the basic exchange rate, macroeconomic, and export policies in a consistent and credible way that made it profitable for efficient firms to maintain and expand their exports. In some industries with substantial economies of scale, export profitability meant building plants that were too large to be profitable solely on the basis of domestic sales. Exports were regularly monitored against targets, and firms strove to meet or exceed them to improve their image and chances of receiving discretionary benefits. The most important of these was favorable consideration in the competition to invest in new plants for exports, together with credit for expansion. Some firms received valuable import licenses and government contracts as well. In some cases, relatively low export targets were agreed on for firms pioneering new processes or products, and for a few years these firms were permitted to sell most of their output at high and profitable prices in the domestic market. Thereafter, however, their export targets usually increased year after year until they exceeded their domestic sales. The pressure on such firms was further increased by allowing investments in the same product line by competing firms soon after the initial investments appeared to be successful. Capacity soon exceeded domestic demand, and its utilization was therefore dependent on direct or indirect exporting.

The rapid growth of manufactured exports often meant that, at the level of individual industries, the purely domestic market (as distinct from the domestic market for indirect exports) became a residual market and that the principal focus of competing firms was on exports. But export markets were highly competitive and risky, and subject to cyclical influences and protectionist lobbies that could close off or slow down profitable export opportunities. These changing conditions in export markets were reflected in the Korean domestic markets, which were generally highly competitive even though imports were prohibited or tightly restricted and even though seller concentration was sometimes high, especially in the markets for intermediate materials and engineering goods. Firms in such industries, because of fluctuating and not easily predictable capacity utilization arising from their predominant export activities, were seldom able to coordinate their policies and benefit from their potential market power. Studies of effective protection in Korean manufacturing in the 1960s and 1970s reflected these competitive conditions. Because imported raw materials used to produce goods for the domestic market were subject to import duties, domestic ex-factory prices were generally higher than export prices. But, after allowing for the preferential credit and tax advantages of exporters, processing margins in most export industries were broadly similar in domestic sales and exports.

(Box continues on the following page.)

Box 6-1 *(continued)*

Heavy Industry Promotion, 1973–79

In 1973, a new set of policies was superimposed on this basic model, with the objective being the development of heavy and chemical industries, including petrochemicals, steel, metal products, shipbuilding, machinery, and automobiles. Selective and discriminatory policies were followed, including substantial subsidies through long-term lending, tax holidays, accelerated depreciation, and import protection. These policies eventually succeeded for some industries (steel and automobiles) but were expensive failures in others (petrochemicals) and had mixed results in still others (heavy machinery). According to a recent internal Bank study, these policies contributed to an economic crisis in 1980 and, on average, produced low economic returns. Their deficiencies were rapidly recognized, and drastic restructuring of some industries began as early as 1979. These problems influenced the new liberalizing policy direction followed in the 1980s.[2]

Resource Allocation

In Korea, apart from some instances in the heavy and chemical industry episode, there were generally no major longstanding resource misallocations within the manufacturing sector. This in turn was due to Korea's export policies and orientation, in particular to the temporary nature of the special protection given to new exporting industries, the basically nondiscretionary and uniform incentives for manufactured exports, and the competition among exporters in domestic markets, which tended to equalize the profitability of exports and domestic sales. The higher protection of some nonexporting industries in the 1960s became quantitatively less and less important as the shares of direct and indirect exports in manufacturing rapidly increased.

Agriculture, however, was heavily protected, and the level of protection increased over time. This protection was costly for consumers and for the government budget, but was never as serious a brake on efficiency and growth as the more typical promanufacturing and antiagricultural bias of other trade regimes. For one thing, the distortion of consumption resulting from this protection was in part offset by the tariffs on imported materials and equipment, which raised the prices of domestically produced manufactured consumer goods, and also by relatively high indirect taxes, especially on luxuries and durables. For another, most of agriculture was inherently high-cost, and the

---

2. Kim Mahnje (former deputy prime minister of Korea), "Korea's Adjustment Policies and Their Implications for Other Countries," in Vittorio Corbo, Morris Goldstein, and Mohsin Khan, eds., *Growth-Oriented Adjustment Programs* (Washington, D.C.: IMF, 1987).

protection and subsidies it received were always kept below the level that would have produced a surplus on the domestic market and required exports. Thus the protection policies maintained agriculture as a protected import-substitute enclave, but as real incomes rose, agriculture's share in consumer budgets and in GDP declined much more rapidly than its level of protection increased, leading to a correspondingly rapid decline in the relative importance of agricultural protection for the economy and consumers.

Trade Liberalization in the 1980s

The fraction of customs-code items exempt from quantitative restrictions rose from about 60 percent in 1977 to 80 percent in 1985, with a target of 95 percent by 1988. The average tariff was reduced from 41 percent in 1978 to 22 percent in 1985, with a target of 18 percent in 1988. This change was partly in response to pressure from the United States and others to open Korean markets to imports. It also reflected a recognition that previous policies had produced problems and that the economy was becoming more complex and less amenable to selective government intervention—especially in investment. Greatly improved living standards and democratization of the political system also meant that the government was less able to control the activities of interest groups and to administer discretionary controls in the consistent and focused way it had previously. But liberalization of the trade regime and of other policies did not retard the growth of exports and the economy, which after slowing in 1979 and 1980 as a result of policy-induced imbalances and external shocks, continued at a rapid pace during the 1980s.

Lessons from the Korean Experience

One lesson from the Korean experience is the importance of maintaining a real exchange rate that is reasonably stable and adequate for a sustainable balance of payments as well as longer-term growth of exports and output. It also appears that it is critical to prevent import protection from tipping the terms of trade against exports, either directly (by raising the cost of imported inputs) or indirectly (by causing competition for resources). It is not clear that other countries can or should emulate Korea in more specific strategies, however. In particular, for strong export growth to coexist with protection of imports requires conditions that are not likely to be met in many countries. They include investment controls on the local production of luxury and other consumer goods whose import is banned or restricted, the control of rent-seeking and lobbying (by suppressing unions and penalizing executives of companies that misuse their privileges), and control of smuggling. In Korea,

(Box continues on the following page.)

Box 6-1 *(continued)*

all this was facilitated by the authoritarian nature of the regime and a widely shared national pride in the country's growing international status and the increased political security this implied. And even in Korea, incentives targeted to specific industries produced some expensive mistakes, this problem would be compounded in a political system in which rent-seeking is less effectively controlled. Finally, the credit subsidies offered to exports to help offset the effects of import protection are now more likely to be countervailed by developed countries.

that conflicted with the goal of export-oriented development. These economies also offset their protectionist policies with other industry and trade-promotion measures that would be difficult to administer and open to abuse elsewhere and augmented them at times with forms of export subsidies that are now usually countervailed by developed economies.[5] Furthermore, both economies recognized the disadvantages of protection and undertook to liberalize imports. Korea has been engaged since 1967 in a gradual process of import policy reform, which it greatly accelerated in the 1980s. This has resulted in fairly low protection in recent years. The economy's spectacular export growth has continued, and the share of exports in GDP increased during the import policy reforms of the 1980s.

Where import substitutes remain protected, the East Asian experience suggests that exporters should be insulated from the tendency of such protection to raise the prices of inputs above world prices and to reduce their availability and quality. Reliable, tax-free access to imported inputs is best provided by offering at least three alternative schemes at once, as described in the following paragraphs. While each may serve a different set of export requirements, the schemes should be available to all exporters and potential exporters. These schemes are not without cost, however. For one thing, they may at least temporarily reduce government revenue. In an environment of high import protection, such schemes also create opportunities for cheating and abuse. Their design and implementation require the attention of policymakers and consume administrative resources. These costs need to be balanced against the likely economic gains.

The most important of the three alternatives is a scheme that provides duty waivers and exemptions from other restrictions on imported inputs for established exporters of manufactures that import inputs, whether for export or domestic market production, or both. This may be a rebate scheme on account as in Taiwan, a deferred drawback scheme as in Korea, a temporary admissions scheme such as the ones set up or improved in Mexico and Morocco starting in 1983, or duty exemptions as in Indonesia and Thailand and in Korea before 1975. To illustrate, in Indonesia a special government unit gives out import licenses for the imported inputs required by manufacturing enterprises exporting directly. To obtain a license, an exporter must submit an export plan that includes technical coefficients for the inputs required, together with a bank guarantee for the value of the duties that must be paid if the exports are not realized within the period allowed. Manufacturers who export 85 percent of their output receive licenses for 100 percent of their imported inputs. Generally similar are the import entitlements scheme introduced in Turkey in 1980 and the advance licenses scheme started in India in 1978 and then greatly improved in the late 1980s.

What is administratively difficult in such schemes is, first, to extend them to indirect exporters, thereby making domestically made inputs competitive with imports and increasing the net value of exports, and, second, to ensure that (to the extent desirable) exporting firms get tax-free only as much of each input as is needed for export production. This approach safeguards government revenue and prevents imported inputs from spilling over into the domestic market and penalizing local production of the same inputs. For this second challenge, one solution, efficiently used in Korea and Taiwan, is to determine and routinely apply published technical coefficients for each of the usual export products (see box 6-2). Technical coefficients are used in a similar way for firms sponsored by the Board of Investments in Thailand. The approach has recently been expanded in Bangladesh, India, and Pakistan with encouragement from the World Bank, but it is still almost unknown outside Asia. Another approach, used for example in Morocco, is a system of rebates based on declarations by exporters, with verification by customs officials within six months.

Such schemes need to ensure both that sufficient quantities of inputs can be imported to satisfy all of an exporter's needs for export production and that these imports cannot be sold at high prices in the protected domestic market. If either of these conditions fails to be met, the shadow price of the imports will still be the (protected) domestic price and the objective of encouraging exports by providing imports at world prices will not be achieved.

A second arrangement is needed to meet the needs of small or occasional exporters and for materials required in small quantities. A quick, reliable system of drawbacks or rebates of duties and indirect taxes actually paid is essential so that exporters can buy their inputs duty paid

Box 6-2. *Duty Rebates in Taiwan*

Since 1955, Taiwan's support for exports has included rebates of import duties and other indirect taxes on inputs used directly or indirectly to produce manufactured exports. A firm that is a major, regular, law-abiding manufacturer-exporter is allowed to put its duty liabilities "on account," to be canceled against evidence of subsequent exports. Firms must furnish a bank guarantee that the duty plus penalties will be paid if the exports are not produced within eighteen months. Since 1965, exporting firms have had the further option of locating in an export processing zone or becoming in-bond manufacturers, but these schemes account for only modest shares of the economy's exports. Firms (including trading firms) not involved in either of these schemes must pay duties on their imported inputs. These duties are reimbursed or canceled for exporters by the customs administration following presentation of documentation showing completed exports, receipt and appropriate disposition of foreign exchange proceeds, and the amount of the rebate to which the firm is entitled. The customs administration handles more than half a million rebate applications a year with a staff of about 200.

Either the direct exporter or one indirect exporter collects the entire rebate. The indirect exporter (for example, a firm supplying inputs for exports) can collect the rebate only if the direct exporter signs over the necessary documents. Often, a large supplier of inputs that is dependent on imported raw materials systematically acquires these documents from its small exporter customers and collects the rebates. Typically, it sells to direct exporters (or extends them credit by accepting postdated checks) at a duty-free price, but it also requires a postdated check covering the duty. This check is returned uncashed once the exporting firm signs over its documents.

Rebates on new products are calculated on a case-by-case basis, whereas rebates for established products are determined on the basis of published fixed rates. Both methods involve the systematic application by customs rebate officials of preestablished input coefficients for each physical unit of output.

To export a product not previously exported, an exporter must obtain an export license and a list of the product's physical input-output coefficients. To work out the coefficients, government staff or consultants visit the fac-

and later get the duties back, rather than having to import inputs in small lots or pay duties. This alternative is built into rebates in Taiwan and drawbacks in Korea, while other countries such as India, Indonesia, and Thailand offer drawbacks as a separate alternative. Collecting duties and giving them back later is administratively more expensive than waiving duties, however, and drawbacks do not offset nontariff barriers against imported inputs. For administrative simplicity and the

tory, inspect its records, and examine or test the product. The list is then certified and supplied to the customs administration within a month of the exporter's application. To get a rebate, the exporter must then provide evidence on the source and quantity of all imported and dutiable inputs used. To save administrative time, any input valued at less than 1 percent of the value (FOB) of the exported product is dropped from the calculation of the rebate.

Once a product has had a long enough production history for its input and output coefficients to be fairly stable, it is switched over to the fixed-rate method. To work out the fixed rate, the customs administration calculates the duties rebated on all inputs (direct or indirect) into the product over the previous twelve months compared with the combined value or volume of the corresponding exports for all makers of the product. The result is a standard rate based on value or a physical unit such as weight. Where technical processes and input coefficients of different firms vary widely, their exports are defined as different products with their own fixed rates. Fixed rates on about 6,000 products are published each July, reflecting changes since the previous year in prices, duties, and sources of inputs.

Once a fixed rate is in effect, exporters receive the stipulated amount of rebate only after providing evidence that they paid (directly or indirectly) duties and indirect taxes equal to that amount. Otherwise, they receive rebates equal only to the amount they actually paid. However, details are no longer examined. If an exporting firm shows that its actual payments were more than 20 percent higher than the standard rebate, and it can give good reasons why it needs these extra imported inputs, it can apply to an interagency committee for a redefinition of its export as a separate product eligible for a higher rebate.

The system described began to be partly dismantled, along with protective tariffs, after the mid-1980s. The description is of the system in operation around 1984.

Source: Robert Wade, "Taiwan, China's Duty Rebate System," Trade Policy Division, Country Economics Department, World Bank (Washington, D.C., 1988).

---

convenience of exporters, the scheme should offer a standard drawback for each product regularly exported and also allow each exporter the option of presenting evidence to justify a considerably higher individual drawback.

Third, at least one duty-free scheme can usefully be provided for firms specializing in exports. It should serve to move shipments in and out quickly and at little expense to the firms involved. The most flexible approach is in-bond manufacturing for export, which entails bringing in the inputs and shipping the outputs under customs seal. Bonded factories can be located practically anywhere. An example is Mexico's *maquila* in-bond assembly plants. Modern, streamlined in-bond schemes involve only minimal bonding and customs expenses for enterprises, in contrast to antiquated procedures, still widely practiced, that involve having customs officers on duty in a warehouse and expensive bonds for every shipment. Mauritius's export processing zone is based on a streamlined duty exemption system that functions wherever an exporter wants to locate.

The main alternative to these systems is to have physically separate export processing zones. Each is an industrial zone specializing in exports, with its own customs office to provide the enterprises inside with duty-free trade and quick customs clearances. At least thirty developing countries now have export processing zones of this type. Many of these zones have proved to be poor investments as a result of an unfavorable location, high investment costs, mediocre management, or uncooperative customs officials, but a few (some private) have done well. Manufactured exports from Malaysia and, on a much smaller scale, from the Dominican Republic and Haiti come mainly from such zones. China's special economic zones, all created since 1979, are larger versions with people living in them. A comparison of successful East Asian exporters with other countries that have tried this approach shows that the zones tend to be successful where they are part of an overall favorable environment, rather than a substitute for such an environment.[6]

Export production, like other economic activities, benefits from well-designed and well-located infrastructure, including telecommunications, power grids, ports for containerized cargo, highways, airports, and industrial estates (parks). Exporters have a special need for access to foreign exchange for marketing and service expenses abroad as well as for imports. They also have a variety of service needs, starting with ready access to preshipment credit for working capital and term finance for investments. Capital markets that function well are therefore important. In addition, exporters benefit from restriction-free access to imported capital equipment and technology and from low import duties and indirect taxes on machinery. They also benefit from investment procedures—including those governing foreign investment—that are transparent and efficient.

Attracting foreign direct investment is crucial for success in very small countries that have little industry. Results have been strongest where the investment promotion authorities are also responsible for the development and operation of state-owned industrial estates and can help ensure the availability of sites and infrastructure. This has been the case in Singapore since 1961 and in Mauritius since the World Bank helped to launch the Mauritius Export Development and Investment Authority in 1983. (Foreign direct investment is discussed in more detail in chapter 8.)

Judging by what has been done in East Asia, it also pays to adjust some other—often politically sensitive—regulations and administrative procedures, not just for exporters but for all firms. Labor regulations on laying off workers, fringe benefits, minimum wages, collective action, and the like are important and may need to be adjusted to reduce labor costs and increase flexibility at the enterprise level. Industrial location and regional development policy may have to be changed—exports cannot be expected from underdeveloped areas with poor infrastructure. Measures to quicken competition and facilitate rapid economic change, such as those discussed in chapter 7, can indirectly contribute to the expansion of exports.

Successful Asian economies also strive to make world-quality services available to exporters, including, for example, design, trade information, and consultant services. Organizations initially funded by government in close collaboration with private industry offer consulting services to manufacturing firms to help them improve productivity, technology, and quality control. Korea and, to a lesser extent, other economies have also fostered large trading companies that organize and market exports from smaller firms through a network of offices overseas. Korea and Taiwan have systematically fostered the establishment of industries that supply intermediate industrial inputs at world (or lower) prices. This has been achieved by building well-located, large-scale, state-of-the-art plants and by stimulating competition to attain excellence in each production process.

Unsatisfactory Means of Increasing Exports

Numerous examples show that unsatisfactory methods can achieve minor, but usually only temporary, increases in exports. Most common are high export subsidies or a severe recession. Contractionary macroeconomic policies often serve to increase some exports rather quickly as domestic demand shrinks, but the effect is reversed as the economy recovers. Other generally unsatisfactory means include barter trade agreements or pressuring foreign-owned enterprises to export as a condition of being allowed to retain a profitable share of the domestic market. Several episodes in Latin American countries in which manufactured exports began to rise and then fell back involved heavy dependence on these methods, although economywide influences have also contributed to the downturn.

Export subsidies have been used in lieu of devaluation and to try to offset domestic protection. Results are generally disappointing. Used as a temporary measure, however, with appropriate macroeconomic and exchange rate policies and access to imported inputs, subsidies can have a direct and immediate impact on exports—as in Turkey, for example. Many countries have also tried to promote exports by providing subsidized credit, sometimes with positive effects on exports. These subsidies have not proved as important, however, as ensuring that exporters have ready access to preshipment credit.

In general, subsidies—including income tax rebates, which have long been used in Latin America—have not had satisfactory effects on exports. One study that reviewed the experience of seven developing countries found export credit and insurance subsidy schemes to be ineffective by and large.[7] High subsidies have also usually resulted in cheating to get the subsidies and in wasteful rent-seeking, as experience in Sri Lanka, Turkey, Yugoslavia, and other countries illustrates.[8] Furthermore, the heavy fiscal burden of the high subsidies needed to offset a strong antiexport bias may generate macroeconomic disequilibrium and an external debt problem, as in Yugoslavia, or hinder efficient export sectors, as in Argentina.[9] In Sri Lanka, the export subsidies were financed through a surcharge on imports—hardly a positive step toward reducing the antiexport bias of the trade regime. In most countries the subsidies are targeted only to certain export sectors, moving the incentive structure further from neutrality among sectors. Policies involving special treatment of exporters, including subsidies, foreign exchange retention allowances, and favorable exchange rates, can also cause problems and a dubious allocation of resources in socialist countries. For example, according to a World Bank report on adjustment lending, China's success in achieving rapid aggregate export growth seems less dramatic in view of the possibility that a significant proportion of exports may have been economically unprofitable because of excessive incentives (resulting from competitive subsidies between provinces and regions) and a highly distorted price system.[10]

Most economies that have recorded strong export growth have avoided serious disincentives to exports by following a combination of exchange rate, export, and import policies. Some of the fastest and most sustained growth rates in exports have been attained in Japan, Korea, and Taiwan within policy frameworks that included sound macroeconomic management as well as targeted interventions to develop manufactured exports. Industrial policy involving selective interventions, however, has proved costly and unsuccessful in most economies; in Korea, as well, the results have been mixed (box 6-1).[11]

Technical Assistance

Technical assistance provided to official trade-promotion organizations to improve their information services and their support for export marketing has had especially disappointing results. The components of World Bank loans earmarked for this purpose in more than fifteen countries seem to have been ineffective in expanding exports. More promising approaches for improving support services need encouragement. These include partial subsidies to firms in export industries for production-related assistance from consultants of international caliber, for example, by the establishment of funds (as in India) offering matching grants to firms to purchase services from consultants and suppliers of their choice, whether domestic or foreign, as a component of a firm's export expansion program. They also include the systematic fostering of a broad range of competitive private service suppliers, including experienced foreign firms. Examples would be management consultants, engineering consultants, accounting firms, banks, insurance companies, business publishers, trading companies, foreign firms' purchasing offices, export market research firms, product inspection firms, and testing laboratories.[12]

Many countries have sought to improve the availability of preshipment export credit for working capital, but with only limited and mixed results. Revolving fund arrangements for imported inputs, as in Mexico or Zimbabwe, have proved to be unneeded or have turned into giveaway programs. Some reforms inspired by Korean examples have yet to work well outside Korea. These include automatic guarantees to banks for preshipment export credit, to ensure that exporters with suitable letters of credit receive access to this form of credit, and the use of domestic (inland) letters of credit by exporters to order inputs from local suppliers. The domestic letters of credit are meant to identify the recipients as indirect exporters eligible for export credit and other perquisites of exporting.

The creation or improvement of duty waiver or temporary admissions schemes has yielded the most satisfactory results with regard to exports from reforms supported by World Bank advice and technical assistance. The best examples are India, Indonesia, Mexico, Morocco, and Turkey. Positive export effects also followed an increase in the range of tax-free imported inputs allowed in Brazil beginning in 1983, until this reform was reversed. Argentina, Tunisia, and Uruguay have taken a broadly similar approach. By contrast, results for manufactured exports have been disappointing where the goal appears to have been to set up or improve drawback systems (as in Chile, Ghana, Jamaica, Nepal, Senegal, or Zambia). Despite this experience, many

World Bank loans in 1988 and 1989 supported drawback schemes that had no provisions for exempting exporters from the effects of non-tariff barriers to imported inputs. The outcome has been no more than partly satisfactory where the effort has concentrated on in-bond systems and the use of technical coefficients by customs officials (as in Bangladesh and Pakistan).

Export subsidies for manufactured products are generally subject to countervailing duties. For this reason, and because of concern over potential abuses, the World Bank has seldom recommended export subsidies except as part of a surrogate devaluation (as in the Côte d'Ivoire structural adjustment loan [SAL] II; see also box 3-3 in chapter 3). The World Bank has sometimes supported reform or continuation of an existing subsidy scheme as a temporary measure to offset an antiexport bias (Kenya SAL I; Turkey SALs I, II, and III; Turkey began to scale down the subsidies under SAL V). Measures to help exporters with services, to rebate indirect taxes to them, or to give them better infrastructure, inputs, services, and credit access are not usually considered subsidies under international trade rules. However, giving exporters better prices or interest rates than other domestic firms is not generally recommended in view of the costs and complications involved. Consequently, in some operations (Korea SAL II) the World Bank has supported their phaseout.

Primary Sector Exports

Growth in exports from primary sectors is constrained to some extent by protectionist policies in developed countries (see chapter 8). Low demand elasticities abroad are sometimes cited as constraints to African primary exports, although the evidence is far from clear (see box 6-3), especially when it is recognized that real income may be increased by greater exports, even if revenue declines.

In addition, primary exports are depressed in most developing countries by excessive protection of the country's own manufacturing industries and by a heavy drain of national resources to support industry, urban areas, and the public sector. One usual effect is to turn the terms of trade severely against agriculture while also diminishing the range and quality of products offered in exchange for farm output. Burdens commonly borne by primary exporters include currency overvaluation, restrictions on primary exports, taxes on exports or production, artificially low administered prices, and inefficient monopolistic government production or marketing enterprises. Laws that discourage investment (especially foreign investment) in the primary goods sector also reduce primary sector exports. In some countries the cumulative effect of distortions has been to depress agriculture so severely that the forgone exports are a major macroeconomic cost. In Argentina, where agriculture provides about 75 percent of exports, agricultural exports might be twice as high were it not for the antiexport policy bias.[13]

Malaysia in the 1960s and Chile in the late 1970s achieved good results with comprehensive programs to create a positive policy environment for primary exports. Chile's reforms helped reinvigorate the export-oriented mining sector, largely by encouraging foreign private initiative. They also led to a spectacular increase in agricultural and wood product exports, which grew from US$44 million in 1972 to US$1,102 million in 1986.[14] Low protection in manufacturing was a central feature, along with a realistic exchange rate, in both countries.

In the 1980s, reform programs for primary exports have been more modest, with important exceptions. Bolivia and Ghana have followed Chile's example and opened up mining to foreign investment. In agriculture, prices for leading primary product exports have been improved (Côte d'Ivoire, Malawi, and Turkey). Taxes on agricultural exports were significantly reduced in Argentina and Uruguay as part of operations connected with adjustment loans to the agricultural sector, although this policy was quickly reversed in Argentina. Regulatory controls on exports have been abolished or greatly reduced (as in Colombia, Mexico, and Morocco, for example), and taxes on many exports have been eliminated (as in Bangladesh, Côte d'Ivoire, Ghana, Madagascar, and the Philippines, for example).

Malaysia and Thailand have sustained strong growth in primary exports by consistently avoiding major currency overvaluation, heavy taxation of the sector, and high protection for manufactured exports. Especially since 1986, Indonesia has generated booming manufacturing and nonfuel primary exports through devaluation supported by sound macroeconomic policy. Correction of overvalued exchange rates and establishment or improvement of foreign exchange retention schemes for exporters have played a central role in reviving primary exports from Ghana and Tanzania and nonoil exports from Nigeria.

A number of trade policy reforms have included eliminating public sector marketing boards or stripping them of their monopoly procurement powers, as in Ghana, Mali, Morocco, Nigeria, and Senegal. In Africa, these reforms were intended to raise producer prices of export crops, which had been reduced by the boards to levels far below border prices and so constituted a heavy implicit tax on production. In the case of export crops, the implicit tax was mainly a revenue-generating device for the marketing boards and the government budget; for import crops (such as rice in Madagascar), producer prices were depressed to keep prices low for urban consumers. In Latin America, where producer prices have not been seriously depressed by the marketing

---

**Box 6-3.   *Structural Adjustment and External Demand:
Constraints on Agricultural Exports in Africa***

A consequence of adjustment programs is likely to be an expansion in the production of tradables, including agricultural commodities, especially in Sub-Saharan Africa. One important concern, however, is that the simultaneous expansion of agricultural exports by several countries may lead to a reduction in world prices, which may, in turn, reduce export revenues and possibly the real incomes of the adjusting countries.

At the global level, the impact of an increase in export volume on the total earnings of all exporters of a commodity will depend on the elasticity of world import demand for that commodity. Aggregate export revenues will rise if the elasticity is more than one or fall if it is less than one. How does that translate to the regional and country levels, and what does it imply for the World Bank's policy advice?

The elasticity of demand facing Africa's exports is larger than the elasticity of world import demand, but for several commodities Africa's share in world exports is large. So for some commodities, Africa may face an elasticity of demand for its exports that is smaller than one, and an increase in the exports of these commodities may lead to a fall in export revenues. This concern may be valid for certain commodities such as cocoa (Africa had about 61 percent of world exports in 1985), palm kernels (53 percent), sisal (43 percent), coffee (22 percent), and groundnut oil (21 percent). It may apply to a lesser degree to tea (15 percent), cotton and tobacco (9 percent), and groundnuts (7 percent).[1]

It is much less likely that the elasticity of demand facing an individual country's exports will be smaller than one, so the expansion of exports by one country should lead to larger export revenues for that country in most cases. Thus, correcting distortions in incentives, improving efficiency, and letting the market work (possibly with some export taxation) would seem to be the

---

1. Ulrich Koester, Hartwig Schafer, and Alberto Valdes, "External Demand Constraints for Agricultural Exports: An Impediment to Structural Adjustment Policies in Sub-Saharan African Countries?" *Food Policy* 14, 3 (1989):274–83.

---

boards, such reforms were intended to increase the efficiency of marketing and alleviate the fiscal drain on the government.

While the vagaries of weather and international price fluctuations make the effects of these reforms difficult to verify, in at least some cases the results have been impressive. Nigeria's abolition of marketing boards for palm oil, cocoa, rubber, cotton, and groundnuts, together with exchange reforms in 1986, led almost immediately to a 6 percent increase in cash crop production in 1987 in spite of bad weather. In

optimal policy from an individual country's viewpoint, assuming that the policies of other countries remain unchanged.

The World Bank, however, is advising many countries in Africa (and elsewhere) to correct price distortions, including currency overvaluation, and remove inefficient controls. This is likely to result in a simultaneous supply response in a large number of countries and may lead to a fall in export revenues for some important commodities. But the advice to correct basic relative price distortions, remove controls, and improve overall economic and productive efficiency is generally sound because it will ensure that countries produce the goods they can produce most cheaply. When increased production results from reductions in cost, real incomes may rise even if revenues fall. But the problem remains that this may lead to losses in export revenues and income at the regional level for some commodities.

Moreover, this problem may be more severe for countries whose exports are concentrated in a few commodities for which Africa's share is large (for example, Côte d'Ivoire, which exports coffee and cocoa) than for countries with a more diversified export base. Also, improvements in productive efficiency (say, through liberalization of markets and marketing functions) should lead to regional income gains, but may result in losses in countries where the improvement in efficiency is below the average.

In promoting greater market orientation, the question then is whether the World Bank should support individual countries' policies with respect to the commodities in question, or whether it should support efforts at regional coordination of policies with respect to these products. The evidence on the importance of this phenomenon is scarce, and the analytical, empirical, and implementation problems underlying it deserve further analysis. It should be noted, however, that coordination of production among primary exporting countries has been tried many times, with very few successes.

Source: Background note by Maurice Schiff, Trade Policy Division, Country Economics Department, World Bank.

Madagascar, the marketing role of the rice board was replaced by a well-designed buffer stock scheme, supplemented by modest imports. The results were higher producer prices for rice, rejuvenation of the rice-producing sector, and rapid development of private marketing channels.

Marketing boards are also intended to stabilize domestic prices by insulating domestic producers and consumers from at least some fluctuations in international prices. Although their record of success in this regard is mixed,[15] there is little question that governments consider this goal important. Consequently, it may be difficult to eliminate or reduce the role of these boards unless some alternative means is substituted to achieve the stabilization objective. The agricultural sector adjustment loan to Ecuador called for the abolition of a marketing board without proposing an alternative system to stabilize prices; this reform was never implemented.[16] By contrast, in Madagascar, a marketing board is being successfully phased out, in part because a buffer stock and import scheme has served the stabilization role. Other potential models include the Revenue Stabilization Fund for copper in Chile, the buffer funds for agricultural exports in Papua New Guinea, and the coffee stabilization policy pursued in Colombia (see box 6-4). The arrangement in Chile partially sterilizes changes in budget resources as a result of movements in copper prices outside a predetermined band in order to reduce fluctuations in the exchange rate and public sector consumption. The scheme in Papua New Guinea relies on moderate taxes when world prices are high, which are then used to fund subsidies when prices are low, but the scheme tries to maintain average prices to exporters at their long-run international levels.

Cross-country evidence suggests an exchange rate supply elasticity of primary exports for all developing countries of 0.68, which is almost as large as that for all merchandise (including primary) exports (0.77).[17] For Sub-Saharan Africa, the elasticity for agricultural exports (1.35) is even larger than that for all exports (1.01). Ghana and, more recently, Nigeria and Tanzania have substantially increased primary exports in response to incentives. In a number of markets (cocoa, coffee, palm oil, rubber, copra, tea, and cotton), African countries have lost market shares during the past twenty years to countries (especially in Asia) that have more liberal price and marketing regimes and that have encouraged private investment and improved productivity. These pieces of evidence, together with the continuing existence of significant distortions in the sector, indicate that policy reform aimed at primary sectors (particularly agriculture) can play an important role in adjustment programs by quickly increasing exports.[18]

Perhaps the most important of the policy reforms in Africa are those aimed at increasing the role of the private sector in pricing and marketing agricultural imports and production.[19] One important reform is to eliminate or reduce the power of state marketing boards. Persuading the private sector to enter these markets may require other changes in policies affecting pricing and subsidies to ensure that price margins for transport and storage can cover costs. Another important reform is to encourage the development of informal rural credit markets and to attract commercial banks into agricultural lending by freeing interest rates. Other priorities to improve the efficiency of agriculture are encouraging the use of new technologies to increase productivity, enhancing environmental protection, developing infrastructure (particularly transportation), encouraging rural participation (including women) in decision-making, and improving the security of land tenure.

Summary and Conclusion

Manufactured exports from developing countries grew rapidly in the 1980s, but performances varied greatly from country to country. With some exceptions, primary exports have grown more slowly. Two conditions have been particularly important for expanding manufactured exports: macroeconomic stability around a real exchange rate that is compatible with long-term expansion of exports and output, and access to inputs at tax-free international prices for exporters. One way of ensuring the latter is to have no tariffs or other barriers on imported inputs, as in Hong Kong and Singapore, which are virtual free-trade zones. Otherwise, some means should be used to give exporters quick, duty-free access to imported inputs, such as duty waivers, temporary admission, in-bond manufacturing, export processing zones, or a combination of these. Drawback or rebate schemes can be helpful where tariffs raise the prices of inputs, but they do nothing to offset the effects of nontariff barriers. Reforms intended to improve or create duty waiver or temporary admission schemes have generally shown the best export supply response. Other important measures include reforms of the institutional, legal, regulatory, labor, and industrial policy frameworks.

Expanding manufactured exports requires sustained, vigorous, and many-sided efforts on both macroeconomic and microeconomic levels. Reviving primary exports calls for attention to macroeconomic stability, price incentives (such as appropriate real exchange rates and reduced export taxes), investment and other policies that raise productivity and reduce costs, and institutional changes, such as eliminating the monopsony power of marketing boards. It has proved difficult to develop strong export sectors while maintaining high import protection, which usually produces an overvalued exchange rate. The higher the protection, the more difficult it is to counteract the adverse effects on exports. The few countries with protective import policies that have been successful exporters (for example, Korea) have avoided exchange rate overvaluation and antiexport bias. Korea's approach during the 1960s and 1970s would be difficult to replicate, for a number of reasons.

Box 6-4.   *Dutch Disease and Policy Response: Lessons of Experience*

When export earnings from a commodity constitute a large fraction of a country's supply of foreign exchange, booms and busts in its price (or output) can have significant economic effects. Increases in the price or volume of an export cause the country's real income to rise, but do not affect all sectors equally. The increased foreign exchange earnings tend to generate an appreciation of the real exchange rate, thereby reducing producer incomes in tradable goods sectors except for the booming sector itself or sectors whose prices are delinked from world prices (by nontariff barriers to trade, for example). This adverse effect on other sectors has come to be known as the Dutch disease, after the effect on the Dutch economy of such changes in its natural gas exports. Similar effects have occurred in other commodities and countries.

In spite of the pejorative label, Dutch disease is not necessarily bad. Appreciation of the exchange rate sends the appropriate signal that a change in relative prices in external markets should lead to a change in domestic resource allocation. However, inappropriate macroeconomic policy responses that treat temporary increases as if they were permanent can have serious, adverse macroeconomic consequences. In response to the oil booms, governments of a number of oil-exporting countries greatly increased consumption spending and foreign borrowing, on the assumption that the debt could be repaid with future oil earnings. Pinto, for example, has documented that such a response in Nigeria exacerbated the appreciation of the real exchange rate resulting from the oil boom, devastated the agricultural sector, and created severe macroeconomic imbalances after the boom ended.[1] Similar responses to commodity booms in Côte d'Ivoire (coffee and cocoa) and Senegal (phosphates) had the same effects.[2] Trade policy can also play a role in determining the effects of a boom. When restrictions prevent foreign exchange from being spent on increased imports, the negative effect on the exchange rate (and exportables sectors) is that much more severe, while the incentives for the production of import substitutes increase. Restrictions also may create unforeseen distributional consequences. Higher coffee prices in 1976–79 initially greatly improved producers' incomes in Kenya, but restrictions on imports and capital controls increased rents to suppliers of capital and consumer goods so that much of the gain ended up going to urban areas.[3]

---

1. Brian Pinto, "Nigeria during and after the Oil Boom: A Policy Comparison with Indonesia," *World Bank Economic Review* 1 (May 1987):419–45.

2. Shantayanan Devarajan and Jaime de Melo, "Adjustment with a Fixed Exchange Rate: Cameroon, Côte D'Ivoire, and Senegal," *World Bank Economic Review* 1 (May 1987):447–87.

3. D. L. Bevan, Paul Collier, and J. W. Gunning, "Consequences of a Commodity Boom in a Controlled Economy: Accumulation and Redistribution in Kenya, 1975–83," *World Bank Economic Review* 1 (May 1987).

The Experience of Colombia

A comparative study of Colombia's two recent coffee booms (a major one in 1976–80 and a smaller one in 1985–86) provides some interesting lessons.[4] In the first boom, both fiscal and monetary policies magnified the expansionary effect of the boom. Government expenditures began to grow rapidly in 1977 and accelerated even after prices peaked in 1978. On average, they grew at an annual rate of 38.5 percent during 1977–80. Most of the increase was in government consumption, which rose from 7.7 percent of GDP in 1977 to 10.1 percent in 1980. Meanwhile, revenue grew modestly in comparison, and the fiscal deficit expanded, financed in large part by foreign borrowing. Monetary policy was basically expansionary, with little or no reduction in government net credit to offset the large buildup of foreign assets. The monetary base expanded rapidly. Eventually, trade policy was liberalized somewhat, but the reform was slow and was reversed in 1983–85 as reserves fell. The rapid fall of reserves was apparently at least partially due to rapid spending on imports as it became clear that the liberalization would be only temporary.

The net effect of the shock and subsequent policies was a significant appreciation of the real exchange rate. The trade-weighted real effective exchange rate appreciated almost 30 percent between 1975 and 1982, before beginning to depreciate.[5] Noncoffee exports fell from 7.7 percent of GDP in 1976 to 4.3 percent in 1983, completely reversing the diversification of the export base that had occurred between 1967 and 1974.

When prices again rose at the end of 1985 and early in 1986, the government responded with a much less expansionary fiscal and monetary policy. Relatively small portions of the increased revenues were passed on to producers (in the form of higher prices) or taxed away directly by the central government. By an agreement between the central government and the National Coffee Fund, most of the increase was retained by the fund to be used for strengthening its finances and for supporting several development programs. The fund was to use a fraction of the proceeds to invest in dollar-denominated instruments, a fraction to purchase bonds from the central bank, and a fraction to repay external debt, both directly and by lending to public entities that would in turn repay their debt. The net effect was to sterilize about 60

---

4. W. Easterly and J. Cuddington, "Management of Coffee Export Booms in Colombia," Macroeconomic and Growth Division, Country Economics Department, World Bank (Washington, D.C., 1986).

5. Vinod Thomas, *Linking Macroeconomic and Agricultural Policies for Adjustment and Growth: The Colombian Experience* (Baltimore, Md.: Johns Hopkins University Press, 1985).

(Box continues on the following page.)

Box 6-4 *(continued)*

percent of the windfall by external debt repayment and about 20 percent by the second mechanism cited above, which was equivalent to an open market operation. Thus, only 20 percent of the increased revenue entered the money supply. On the fiscal side, the increased coffee tax revenues were used to turn the public deficit of 5.2 percent of GDP in 1984 into a small surplus in 1986.

Alternative Mechanisms

The mechanism used in Colombia in 1985–86 was helpful in controlling the fiscal and monetary response to the boom. But it was complex and had costs of its own, including the segmentation of financial markets through the use of various special financial instruments carrying nonmarket interest rates. Furthermore, it was specifically designed for the circumstances of the period. Other mechanisms have been used in other countries to accomplish similar goals in a simpler and more automatic manner, and they deserve further study. Chile, for example, has established a revenue stabilization fund for government receipts from copper exports, with rules of operation that allow withdrawal of only a part of the annual earnings in a boom year. Papua New Guinea operates buffer funds for several commodities, with producer prices taxed or subsidized, depending on whether current world prices are above or below their long-term trends. The taxes or subsidies are withdrawn from or deposited into funds, part of which are required to be maintained in a special foreign currency account that does not constitute a part of the monetary base, thus automatically sterilizing fluctuating earnings.

Notes

1. R. J. Caballero and Vittorio Corbo, "How Does Uncertainty about the Real Exchange Rate Affect Exports?" Policy, Planning, and Research Working Paper no. 221, Country Economics Department, World Bank (Washington, D.C., 1989).

2. Combined with other measures, a real depreciation of the exchange rate has played a major role in increasing exports, as in Chile and Colombia in the 1970s or, more recently, in India, Mexico, Pakistan, Turkey, and (in some years) China. As an interim measure in situations involving severe exchange rate uncertainty and multiple rates, exporters of manufactures in China, Ghana, Nigeria, Poland, and Tanzania (and in Turkey from 1980 to 1984) have been given the right to use a substantial percentage of their foreign exchange earnings for production-related imports and other payments abroad. Such foreign exchange retention schemes have usually helped increase hard currency exports under disequilibrium conditions.

3. Developing countries are defined here as the low- and middle-income countries in the World Bank's *World Development Report 1989* (New York: Oxford University Press, 1989). Apart from centrally planned economies that are not World Bank members, they include all economies with a per capita GNP of under US$6,000 in 1987 (which is less than that of Ireland or Spain, for example).

4. The last two columns in table 6-1 include estimates of export growth in terms of purchasing power calculated from an index of the unit values of industrial countries' manufactured exports. These growth rates understate the real growth of purchasing power because continuing improvements in the technology and quality of manufactured products (especially of machinery) in industrial countries are not reflected in the price indexes. Furthermore, developing countries are to varying degrees importers of crude oil and primary commodities, and to this extent the overall growth in the purchasing power of their exports was lower than shown during the 1970s and higher than shown during the 1980s until 1987. After 1987, world primary commodity prices recovered, and the purchasing power of exports was again affected in the opposite direction.

5. Bela Balassa and associates, *Development Strategies in Semi-Industrial Economies* (Baltimore, Md.: Johns Hopkins University Press, 1982).

6. J. F. Linn and D. L. Wetzel. "Public Finance, Trade and Development: What Have We Learned?" In Vito Tanzi, ed., *Fiscal Policy in Open Developing Economies* (Washington, D.C.: IMF, 1990).

7. Bruce Fitzgerald and Terry Monson, "Preferential Credit and Insurance as Means to Promote Exports," *World Bank Research Observer* 4 (January 1989):89–114.

8. See World Bank, Country Operations Division, Latin America and the Caribbean Department, "The Timing and Sequencing of a Trade Liberalization Policy: Inferences from Country Studies and Emerging Hypotheses for Further Analysis: Discussion" (edited transcript of a conference in Lisbon, Portugal, June 15, 1986), pp. 65–70 (Yugoslavia) and pp. 77–87 (Turkey); also pp. 66–67 (New Zealand) and p. 72 (Sri Lanka).

9. Oli Havrylyshyn, "Yugoslavia: The Experience of Trade Policy Reform, 1965–1975," in World Bank, "Trade Liberalization: The Lessons of Experience," LAC Regional Series Report no. IDP14, Latin America and the Caribbean Department, World Bank (Washington, D.C., 1988); and Julio Nogués, "Latin America's Experience with Export Subsidies," Policy, Planning, and Research Working Paper no. 182, International Economics Department, World Bank (Washington, D.C., 1989).

10. World Bank, *Adjustment Lending: An Evaluation of Ten Years of Experience,* Policy and Research Series no. 1 (Washington, D.C., 1989).

11. World Bank, "Korea: Managing the Industrial Transition," East Asia and Pacific Country Programs Department (Washington, D.C., 1986).

12. See D. B. Keesing and Andrew Singer, "How to Provide High-Impact Assistance to Manufactured Exports from Developing Countries," Trade Policy Division, Country Economics Department, World Bank (Washington, D.C., 1989).

13. Adolfo Sturzenegger, "Argentina," in A. O. Krueger, Maurice Schiff, and Alberto Valdes, eds., *The Political Economy of Agricultural Pricing Policy*, vol. 1, *Latin America* (Washington, D.C.: World Bank, forthcoming).

14. Data are from World Bank, *World Development Report 1986* (New York: Oxford University Press, 1986), pp. 106–9, and an internal World Bank report on Chile's agricultural sector.

15. For export crops (beverages and fibers), domestic prices and producer revenues were less stable than they would have been had they been determined by border prices in 30 to 40 percent of the cases studied. For cereal grains, this was true in 10 to 15 percent of the cases. Odin Knudsen and John Nash, "Domestic Price Stabilization Schemes in Developing Countries," *Economic Development and Cultural Change* 38, no. 3 (April 1990): 538–58.

16. Odin Knudsen and John Nash, "Agricultural Policy," in Vinod Thomas and others, eds., *Restructuring Economies in Distress: Policy Reform and the World Bank* (New York: Oxford University Press, 1991).

17. Bela Balassa, "Economic Incentives and Agricultural Exports in Developing Countries" (paper presented at the Eighth Congress of the International Economic Association, New Delhi, India, 1986). The paper also found a significant positive supply elasticity of export crops (and total value added in agriculture) with respect to producer prices in Sub-Saharan Africa.

18. Hans Binswanger, "The Policy Response of Agriculture," *Proceedings of the World Bank Annual Conference on Development Economics* (Washington, D.C.: World Bank, 1989).

19. World Bank, *Sub-Saharan Africa: From Crisis to Sustainable Growth, a Long-Term Perspective Study* (Washington, D.C., 1989).

7
Issues in Import Policy Reform

The economic costs of protection include direct resource allocation costs and indirect costs that derive from the nature of the import regime and its administration. The indirect costs are associated primarily with nontariff barriers to imports, because these delink domestic and foreign prices and insulate domestic producers from foreign competition. Removal of these barriers may lead to substantial (but not easily quantifiable) economic gains, even if the level and structure of protection for local industries provided by tariffs remain roughly unchanged.

However, even import regimes based predominantly on tariffs rather than nontariff barriers have indirect economic costs that, although generally lower, may not be negligible. When the system has a wide range of tariffs that change frequently, includes many specific (rather than ad valorem) tariffs, administratively granted exemptions, and antidumping surcharges, and uses arbitrary prices for assessing duties, its protective effects may be obscured and rent-seeking activity encouraged. Furthermore, when the gap between domestic and world prices is large, export mechanisms such as duty-free admission and drawbacks may be difficult to administer and subject to abuse.

A common argument for initially protecting high-cost infant industries is that these costs are justified by the economic benefits that will flow from these industries once they become efficient. Various versions of the argument postulate that costs diminish over time as industries learn by doing but that entrepreneurs and capital markets are unable fully to capture the eventual benefits or they discount them excessively.[1] Systematic evidence and satisfactory empirical research on the subject are lacking, principally because of the need to simulate the counterfactual situation (that is, what would have happened in the absence of policies to promote infant industries). Experience with protection policies in most developing countries, however, suggests that arguments for protecting infant industries are generally used as a rationale by politically powerful, protection-seeking interests. Rarely has serious consideration been given to whether and under what conditions the economic benefits of the protection will exceed its economic costs. Thus the policies seldom recognize that, in order to offset the initial economic costs, the learning-by-doing benefits (weighted for risks and discounted for the opportunity cost of the capital invested) must appear within a period of, say, five to seven years.

In practice, industries and firms that are inefficient previously received high protection for relatively long periods, while those that are efficient (notably exporting industries) received relatively low protection and incentives. Country case studies show the steady deterioration of industrial performance (in terms of production costs, quality, technology, and the like) over prolonged periods of insulation from world markets through protection policies (for example, the steel, glass, and many engineering industries in India). Evidence from Mexico shows that total factor productivity growth across sectors was strongly negatively correlated with the fraction of the sectors' production covered by quantitative restrictions. Thus the evidence indicates that protection is usually not associated with increasing efficiency over time and in fact frequently has the opposite effect.

A few economies—notably Japan in the 1950s and 1960s and Korea and Taiwan in the 1960s and 1970s—have had outstanding records of economic growth while maintaining approximate neutrality in incentives by applying export-developing measures to offset significant protection and quantitative restrictions in the import regimes. It has also been argued that they have successfully followed selective infant industry policies. Some analysts have argued that they provide an alternative trade policy model for developing countries (see box 6-1 in chapter 6). The Korean success was due to a combination of sound and consistent macroeconomic policies, a system of automatic and nondiscriminatory mechanisms for exports, competition between exporting firms in the domestic market, and rigorous and single-minded administration of the discretionary controls over imports and investment in the interests of rapid expansion of manufactured exports. Temporary protection was given to new firms in new industries, but these newcomers were generally pushed to export a substantial share of their output within a short period (four to five years) and to become internationally competitive rapidly, with no guarantee that they would be rescued if they failed to do so. Furthermore, Korea's import policy has moved consistently toward liberalization since the late 1960s, slowly at first and then rapidly in the 1980s following a crisis brought on by policy-induced imbalances and external shocks. Currently, only about 5 percent of Korea's imports are subject to restriction, and the average tariff is about 20 percent.

For most developing countries, given their economic and political conditions and their poor record of administering quantitative restrictions on imports, a growth model based on import protection (even with compensatory treatment of exports as in Korea in the 1960s and 1970s) is unlikely to be successful. With a relatively liberal regime in the 1980s, Korea has been growing as fast as or faster than in earlier periods.[2] The same has been true of other economies, such as Chile, Hong Kong, and Singapore, during periods of liberal import policy. These examples and other arguments have convinced many governments of the wisdom of import policy reform that emphasizes liberalization. The design and implementation of such programs are the subject of this chapter.

Comprehensiveness, Intensity, and Speed

A reform program that is comprehensive, intense, and rapid is usually preferable to one that is not because the benefits are greater and begin sooner. (Arguments in favor of such an approach that are based on considerations of the political economy were given in chapter 4.) Two arguments that qualify this broad conclusion are noted below.

One argument concerns the economic loss from transitional unemployment, which in theory could be larger with radical programs than with programs in which changes are announced in advance and phased in over time. The gradual approach allows enterprises and individuals to begin to adjust before reforms are implemented, thereby reducing transitional unemployment. There are, however, theoretical reasons for believing that rapidly implemented programs could minimize unemployment effects, and there is evidence that labor has in fact been absorbed quite rapidly into expanding industries (see chapter 3), especially when they had excess capacity, were labor-intensive, and required little or easily obtained capital equipment. This finding raises at least some doubt about the severity of the problem of transitional unemployment, whether change is rapid or gradual. Moreover, in import regimes dominated by quantitative restrictions, delays and uncertainties are common in the procurement of raw materials, components, and capital equipment. In some cases the government must approve new investment, which can greatly delay the response to new opportunities. Under such circumstances, introducing import policy reforms gradually could worsen temporary unemployment because firms wishing to expand may continue to face these delays and procurement problems, which would not be the case were reforms more drastic and rapid.

A second argument concerns the credibility of the reform program and the likelihood of its being reversed. Gradual reforms may be preferable if they are more likely to be sustained than radical reforms.

Rapid, radical import policy reform concentrates the disruption of existing patterns within a short period. Whether this is politically more difficult to handle than a less concentrated disruption spread over a longer period depends on the circumstances in each country.

In practice, episodes of reform have followed many patterns with respect to their comprehensiveness, intensity, and speed. Some very successful reforms have been extremely comprehensive and fast, as in Bolivia, where controls were abolished and tariffs drastically slashed virtually overnight. Chile and Mexico reduced the coverage of quantitative restrictions quickly, but reduced tariffs more slowly, over periods of about five and two years, respectively. These reformers have now achieved relatively uniform rate structures (one or two rates) of around 15 percent. Other countries have been quite slow; Korea's very comprehensive reforms have been carried out over twenty years, although the most important reforms have been adopted since 1980. India, although it has not instituted any major reforms, has been slowly relaxing import controls in a low-key but consistent manner since about 1978 (although there were some reversals in late 1990).

An overview of many episodes suggests that although many countries could benefit from more rapid reforms, five to seven years is a reasonable period for moving from massive restrictions to substantially open trade regimes, preferably with strong actions at the beginning of the period. Constraints related to revenue needs or politically sensitive protection may prevent comprehensive liberalization in such a time span, but a reasonable and practical goal would be to phase out quantitative restrictions and reduce tariffs to a range of 15 to 30 percent. Slower reforms have been less successful. For example, several of the programs supported by World Bank trade policy loans in calendar years 1988 and 1989 have been ongoing for a number of years and have been supported by previous adjustment loans, yet they are still chipping away at only the first of several redundant layers of protection (see chapter 2). For the countries involved, it remains unclear how long it will take to reduce protection.

Another important aspect of reform is the manner in which it is begun. Reforms begun with strong measures have more often survived than those begun with weak or tentative steps. There is also evidence that announcing the timetable ahead of the reform, even if the schedule is not rigidly adhered to, enhances the reform's sustainability because it allows economic agents time to adjust to the new order.

Removal of Quantitative Restrictions

When quantitative restrictions are to be reduced in stages, the exchange rate, the existing and the desired structure of tariffs, the relationships among all of these, and the phasing of changes over time must be considered.

The Role of the Exchange Rate

A real devaluation, by increasing the supply of, and cutting the demand for, foreign exchange, makes it relatively easy to drop quantitative restrictions that have been imposed for balance of payments reasons rather than for protection. In addition, by raising the domestic currency price of imports, devaluation reduces the protective effects of quantitative restrictions (that is, the quota premiums). By making imports more expensive in domestic currency, devaluation often makes the restrictions redundant and so reduces opposition to their removal on the part of protected industries. This is one reason reforms involving the rapid removal of a large number of quantitative restrictions have often been preceded or accompanied by large devaluations; for example, in Bolivia (1985), Chile (1974), Ghana (1986), Guinea (1986), Laos (1988), Mexico (1985), Nigeria (1986), Sri Lanka (1977), and Zaire (1986).

Devaluation may also play a key role in reform programs that remove quantitative restrictions on noncompeting imports of capital equipment and intermediate materials but retain them on competing imports, as was the case in the reforms beginning in India in 1978, in Pakistan in 1983, and in Tunisia in 1986. If unaccompanied by devaluation, reforms of this nature can worsen resource allocation by increasing the effective protection of industries that use imported intermediates and capital equipment. Devaluation can not only offset this effect but also reduce the strain on the import licensing system and thereby reduce the quota rents and other associated indirect costs of protection. Insofar as devaluation narrows the gap between the world and domestic prices of import substitutes that are still protected by quantitative restrictions, it also reduces the incentives for diverting duty-free raw materials to the domestic market or otherwise misusing facilities designed to promote exports. Thus devaluation can have a direct impact on resource allocation and an indirect impact resulting from the increased efficiency it permits in the administration of export incentives.

The importance of accompanying the removal of quantitative restrictions with devaluation is underlined by the difficulties encountered by the countries in Africa whose currencies are tied to the French franc. Côte d'Ivoire, in a program initiated in 1984 to remove quantitative restrictions, attempted to compensate for its inability to devalue the nominal exchange rate by using a combination of higher tariffs and export subsidies (see box 3-3 in chapter 3). This strategy proved a poor substitute for devaluation, owing largely to extensive smuggling and an unwillingness to fully finance the export subsidies.

Devaluation and more general exchange rate reforms are also fundamentally important in countries in which the government allocates foreign exchange at officially controlled rates, while a large proportion of foreign exchange transactions takes place in illegal or legal parallel markets. This is the rule rather than the exception in most of the nonfranc-zone countries of Sub-Saharan Africa and occurs frequently in Latin America and in many socialist countries. Such foreign exchange controls are generally accompanied by import controls, but even when they are not, their costs are similar to those associated with import regimes with a unified exchange rate that are dominated by quantitative restrictions. They are typically characterized not only by a general bias against exports, but also by substantial differences in effective protection within both import-substitution and export sectors. Effective protection rates vary also because foreign exchange retention allowances for exporters differ and because the amount of foreign exchange allocated at the official rate is generally not the same for imports of intermediate inputs and machinery as for finished products (see box 2-2 on Poland in chapter 2). To reduce the antiexport bias of such systems and move them toward a more neutral incentive structure, the dual or multiple exchange rates for imports and exports must be unified into a single rate, usually by a substantial devaluation of the official rate (see chapter 5).

Phasing Out Quantitative Restrictions

Phased removal of quantitative restrictions frequently involves various types of transitional problems. Some of these, if not handled carefully, may increase rather than diminish the misallocation of resources and the indirect costs of protection during the transitional period.

For import control systems based on clearly defined product quotas, there are various well-tried methods of phasing out quotas that have the important advantages of being reasonably transparent and open to monitoring.[3] One method is simply to raise the quota ceiling, preferably according to a preannounced schedule, until the quotas become redundant and can be abolished. This method was used by the original members of the European Economic Community (EEC) and has also been used in Australia and New Zealand. Another method, also used in Australia and New Zealand, is to replace quotas with tariff-quotas. Tariff-quotas permit imports of a specified amount (usually the original quota amount) of a product at the going tariff rate and an unlimited amount at a higher, initially prohibitive tariff rate. The high rate is then reduced in steps until the two rates are identical. This method has the advantage of clearly indicating the declining level of protection during the transition phase. A third method, used in Australia, Brazil, and New Zealand, is to auction import quotas, steadily increasing the amount auctioned until the bids fall to a level at which the quotas appear to be no longer binding, at which point they can be abolished. Alternatively, the auction prices can be viewed as a proxy for the tariff equivalent of the quota and can be used to set quota-replacement tariff levels, which can then be progressively reduced. These mechanisms have proved effective in some industrial countries, but have yet to be tried in developing countries except for Brazil and Colombia.

Most developing countries have import control regimes based on import licensing rather than explicit quotas. These systems generally operate on the basis of product lists of various types, usually lists of banned products, of restricted products that require licenses, or of uncontrolled products. Part of the cost imposed by such systems derive from the uncertainty, excessive paperwork, and rent-seeking that accompany a system in which licenses are issued at the discretion of the relevant authorities. Without any change in the value of licenses issued, the restrictiveness of licensing in these systems can be reduced by broadening the list of products for which individual licenses can be used and by making the licenses transferable. Under a license-based system, the phasing out of import restrictions usually consists of shifting products from banned and restricted lists to unrestricted lists.

If pursued consistently and completed in a reasonably short period, this method can be effective in eliminating import licensing. If the process is slow, however, problems involving important economic costs can arise. For example, if governments remove licensing requirements for imports that do not compete with domestic production (often industrial raw materials and machinery) but leave decisions on when to remove restrictions on competing imports to a distant (often indefinite) future, the effective protection of local import-substitution industries will tend to increase and resource allocation will tend to worsen. Or, less commonly, if competitive imports are allowed, but imports of intermediate materials and machinery are not liberalized and these goods must continue to be purchased locally, economically efficient industries may be penalized by a large decline in their effective protection. Both of these results can be offset by devaluation and temporary tariff increases, although once tariffs have been raised it is often difficult to reduce them later.

Another issue in import licensing concerns the nature of the product lists. In systems that list both products subject to licensing and products not subject to licensing, many products will be on neither list and fall in a no-man's-land where the need for a license is uncertain. This uncertainty increases the discretionary component of such systems and leads to a corresponding increase in delays. Switching to a negative-list system, which permits unrestricted imports of all products not listed as subject to licensing, can on its own constitute an important liberalization. Apart from reducing the scope of discretionary decisions, this change shifts the burden of import control lobbying away from importers trying to get controls removed and onto local producers trying to get controls installed on new classes of import products. This change has been a key step in freeing import licensing in a number of countries and is a standard element in approaches to import policy reform taken by both the IMF and the World Bank. It also facilitates the monitoring of reform programs, which is preferably based on data on the proportion of domestic production in product categories whose imports are subject to quantitative restrictions.

Various transitional issues also arise in liberalizing imports that are controlled by government monopoly trading organizations. One way to liberalize such imports is to reduce the number of products that these organizations can import, as was done in India. Another way is to establish operating rules that remove or reduce the organizations' discretionary behavior in areas that can distort competition between imports and domestic production; for example, they can be instructed to import on behalf of all customers, subject only to commercial criteria such as solvency. In practice, however, some discretionary behavior is likely to continue as long as the legal right to import is limited to the monopoly trading organizations. Consequently, the introduction of competitive conditions in importing activities will generally be an important step in the removal of quantitative restrictions under such systems. Many governments have been reluctant to take this step for some products, however, especially agricultural commodities, because it involves important changes in domestic policies, such as price support and stabilization policies for agriculture.

Local-content or "indigenization" programs to force the use of domestic inputs are another type of nontariff barrier that has proved difficult to remove. These barriers remain even in Chile and Mexico, which have removed virtually all other nontariff barriers against manufactured imports. The difficulty lies in the origins of these arrangements, which are usually part of agreements concerning the investments of individual firms and are not directly related to the country's import policies in general. Removing them, whether abruptly or gradually, may conflict with the desire to maintain a favorable climate for investment, especially by foreign firms. One approach is to renegotiate the agreements and replace quantitative local-content requirements with tariff-quotas having low and high rates that are progressively merged.

The Role of Tariffs during the Removal of Quantitative Restrictions

The removal of binding quantitative restrictions will lead to a reduction of protection. Consequently, tariffs have been used as a transitional measure to allow the reduction to take place gradually. One approach is to set tariffs at approximately the level of the difference between domestic and international prices before removing quantitative restrictions, and then to reduce the tariffs in stages. In some reform programs (as in the Philippines in 1977 and Nigeria in 1988), the future tariff rates were written into the new tariff schedule, whereas in others (for example, in Côte d'Ivoire in 1984) they were published in advance, while temporary but declining tariff surcharges were imposed on products for which domestic prices exceeded world prices by more than the amount of the published tariffs. Announcement ahead of time makes the future rates clear and enables businesspeople and investors to make informed decisions.

While replacing quantitative restrictions with tariffs can reduce the initial impact of the removal of quantitative restrictions, there are many difficulties in measuring the actual difference between domestic and world prices. These include product complexity, lack of information on world prices (especially if imports have been banned), and differences between domestic and imported products with respect to credit, service, and other selling conditions. Also, tariffs cannot replicate all the effects of quantitative restrictions, nor would this be desirable, as the following examples of their differences indicate.

First, inefficient firms that received import licenses under a regime of administratively allocated and nontransferable licenses will not be able to afford them under a reformed system if they have to pay the tariff equivalent of the economic rent they previously received. They will have to either increase efficiency or go out of business. This improvement in the efficiency of allocation will occur unless different, firm-specific tariffs are charged for the same products. Second, quantitative restrictions cut the link between world and domestic prices, whereas tariffs permit world and domestic prices to move together. Third, a quantitative restriction on a particular product will generally cover a wide range of product qualities and specifications; thus the effects of quantitative restrictions on domestic prices will depend on how import licenses are allocated and will vary by product quality and specifications and from period to period. Such diverse effects are impossible to replicate with tariffs. Finally, quantitative restrictions, especially when haphazardly administered, have a greater deterrent effect on importers than do tariffs because importers are reluctant to invest in distribution networks and marketing if the markets they develop can be arbitrarily closed off.

Domestic industries protected by quantitative restrictions are largely insulated from fluctuations in world markets and from temporary episodes of world surplus and low prices. When the restrictions are removed, local industries are exposed to these fluctuations, and strong pressures are often exerted to implement special protective measures against dumping. Such pressures have become a major problem and threaten to undermine or at least reduce the favorable economic impact of many import policy reforms. In countries in which customs administration is weak and underinvoicing of imports to reduce duty payments is prevalent, the pressure to base import duties on reference or check prices, as in Morocco, is particularly strong. A reaction along these lines, or the introduction of antidumping procedures as permitted by the GATT, although not desirable in itself, is preferable to the reintroduction of quantitative restrictions, for which many affected industries have pressed. Where the customs service is a problem, a better solution might be the use of preshipment inspection firms to control underinvoicing and other forms of tariff evasion.

Tariff Reform

Import tariffs instituted for protectionist purposes typically have several major deficiencies. Often, tariffs on products whose domestic production is being favored give very high protection, raising prices to consumers and frequently leading to smuggling and corruption. Tariffs on products that are important to influential consumers or enterprises are low, discouraging or preventing their domestic production. The tariff structure is generally escalated, with tariffs rising according to the degree of processing. This increases the effective protection of later-stage processes above the nominal protection afforded by tariffs on the finished product, while providing low or negative effective protection to earlier stages in the processing chain. Big differences between tariff rates on substitute goods artificially encourage the consumption of those with the lower tariffs. In addition, the tariff structure is often greatly complicated by a complex array of special provisions introduced in response to lobbying pressures. In many cases, the effects of the tariff structure are determined more by the exemptions than by the nominal structure.

The Level and Structure of the Target Tariff System

The lower the general level of tariffs, the less severe all these problems become. A major lesson of experience is that tariff reforms should aim at an eventual tariff structure with levels as low as possible. Sometimes, however, other needs conflict with this goal, including political constraints, the use of tariffs as a surrogate for exchange rate policy (as in the franc zone in Africa), or budgetary constraints (see chapter 5). In cases where tariffs cannot be lowered, priority may be given to eliminating exemptions and imposing (or increasing) taxes on the domestic production of goods protected by high tariffs on competing imports. This response has the dual advantage of reducing the distortionary effects of tariffs and raising revenue. If the need for revenue is a binding constraint, such taxation would allow further reduction of tariff rates or, if necessary, permit transitional assistance to help restructure the economy in line with the changed incentives. The domestic taxes, of course, should not be at rates higher than the tariff rates, nor should the tax apply on top of the tariffs because this would tax imports twice.

More generally, reform of the tariff structure and reform of the domestic tax system should proceed simultaneously wherever possible. In countries with the necessary collection apparatus, the system should be designed so that it taxes consumption of products, whether domestically produced or imported, at the same low rate, perhaps through a value added tax or a sales tax collected at the point of import or ex factory, with exemptions for exports and imports (as in Swaziland).[4] An alternative that is less efficient but still preferable to reliance on tariffs alone is a retail sales tax. Malawi, Nigeria, and Togo have begun since 1988 to harmonize tariff rates on imports with tax rates on domestic production of import-competing products.

Another important issue is whether all rates should be equal. Uniformity would be beneficial from an economic point of view if all rates were unified at the level of the lowest rates. A more controversial question is whether, when high rates cannot be reduced to the lowest level, low rates on imported inputs should be raised to achieve uniformity (of course, the lower the top rates, the less important the issue of uniformity; see also the section below on tariff reform during the transition). The answer depends to a large extent on whether a temporary admission or duty drawback scheme is in operation for exports. If not, raising tariffs on inputs *may* increase the antiexport bias because some of the inputs are used by exporters. Without a duty drawback scheme, therefore, the marginal net economic benefits of raising input tariffs (see below) should be traded off against the marginal economic costs resulting from the reduced incentives for export production, to the point where the former fall to level of the latter. This point need not coincide with the level at which tariff rates are uniform, except under special conditions.

Where exporters are ensured duty-free inputs, the case for a tariff structure relatively uniform between intermediate and final goods is more compelling.[5] When the focus is on minimizing the productive efficiency costs of providing a given level of protection or achieving a target level of self-sufficiency in importables, there is also a strong case for uniform tariffs among final goods (see box 7-1). Although in theory a carefully designed nonuniform rate structure could be more economically efficient for raising revenue than a uniform structure, the design of such a system depends on parameters that are difficult to estimate, and in practice such a structure would be more difficult to insulate from lobbying pressures. By contrast, a uniform structure gives the appearance of fairness and is easier to administer. In addition, in complicated, nonuniform systems, concessions to particular firms or groups are less apparent, especially tariff reductions or exemptions on inputs that affect government revenue but not buyers of the finished products.

Some tariff reforms have actually achieved uniformity (Chile's uniform tariff is 15 percent), and others are close (Bolivia currently has two rates, 10 and 17 percent, with the goal of a unified rate by 1991). Most World Bank recommendations for tariff reform have emphasized reducing the dispersion of rates, although only a few have explicitly envisioned a uniform structure as even a long-term goal.[6] It is often not clear whether this reticence results from a judgment that a uniform structure is undesirable or politically unattainable, or from a failure to establish a long-term target.

Tariff Reform during the Transition

When tariff reforms are to be phased in over time, one approach is to proceed industry by industry. Ideally, in such a sequential process governments would first make the changes involving large economic benefits. This may be politically feasible in some cases, especially when it involves increases in protection for previously underprotected industries. But more often it involves reducing tariffs for large, highly protected industries. Thus governments are frequently tempted to leave these difficult cases until the end of the reform program and to introduce tariff changes that have lower political costs and relatively low economic benefits in the early stages. And, indeed, it may be better to postpone dealing with some especially intractable cases to avoid undermining or delaying the whole reform program. Then, once all other tariffs have been reduced and restructured, these cases may stand out in such an obvious way (the "sore thumb" principle) that support can be mobilized to deal with them. In the meantime, it may be possible to limit the costs of delay with regard to resource allocation by using other policies to prevent or slow investment in these industries.

Prior studies of the impact of reform on individual industries are useful. But reforming tariffs industry by industry can create unpredictable problems. Tariff actions in one industry have repercussions for other industries via input-output linkages or through substitution or complementarity in consumption. These repercussions may reduce economic benefits and increase economic costs along the way, and attempting to respond to them may slow or even abort the tariff reform process. Therefore it is better to make general phased changes in all tariffs without discriminating among industries. This approach is even-handed and avoids discretionary decision-making concerning the order of reform among sectors. It also avoids the need for interim measures that might subsequently be removed because of the impact of reforms in industries for which tariffs have not yet been adjusted.

In moving toward overall uniformity, it is beneficial to raise the rates at the low end, which are usually for inputs. First, for the final goods that use these inputs and whose domestic production is protected by higher tariffs on the final goods, raising input tariffs reduces the effective rate of protection.[7] Second, if reform is constrained by the need to raise a target level of revenue or provide a target level of average nominal protection to importables as a group, raising low tariffs on inputs allows tariffs on outputs to be reduced further than they could be otherwise.

Three potential costs should also be noted. First, if importable inputs are produced domestically, the higher protection will increase the flow of resources to these sectors. To the extent that resources coming from nontradable and relatively unprotected sectors (such as exportables) outweigh those coming from heavily protected importable sectors, the net effect is to worsen resource allocation. Second, if these inputs are used in the production of exportables, raising their tariffs may directly reduce profits and production in this sector. Third, if the net effect is an appreciation of the exchange rate, exportables will be further penalized.

If there is a duty drawback scheme that works well, raising input tariffs will have little negative direct effect on the profitability of export production. If inputs are not produced domestically or if they compete more strongly for domestic resources with other, more highly protected importables than with less-protected exports and nontradables,[8] raising their tariffs will not have a net adverse indirect effect. If both these conditions are met, raising low tariffs will improve resource allocation.

Even without a duty drawback system, other conditions can make it more likely that this will be the case. First, if raising low tariff rates means that the higher rates can be reduced further than they could be otherwise (the revenue- or nominal protection–constrained cases), there is no adverse effect on overall protection levels and thus no pressure on the exchange rate to appreciate. Under these conditions it is also likely that a larger share of the resources flowing to the low-tariff

Box 7-1. *Designing a Tariff Structure*

If some level of tariffs is to be retained, countries face two important questions. First, is a uniform tariff structure desirable? Second, should intermediate inputs be subject to import duties, and if so, are export duty drawbacks justified? The answers depend to some extent on whether tariffs are aimed at goals related to self-sufficiency, protection, or revenue. Administrative convenience and political economy considerations also determine the best tariff policy.

If self-sufficiency is the objective, the government wishes to limit the value of total imports of final goods (at world prices) to a specified level. The least costly way to achieve this objective is a uniform tariff, because it equalizes the marginal (distortion) cost of restricting imports in production and consumption across commodities.

If protection is the objective and the government wishes to maintain the value (at world prices) of output of final-good importables at a level above that achieved under free trade, the optimal policy is a uniform output subsidy on these importables, provided revenue can be raised costlessly. If revenue cannot be raised costlessly, tariffs may be used as an instrument of protection. The main difference between output subsidies and tariffs is that the former distort only production, whereas the latter also distort consumption. Therefore, if the distortion in consumption is ignored or can be corrected by a set of commodity-specific taxes and subsidies, optimal tariffs for protection will be uniform across final goods. Otherwise, optimal tariffs for protection will be nonuniform. A better alternative to using tariffs alone is to combine them with output subsidies, reducing the necessary tariffs and therefore the consumption distortion.

If revenue is the objective and there are no other constraints, consumption taxes are usually the best instrument. If, however, adequate administrative machinery to collect such taxes does not exist, tariffs may be the primary source of revenue. Optimal tariffs for raising a specified amount of revenue will generally be nonuniform across final goods. If the cross-price effects are ignored, goods with low elasticity of demand for imports should be subject to higher tariffs than goods with high elasticity. Intuitively, when the import-demand elasticity is low, a high tariff enables substantial revenue to be raised without causing large movements away from the Pareto-efficient equilibrium.

To highlight the potential conflict between protective and revenue-raising tariffs, ignore the distortion costs of tariffs in consumption. Then a commodity with highly inelastic supply is a perfect candidate for raising revenue. But the same commodity is a poor candidate for protection in the sense that a large expansion in the value of its output will be much more distortionary than a similar expansion of an elastically supplied good.

To analyze the issue of whether tariffs should be uniform between intermediate and final-good imports, consider a country producing a final-good importable and an exportable. Assume that the production of both these goods requires an imported intermediate input and that there is a tariff on final-good imports. Then the welfare effect of the introduction of a tariff on the intermediate input depends on several factors. In particular, if the input is more important in the production of the exportable than that of the importable, the change will reduce welfare. If the tariff is combined with a duty drawback scheme for exporters, however, the net effect is unambiguously positive. The tariff on the use of the intermediate input in the production of the importable reduces the output of the latter, which is beneficial. (In fact, if the tariff on the input is raised sufficiently, it can completely eliminate the effective protection of the final good.)

This analysis remains valid in the presence of a revenue constraint. If revenue is to be kept constant, the introduction of a positive tariff on the intermediate input, along with a duty drawback for exports, will enable the tariff on the final import to be lowered, which will further improve welfare. For a given amount of revenue, however, the optimal rate of tariff on the final good may be different from that on the intermediate input.

An important question concerns the effect of a duty drawback when not all exports use the intermediate input. One fear is that the duty drawback for manufactured exports may reduce welfare by expanding the latter at the expense of resource-based exports. If, however, the policy package consists of a small tariff on the imported input, a drawback for exports, and a reduction in the tariff on the final-good import to hold revenue fixed, this is equivalent to a tax on the production of the importable, a consumption tax on the exportable using the input, and a reduction in the tariff on the final import. All three of these changes are normally welfare-improving, in the absence of other distortions.

Special circumstances would temper these conclusions. If smuggling is a serious problem, uniform tariffs may not be optimal because not all goods can be smuggled with uniform ease. Similarly, monopoly power in world markets, domestic taxes, and, most important, economies of scale and imperfect competition may alter the conclusions.

Nonuniform tariffs conflict with administrative simplicity and transparency. It is also extremely difficult to determine the level at which particular tariffs should be set. Nonuniform tariffs also encourage smuggling and are more prone to eliciting rent-seeking and lobbying activities intended to raise tariffs. Under a uniform tariff, the structure of tariffs is nonnegotiable. Therefore, if tariffs are to be raised, all of them must be raised simultaneously. Gains to a particular industry from raising all tariffs are relatively small, so collective action in this direction is unlikely. By contrast, if tariffs are nonuniform, it is much more profitable for a low-tariff industry to lobby for a

(Box continues on the following page.)

Box 7-1 *(continued)*

higher tariff, whereas counterlobbying is unlikely because the costs of raising the tariff on a single industry are diffused. Moreover, it is easier to obtain higher protection when someone else in the economy already enjoys that benefit. Thus, under nonuniformity, tariff rates are likely to escalate and to be determined by the relative political power of interest groups rather than by considerations of efficiency.

Source: Background paper by Arvind Panagariya, Trade Policy Division, Country Economics Department, World Bank.

sectors will come from the high-tariff sectors, so that the negative effect on exportables is at least mitigated. Second, the more dispersed the initial structure, the more likely it is that raising low tariffs on inputs will improve resource allocation. In fact, if input tariffs initially are close to zero while final-good tariffs are much higher, and the reform is revenue-neutral (lowering final-good tariffs while raising those on inputs), the welfare effect will usually be positive even if no duty drawbacks are in effect for exports. However, it is important to keep in mind the eventual goal; if increases will be difficult to reverse for administrative or political reasons, it may be better not to raise tariffs above their eventual target levels.

During transition periods in tariff policy reform, the main objective is to reduce the dispersion and the average level of protection. One way to reduce both (currently being followed in Costa Rica and Guatemala) is the concertina approach, which collapses the structure by reducing the top rate at each step of the transition to the next highest level, while leaving lower rates the same. Another method (followed in Mexico) involves radial or proportionate reduction, in which all tariffs are reduced at each stage to an equal fraction of their previous levels.

A radial reduction is usually superior to a concertina reduction because the latter will have little impact on protection in its initial stages if, as is typical, the top rates are redundant for many products and cover only a small fraction of production. In addition, a concertina reduction may, without offsetting policy changes, send conflicting signals at different steps in the process since each step depreciates the real exchange rate, thereby improving the incentives for all products whose tariffs have not yet been reduced. For example, the price of a product covered by a median-level tariff will increase at each step until midway through the process, at which point it will finally begin to fall.[9] This change in signals may produce first an expansion and then a contraction of each sector, with the attendant costs of resource movement. (If the reform is announced in advance, however, and is widely expected to proceed as planned, these costs will be reduced because long-term planning and investment will be based on the target structure of incentives.) With a radial reduction, the signals are more likely to be uniform for each protected importable product at each step. However, radial reductions are more likely to reduce revenue than concertina reductions, making it more important to ensure that the reform does not exacerbate the budget deficit.

Once a new target tariff structure is in place or a process for reaching it has been put in motion, standard and, if possible, public procedures for dealing with pressures for further changes should be developed. These procedures can be designed along the lines followed by the Australian Industries Commission, which gives opponents of changes a chance to be heard and requires that an objective economic analysis be done. The analysis is made publicly available and must be taken into account before final decisions are made.

Import Policy Reforms and Domestic Reforms

When domestic markets are distorted because of the monopoly power of domestic firms or constraints related to the regulatory, institutional, or infrastructural framework, standard analyses of the effects of trade policy reform must be modified. The traditional gains from reform are magnified with some types of domestic distortions, but in other cases the supply response to reform is reduced.

When domestic firms exercise market power, the gains from trade policy reform may be augmented. In addition to the usual efficiency gains, the liberalizing country benefits from reductions in the monopoly profits of domestic firms. Evidence from Chile's dramatic trade liberalization episode in the 1970s shows that profits declined most in the highly concentrated sectors. The Chilean experience is confirmed by enterprise-level surveys conducted in Morocco following trade policy reforms that began in 1983. Domestic firms that previously enjoyed considerable market power due to limited competition from abroad were induced by liberalization to slash profit margins and increase the efficiency of factor use. Korea's successful reform experience in the 1980s is particularly instructive in this regard. Liberalization in the manufacturing sector emphasized industries with monopolistic market structures, many of which had been encouraged and supported by government policies during the 1970s.

Trade and domestic policies often contribute to fragmented production patterns. High levels of protection have encouraged firms to enter import-substituting sectors (the automobile industry is a classic example), and continued protection has allowed firms operating on inefficiently small scales to remain profitable. In markets where this is the case, trade policy reform may rationalize the market structure. Competition from imports that accompanied reforms in Argentina, Chile, and Mexico led to narrower and more specialized product lines as well as to mergers, consolidations, and plant closings. In Chile, increased exploitation of economies of scale accompanied declining protection. Some firms that were insufficiently specialized and seemed to need high protection before the 1974 reform were able to concentrate on a few product lines and to export after the reform.

Yet in the presence of other types of domestic market distortions, the welfare benefits of trade policy reform can be reduced. In countries as diverse as India and Mexico, domestic regulatory policies that control the market entry and expansion of firms have deterred growth in capacity and the establishment of new firms. For example, Mexico's regulations in these areas slowed the pace of adjustment for several years despite decisive trade liberalization measures. Exit restrictions also reduce the welfare gains of trade liberalization. The impetus given to competition by reform should lead some firms to exit and others to enter; if exit is not possible, inefficient firms remain, and funds that would have been used to enable new firms to enter are diverted to inefficient or failing firms. Regulations that make it costly or impossible for firms to restructure or shut down (including requirements for large severance payments to workers and rules inhibiting liquidation or bankruptcy) have been a factor in failed liberalization attempts in Poland, Turkey (in the early 1970s), and Yugoslavia. By contrast, an absence of exit restrictions was important for the success of the 1974–79 trade policy reforms in Chile, which were carried out concurrently with the reduction or elimination of many regulatory interventions, including those affecting the labor market.[10]

Comprehensive and rigid price controls are by definition incompatible with trade policy reform since its purpose is to alter relative prices. However, even relatively flexible or partial price controls can limit the ability of the economy to respond. Wage and employment controls can also reduce the benefits of trade liberalization. In the presence of minimum wages set above market-clearing levels, whether by law or collective bargaining, firms may have to shed labor or close down in response to import competition even though workers could have been profitably employed at lower rates; at the same time, expanding industries may find it difficult or expensive to bid labor away from contracting sectors with high minimum wages.

Other policies and conditions that can inhibit a supply response to trade policy reforms include the centralized allocation of major material inputs (as in many socialist countries); lack of competition and poor performance in transport, banking, and telecommunications; and excessive or poorly managed regulation of financial markets. For example, when banks are not allowed to write off bad debts from inefficient import-competing firms, new credit may not be available for the firms that should be expanding after the trade policy reforms (see box 5-2 in chapter 5). Another example is Mexico's transport regulations, which have made it costly and difficult for exporting manufacturers to ship their products to ports or to the U.S. border.

The structure of the public sector or policies relating to the sector may affect trade policy reform or be affected by it. The desire to protect state-owned manufacturing enterprises has interfered with liberalization programs in a number of countries, including Argentina, Bangladesh, and Peru (see chapter 4). In other cases, when governments have privatized unprofitable firms instead of liquidating them, the buyers have required guarantees of continuing high protection, as when the government of Togo privatized its steel mill. The structure of the public sector in socialist countries is such that trade policy liberalization would accomplish little unless accompanied by significant changes in other policies (see box 2-2 on Poland in chapter 2).

In agriculture and agroindustry, unintended effects may result from interactions between trade policy reforms and existing interventions in input and output markets. Many of these are indirect effects on the welfare and budgetary costs of agricultural price policies.[11] Liberalization of imports of agricultural commodities, for example, can increase the budgetary cost of output price supports and reduce the budgetary cost of input subsidies. To take another issue, parastatal domination (or other distortions) of crop output markets might mean that a devaluation would affect producer prices very slowly, while causing input prices to rise quickly. Or a protected processed product (for example, textiles) may rapidly become unprotected if its tariffs are reduced while its input (cotton) price remains high because it is determined by a monopolistic parastatal. Meaningful trade liberalization in such cases may necessitate abolition of the parastatal (as called for in the Ecuador agricultural sector adjustment loan, but never implemented) or elimination of its legal monopoly in the import market (as in the Mexico agricultural sector adjustment loan).

Public sector policies or characteristics, by increasing the costs of importing and exporting, may have the effect of taxing trade. One obvious way this can occur is through an inefficient or corrupt customs service (as in Guinea and Madagascar; see box 7-2). Excessive paperwork requirements can have the same result: not only do documenta-

Box 7-2.   *Constraints to Economic Adjustment to Trade Policy Reform in Madagascar*

The recent experience of Madagascar illustrates how the potential salutary impact of trade policy–related reforms can be much reduced by domestic regulatory constraints.

Foreign Exchange Market

Madagascar introduced a new system to improve the foreign exchange market, but the system, as implemented, is highly inflexible and limited. Foreign exchange requests have to be specified at the ten-digit product classification level, and product substitution is not permitted. Average processing time for an application is four weeks—six weeks if even a minor mistake is made on the application. The system covers imports of goods only, not services. The unavailability of foreign exchange for business travel or for the purpose of participating in international product fairs has become a major barrier to entry in the export markets. Exchange regulations clearly increase the risks of doing business in an export market. Foreign currency from export proceeds must be repatriated within ninety days of the date of export. Exporters who fail to do so—even for reasons that are beyond their control (theft or damage of merchandise or lack of payment from clients)—are subject to prosecution and imprisonment. These regulations are designed to reduce foreign exchange outlays, but their effect is the opposite. Entrepreneurs establish foreign exchange buffer funds abroad (by transfer pricing) to cover future risks in the export market or to withdraw dividends and capital.

Labor Regulation

Restrictions on closing down public as well as private enterprises result in continued operation of a number of unprofitable firms, while deterring entry and expansion by others. Government permission is required for the release of employees, even temporarily. Laws prohibit firms from closing if this would result in the firing of permanent employees. Closure is further circum-

tion requirements impose the direct cost associated with filling out the forms, but processing delays may cause imports to pile up on ships or at the docks and exports to pile up in company warehouses. This has been identified as a significant problem in Morocco, where the World Bank is sponsoring research to ameliorate the problem.

Infrastructural inadequacies and lack of important services are particularly important constraints on the response to trade policy reforms, especially in low-income countries. In many instances, publicly owned

scribed by the banking system because firms with outstanding loans cannot close without the agreement of their creditor.

Import Tax Administration

Although import taxation has been reformed and export procedures have been simplified, the positive effects of the reforms are obstructed by inefficiencies in tax administration and corruption in the customs service. Most firms surveyed claimed that customs employees will work only if paid directly by the importing or exporting firm. Rent-seeking is fueled by the numerous formalities of customs and the excessive documentation required for temporary admission (fifty-one documents need to be stamped and verified three times, on average). Exporters normally employ a specialized firm to deal with customs requirements, at a fee equivalent to about 1 percent of the value of the export. Some exporters use their own employees for this purpose, which requires three days of full-time work by one employee for a normal merchandise expedition. Large-scale customs tax evasion is also widespread; for example, the Ministry of Commerce regularly imports products without having to pay import duties. Such practices partly explain the discrepancy between the nominal import tariff of about 35 percent in 1987 and the actual tariff collection rate, which did not reach 10 percent.

Infrastructure

A survey of industrialists found that, in addition to such policy-created constraints, poor infrastructure was a concern. In particular, the respondents cited poor road maintenance, the condition and administration of the ports, the poor telecommunications system, and the scarcity of industrial buildings as constraints to starting or expanding a business.

Source: South-Central Africa and Indian Ocean Department, World Bank.

utilities provide inefficient service, imposing large costs on businesses and forcing those that can afford them to install their own electric generators, water supply systems, and communication equipment. A study in Nigeria found that virtually all firms were hooked to (and paid for) the public power grid, although every one with more than twenty employees had its own generator.[12] In some countries fewer than 20 percent of all telephone calls and 10 percent of international calls are completed. Lack of road maintenance increases costs to vehicle owners and shippers (by up to 50 percent on paved roads and even more on unpaved roads). Adjustment to international competition is made more difficult by these added costs.

Human infrastructure is also deficient in many respects. Hostile policies toward the private sector in general and middlemen brokers in particular in the past discouraged the development of entrepreneurial talent. At least partially for this reason, in Guinea new private investment remains very weak, notwithstanding significant reform of the trade regime. Education in some countries has been concentrated too heavily on upper levels, providing a labor pool mismatched to job opportunities. Correction of these problems will require major changes in official policies and attitudes, and considerable time.

The importance of domestic market distortions suggests that action to remove them or reduce their incidence and severity should accompany trade policy reform. A recent assessment concludes that sufficient emphasis has not been placed on reforming domestic regulatory barriers.[13] The World Bank's lending operations have emphasized the importance of import competition but have neglected the influence of industrial regulatory policies. For example, only 2 percent of adjustment operations have included specific conditions related to entry and exit policies. Yet the evidence suggests that policy action in the area of trade reform should, whenever possible, include a consideration of domestic regulatory reform.

In practice, however, political considerations and administrative capacity greatly constrain what can be achieved in a given time. Thus some trade policy reforms will precede some domestic reforms and vice versa, but most of these choices have their attendant costs. For example, if domestic investment and price controls are removed before trade is liberalized, new investment and expanded production may occur in highly protected sectors, making it more difficult to reduce this protection when trade policy reforms are introduced. The economic cost will be even greater if there are economies of scale in the industry but new high-cost plants of suboptimal scale are established. Similar considerations apply to infrastructure. On the one hand, new investments and other measures to expand and improve infrastructure that are undertaken before trade liberalization takes place may not be appropriate for the patterns of production and demand that emerge after liberalization. On the other hand, when trade liberalization precedes actions to extend and improve infrastructure and such services as ports, roads, railways, electricity, and telecommunications, infrastructure deficiencies can slow the desirable reallocation of resources.

Many regulatory reforms and infrastructure improvements can increase economic efficiency both before and after trade liberalization. Such actions include increasing competition in domestic financial markets and facilitating the closing or restructuring of firms. To some extent it may also be possible to design domestic policies that will support future trade liberalization. But such policies may be difficult to implement, especially if it is uncertain whether and when previously announced trade measures will be introduced. Furthermore, it is extremely difficult to predict the pattern of production that will develop after a substantial liberalization. In many cases large industries have emerged that did not exist before reform or that existed only in embryonic form (such as fresh fruit exports in Chile and cut flowers in Colombia and Mexico) or that are based almost entirely on foreign demand (such as the cutlery, fur, and color television industries in Korea). Because of this unpredictability, it is difficult to undertake the required complementary domestic policies or infrastructure investments until the need becomes manifest following the trade policy reforms.

For this reason there are advantages in implementing domestic regulatory and trade policy reforms concurrently. The uncertainties make it unwise to postpone trade policy reforms until all the domestic reforms and infrastructure investments expected to be required are in place. (Furthermore, arguments of this kind may be used to postpone trade liberalization indefinitely.) A similar argument can be made against delaying domestic regulatory reform. If domestic reforms are postponed until after trade liberalization occurs, industry avoids adjustment to a more competitive environment. The transition from a protected to a more open regime may be smoother if firms are exposed to domestic competition while or before trade barriers are reduced.

It is also sometimes argued that trade liberalization should await the success of policies intended to make domestic industries "internationally competitive." A basic problem with this argument is that every industry cannot become internationally competitive. A general trade liberalization by definition will lead to the contraction of some activities and the expansion of others—even if, at some sufficiently devalued exchange rate, all of them would appear to be internationally competitive. Furthermore, if an economy is starting from a situation of greatly dispersed effective protection, not all existing industries would pass this test. If this condition had to be met, trade liberalization would never take place, or it would consist only of the liberalization of imports competing with the country's lowest-cost industries, with high protection remaining for the least competitive. Such a "cost plus" criterion for protection is the opposite of neutrality and is incompatible with any reform intended to improve the country's ability to benefit from the opportunities of international trade.

Finally, there are practical political arguments for initiating reforms wherever possible. Trade liberalization undertaken in advance of domestic reforms can help create the effective demand and mobilize political support for domestic reforms that might not otherwise be introduced—even if their need could be foreseen. For example, in a typical import-substitution regime with high protection of manufacturing and discrimination against exports and agriculture, there may be little demand for expanded and improved transport and communication services, technical education, or banking, accounting, international marketing, extension, and other services required by manufacturing firms and agricultural industries. Once the trade policy reforms are implemented, however, the bottlenecks and deficiencies may become obvious and generate pressure from interested groups to remedy them. Conversely, however, insofar as domestic regulatory reforms reduce costs and improve industrial performance, resistance to allowing competition from imports may decline.

Thus it is counterproductive to suggest that all trade policy reform should always precede domestic reform, or vice versa. Rather, they should be viewed as complements. As the reform process advances, changes in specific trade and domestic policies that are highly complementary should be made simultaneously.

Summary and Conclusion

Import protection dominated by quantitative restrictions leads to inefficiencies and rent-seeking. Many developing countries have attempted to reform their import regimes by liberalizing quantitative restrictions and reducing tariffs. By reducing rent-seeking, the liberalization of quantitative restrictions can substantially improve economic efficiency, but liberalization should be coordinated with exchange rate and tariff reform. Comprehensive, intense, and reasonably rapidly implemented reforms are preferable—providing they can be sustained—because the economic benefits are larger and come sooner than with slower, less intensive reform.

Allocative efficiency can be improved by replacing quantitative restrictions with tariffs even if domestic prices are kept at roughly the same levels. However, the full benefits of reform can be realized only by decreasing tariff rates and their dispersion. There are practical advantages to aiming for as low and as uniform a tariff structure as is sustainable politically and is consistent with revenue needs. Preannounced tariff reductions applied across the whole tariff structure are preferable to an industry-by-industry approach.

Domestic pricing policies and market structure, the state of infrastructure, and regulation of market entry and exit of firms can magnify or reduce the economic gains of import policy reform. For example, the benefits are greater when import liberalization provides competition to a domestic monopoly. Conversely, domestic price controls and entry or exit regulations reduce the gains from import liberalization. Generally, however, import policy reforms ought not to be delayed pending domestic reforms, because the infrastructure and domestic reforms required to support the new configuration of the economy after import liberalization are not easy to predict and such concerns may be used as an excuse to postpone trade policy reforms indefinitely.

Notes

1. A recent review of arguments concerning infant industries is given in G. M. Grossman, "Promoting New Industrial Activities: A Survey of Recent Arguments and Evidence" (paper prepared for Economics and Statistics Department, OECD, Paris, 1989).

2. From 1965 to 1980, GDP growth in Korea averaged 9.5 percent a year. From 1983 (the year of the second structural adjustment loan) to 1987, growth averaged about the same. Following the completion of the second phase of adjustment (1985), GDP grew by 11.9 percent in 1986 and 11.1 percent in 1987. See World Bank, *World Development Report 1988* (New York: Oxford University Press, 1988); and World Bank, *Adjustment Lending: An Evaluation of Ten Years of Experience,* Policy and Research Series no. 1 (Washington, D.C., 1989), pp. 79 and 92.

3. These and other gradual methods of removing import quotas are discussed in W. E. Takacs, *Alternative Transitional Measures to Liberalize Quantitative Trade Restrictions,* UNDP/World Bank Trade Expansion Program Occasional Paper no. 3 (Washington, D.C.: World Bank, 1989).

4. See Zmarak Shalizi and Lyn Squire, "Tax Policy for Sub-Saharan Africa," Country Policy Department, Resource Mobilization Division, World Bank (Washington, D.C., 1986); and a background paper for this book by Robert Chambers, "Tariff Reform and the Uniform Tariff," Trade Policy Division, Country Economics Department, World Bank (Washington, D.C., 1989).

5. However, if different productive sectors are taxed at different rates by nontariff measures, the optimum tariff structure may be one that places a lower tariff on sectors that are taxed the most through other instruments. In Ghana, a study found that because of other taxes a uniform import tariff of 30 percent would result in rates of effective protection varying from 0 to 50 percent. See Shalizi and Squire, "Tax Policy." In cases like this, it is particularly important to coordinate reforms of the domestic and trade tax systems. Other constraints may prevent a country from achieving a uniform structure. For example, when for political or other reasons the protection for local producers must be higher than would be provided by a low uniform rate, the desirability of uniformity may need to be balanced against the ability of the customs administration to control smuggling and corruption. If noncompeting intermediate inputs are subject to low or zero tariffs, a desired level of effective protection can be given to domestic producers with relatively low final-product tariffs. But if input tariffs are higher—especially if all tariffs are

uniform—the final-good tariffs required to achieve the desired level of effective protection must also be higher.

6. Anand Rajaram, "Tariff and Tax Reforms: Do Bank Recommendations Adequately Integrate Revenue and Protection Objectives?" Public Economics Division, Country Economics Department, World Bank (Washington, D.C., 1989).

7. If a duty waiver system is in effect for exporters, the distortionary effect can be eliminated entirely by raising input rates to a level higher than the final-good rate. See A. C. Harberger, "Issues in the Design of Tariff Reform," Trade Policy Division, Country Economics Department, World Bank (Washington, D.C., 1988).

8. This is likely to be the case for at least two reasons. First, in many developing countries, a large number of intermediates are not produced domestically. Second, the basic principle of comparative advantage indicates that import substitutes are likely to be intensive users of the same or similar resources as imports, rather than of the resources used by exports.

9. See A. C. Harberger, "Notes on the Dynamics of Trade Liberalization" (paper prepared for a conference on trade liberalization sponsored by the World Bank and Fundaçao Getulio Vargas, Santiago, Chile, October 1974).

10. See Dominique Hachette, "Chile: Trade Liberalization since 1974" (paper prepared for the conference "Toward a New Trade Policy for Brazil," São Paulo, Brazil, April 1988), in "Trade Liberalization: The Lessons of Experience," LAC Regional Series Report no. IDP14, Latin America and the Caribbean Department, World Bank (Washington, D.C., 1988).

11. For an analysis and application to Bangladesh, Korea, Thailand, and Venezuela, see G. S. Tolley, Vinod Thomas, and C. M. Wong, *Agricultural Price Policies and the Developing Countries* (Baltimore, Md.: Johns Hopkins University Press, 1982).

12. World Bank, *Sub-Saharan Africa, from Crisis to Sustainable Growth: A Long-Term Perspective Study* (Washington, D.C., 1989).

13. See Claudio Frischtak, Bita Hadjimichael, and Ulrich Zachau, "Competition Policies for Industrializing Countries," Industry Development Division, Industry and Energy Department, World Bank (Washington, D.C., 1989).

8

External Constraints and Opportunities

Changes in protectionism abroad affect attitudes toward domestic trade policy reform. In the Uruguay Round of multilateral trade negotiations, several groups have been established to deal with trade policy issues of concern to developing countries, and these countries in turn need to ensure that the negotiations take their interests into account. A related issue is whether developing countries would benefit more by undertaking unilateral liberalization measures immediately or by waiting to negotiate multilateral liberalization measures later. Another important external influence on trade policy in developing countries is foreign direct investment, which has significant benefits in improving access to export markets, transferring technology and management skills, and increasing production efficiency and competition. Finally, trade links with neighbors also have a strong influence on the trade policy of developing countries. Hoping to gain the benefits of a greater outward orientation while retaining a considerable measure of protection against much of the world, many developing countries have participated in regional integration schemes. For reasons discussed in this chapter, however, most of these schemes have disintegrated, stagnated, or failed to increase intraregional trade.

External Factors Affecting Trade Policy

Although economic analysts may argue that protection in export markets does not affect the gains from increased trade, higher trade barriers against a country's exports make protection for the domestic market more attractive politically, and international liberalization increases the attractiveness of outward-oriented trade policy reforms.

Changes in External Protection

During the past four decades a major, positive external factor has been the general reduction of tariffs in the industrial countries. Through a

Table 8-1. Trade Indexes for Major Product Groups Affected by Nontariff Barriers in Industrial Countries

(1966 index, percentage of imports affected by nontariff barriers; 1966–86 change, percentage points)

Country	All foods		Agricultural raw materials		Fuels		Ores and metals		Manufactures		All goods	
	1966 index	1966–86 change	1966 index	1966–86 change	1966 index	1966–86 change	1966 index	1966–86 change	1966 index	1966–86 change	1966 index	1966–86 change
All industrial countries	56[a]	36	4	37	27	0	1	28	19	39	25	23
EC	61[b]	39	3	24	11	26	0	40	10	46	21	33
Finland	n.a.	70[c]	0	55	67	28	4	–1	8	20	15	36
Japan	73	26	0	59	33	–5	2	29	48	2	31	12
Norway	43	52	3	13	0	0	0	15	38	–16	31	–8
Switzerland	53	37	4	51	0	99	0	9	15	24	19	31
United States	32	42	14	31	92	–92	0	16	39	32	36	9

n.a. = Not available.

Note: The table shows the value of trade affected by nontariff barriers. A nontariff barrier applied to one or more tariff lines within a four-digit Standard International Trade Classification group is held to affect all trade in the group because exporters often modify trade to halt the spread of barriers. See Laird and Yeats for a list of the nontariff barriers included in these tabulations.

a. Finland, Greece, and Ireland are excluded from the totals because complete information on their agricultural trade barriers was not available in 1966.

b. Ireland and Greece are excluded from the EC totals because complete information on their agricultural trade barriers was not available in 1966.

c. Since data are not available for Finnish nontariff barriers and imports of food in 1986, the number is the actual share of trade affected by nontariff measures in 1986.

Source: Laird and Yeats, "Nontariff Barriers of Developed Countries."

series of multilateral negotiations, the average most-favored-nation tariff in the OECD countries has been progressively lowered from approximately 40 percent in the late 1940s to less than 5.5 percent today. Another strong stimulus for outward-oriented trade policy reforms has been the high growth rates in the OECD countries during most of this interval, which generated a strong and persistent demand for imports from developing countries.

While tariffs have been steadily reduced, nontariff barriers have assumed increased importance.[1] Overall, the proportion of OECD imports affected by nontariff barriers nearly doubled during 1966–86 (see table 8-1). Foodstuffs recorded one of the largest increases, and more than 90 percent of OECD imports of foodstuffs are now affected by some type of nontariff barrier.

External protection can influence not only trade levels but also the composition of developing countries' trade. For example, the structure of tariffs and other trade barriers in major industrial countries is frequently biased against imports of processed goods relative to unprocessed goods, thereby discouraging domestic processing in developing countries. Although low tariffs are generally applied to industrial countries' imports of primary (unprocessed) commodities, duties increase as products undergo increased fabrication. Such tariff escalation is sometimes reinforced by nontariff barriers as well.

Protectionism and subsidization of exports (particularly of primary agricultural products) in industrial countries have a major impact on international markets. That impact can invoke a trade policy response by developing countries.[2] For example, high domestic price supports for such items as sugar, dairy products, beef, and veal in the United States, Japan, and the European Communities (EC), coupled with export incentives and restrictive trade barriers, have had a destabilizing and depressing effect on world prices. Domestic producers in developing countries who could compete with foreign agricultural goods in freer markets may be uncompetitive because of the influence of such external factors. This problem is particularly acute in the case of sugar. Extensive export subsidies have often pushed world prices below the costs of production in efficient Caribbean countries. Under these conditions, Caribbean producers would be displaced in their own domestic market by foreign (subsidized) exports if their governments did not restrict sugar imports. Recent evidence suggests that the nontariff trade control measures frequently applied to foodstuffs in developing countries (variable levies, licensing arrangements, and minimum import prices) are often intended to shield domestic markets from this induced external instability.[3]

Analyses of goods produced by developing countries that are subject to nontariff barriers suggest why making progress in liberalizing agricultural trade barriers under the Uruguay Round is of such vital interest to so many developing countries. One study tabulated the total value of thirty-one food exports from developing countries to the EC and computed the value and share of this trade subject to major forms of nontariff barriers.[4] Approximately one-third of Argentina's agricultural exports were found to be subject to quotas and variable levies, and more than 90 percent of those of Barbados, Botswana, Colombia, Mauritius, and Uruguay were found to face similar barriers. Projections in another study indicate that developing countries experience large losses of export revenue as a result of such barriers, with the rural poor experiencing the greatest direct, immediate economic impact.[5] Of course the gains from eliminating all barriers —on manufactured as well as agricultural products—would be even greater than the gains from eliminating only those on agricultural products. Finger and Messerlin,[6] citing other studies, estimate that elimination of trade restrictions imposed by industrial countries could increase developing countries' exports by 10 percent[7] and their GNP by 3 percent[8] (4 percent for manufactured exports and 2.0 to 2.5 percent for other exports).[9] As Finger and Messerlin point out, these estimates are conservative.

Discriminatory Trade Measures

Some trade-restraining measures are applied in a discriminatory manner to exports of a specific developing country or group of countries. Some of these discriminatory trade measures, such as voluntary export restraints, quotas (bilateral or global), and international commodity agreements, often require complicity on the part of the developing countries (contrary to GATT article XIII) in adopting measures that limit the supply of goods or control the price at which goods are traded. In addition, these restrictions are often accompanied by measures intended to upgrade the quality and cost of the affected product in order to increase export revenues or divert trade to markets not covered by the restraint arrangement.

Voluntary export restraints are typically quantitative restrictions that have been negotiated bilaterally and are enforced by the exporting country's government. These "negotiations" generally involve an implied threat by the importing nation's government that it will apply more restrictive trade control measures unless agreement is reached on the voluntary export restraint. World Bank tabulations show that voluntary export restraints (excluding the Multifibre Arrangement) constituted, on average, the most important of sixteen categories of nontariff barriers in 1986. In the United States, for example, 14.5 percent of imports were affected by voluntary export restraints, which is more than four times higher than the next most significant nontariff barrier. In the EC countries, 7.2 percent of imports were affected by voluntary export restraints, second only to nonautomatic authorizations.

Garment and textile exports from developing countries are restricted by an enormously complex system of bilaterally negotiated voluntary export restraints under the Multifibre Arrangement.[10] This framework, although encumbering, does have several aspects that mitigate its impact on developing countries. First, it allows countries to establish themselves as exporters of textile products before being hit by quotas, which are subject to predictable rules and international scrutiny. Second, the quotas transfer many billions of dollars of quota rents from consumers in North America and Western Europe to efficient producers organized to capture these rents, thereby helping them to finance investments in promising exports. Third, the quota system creates pressures to diversify exports both within and away from textile products, thereby accelerating the learning associated with exports. Finally, the system induces established firms in leading developing economies to set up production in other developing economies before they are seriously restricted by quotas. Despite the quota system, China has attained rapid export growth and has become one of the biggest exporters of textiles and garments.

The negative aspects of the Multifibre Arrangement also loom large. Populous, low-income developing countries outside Africa are all subject to slow-growing quotas. The system is becoming ever more restrictive and has been extended to additional products and fibers. The system favors imports from developed countries over those from developing ones and safeguards the exports of major, established suppliers in developing countries at the expense of new suppliers (once the new suppliers become large enough to represent a significant threat to existing ones). It thus prevents changes in market shares through open competition, which would improve the position of the more efficient producers. The bilateral quota agreements oblige governments to allocate quotas among firms, an inherently arbitrary process, and to monitor and regulate exports of textile products in great detail. Usually the bulk of the quota is given out on the basis of previous exports while allocation of the rest is contested.

Special tariff provisions imposed by industrial countries also influence trade policies and reforms in developing countries. One type of measure includes the Generalized System of Preferences (GSP) and related schemes such as the EC's Lomé Convention and the U.S. Caribbean Basin Initiative. Under these schemes, goods from developing countries are imported at lower than most-favored-nation rates. Each program has its limitations, such as value limits or applicability to certain commodities only. A second type of measure relates to offshore assembly provisions that allow domestically produced components assembled abroad to reenter the country under tariffs that apply only to the value added. The EC has also established similar beneficial tariff provisions for many intermediate goods. Developing countries, on their part, have adopted trade policy reforms to utilize such external incentives effectively. These have included development of required infrastructure and liberalization of barriers facing production inputs. Also, some developing countries have attempted to utilize offshore assembly provisions by establishing export processing zones and supportive trade policy measures, while others have enacted reforms that enable domestic producers to take better advantage of existing preferential trade arrangements.

The GATT Negotiations and Unilateral Reform

For countries liberalizing their trade regimes, there are strong reasons to participate fully in the GATT. One study has identified at least four ways in which GATT obligations can influence trade policy reforms in developing countries positively.[11] First, respect for international legal obligations can strongly influence some government officials with respect to their position on trade policy reforms, especially those officials new to the process or otherwise undecided. Second, international legal obligations can serve as an acceptable public explanation for decisions that might be difficult to defend politically. Third, international legal obligations may be a concise way of defining the bounds of policy for government officials. Liberal trade policy might not fare too well if every new administration were permitted to review the case for free trade, especially in the context of new political obligations to their constituencies. Fourth, international legal obligations can be an effective warning against investing too much in trade-distorting measures and can provide effective ground rules for making trade, investment, and production decisions. In addition, these obligations would almost certainly raise the cost of reversing reform measures and therefore give the reforms added credibility.

In the Uruguay Round of negotiations to revise the GATT, special committees and negotiating groups have been established to deal with the trade policy issues that are of major concern to developing countries. It is important that developing countries use these arrangements effectively and work to ensure that the negotiations take their interests into account. If developing countries emerge from the multilateral trade negotiations with the belief that their interests have been neglected, their incentive to negotiate bilateral deals or to adopt trade and production policies geared toward the (more secure) domestic market may be strengthened.

Several factors influence a country's relative preference for multilateral, bilateral, or unilateral trade policy reforms and its ability to use GATT arrangements to the best advantage. These factors include differences in relative bargaining power, differences in the effects of external protectionism on individual countries, how the issue of credit for unilateral reform is resolved (see below), and how developing countries perceive the costs incurred in joining the GATT.

Differences among Developing Countries in the Negotiations

A major influence on a developing country's position in trade negotiations is its relative importance in world trade. Thus, the newly industrialized economies (NIEs) will come under pressure from industrial countries to act as full participants in the multilateral trade negotiations because of their importance in world trade.[12] For example, in 1987 the value of manufactured exports to industrial nonsocialist economies from Taiwan, China (US$41 billion), Korea (US$33 billion), Hong Kong (US$21 billion), China (US$14 billion), Mexico (US$14 billion), and Brazil (US$9 billion) exceeded that from industrial countries such as Denmark and Finland (about US$12 billion each), Norway (US$6 billion), or Australia (US$4 billion). Also, several of the newly industrialized economies have been running large and persistent trade surpluses with the industrial countries, which has been a major point of contention. In 1987, for example, Korea ran a total surplus on all goods of more than US$6 billion, while the trade surplus of Taiwan, China was about US$21 billion. These imbalances have led industrial countries to exert direct economic pressure on the NIEs to negotiate bilateral deals and to participate fully in the international negotiations. The implication is that the industrial countries will request the NIEs to reduce import barriers as the OECD countries have done.

Newly industrialized economies such as Argentina, Brazil, Mexico, Korea, and Taiwan, China are among the economies that have been most frequently subject to antisubsidy action in the 1980s.[13] Their export products are also among the goods most heavily affected by various forms of nontariff barriers. Thus these countries have an additional incentive to enter fully into the multilateral trade negotiations on nontariff barriers.

In contrast, some other developing countries appear to have less to gain from full participation in the GATT. These countries are usually eligible for trade and aid preferences because of their low income levels or for other reasons (for example, by virtue of the U.S. Caribbean

Basin Initiative). They figure insignificantly in world trade[14] (and therefore are not subject to discretionary protection), and they are exporters of primary products that do not compete directly with OECD products. Although they would benefit from market-opening reforms by the newly industrialized economies, their main interest in the negotiations may be to protect the preferences they receive and to ensure that they are compensated if the value of the preferences is eroded by cuts in most-favored-nation tariffs. For most of these countries, domestic supply-side constraints are normally far more important than external trade barriers in determining their exports. All these considerations argue that, for these countries in particular, immediate unilateral reform should receive priority over future multilateral negotiations.

To exploit the multilateral negotiations effectively, developing countries whose major concerns relate to agricultural trade barriers may need to rely on somewhat different strategies than developing countries concerned primarily with manufactured goods. Size is an important factor, since the value of agricultural exports from individual developing countries is quite small. For example, foodstuff exports from Argentina, India, Malaysia, Mexico, and the Philippines range from US$1 billion to US$3 billion, amounts exceeded even by Denmark, at US$6.4 billion. Countries such as these would not appear to have sufficient leverage to extract meaningful agricultural concessions unless new negotiating positions or coalitions are formed. Indeed, even developed countries such as Australia and New Zealand essentially withdrew from the Tokyo Round negotiations because of the lack of progress on agricultural issues. More recently, a major positive effort to advance serious negotiations on agriculture has come from a coalition of developed and developing countries known as the Cairns group (Australia, Argentina, Brazil, Canada, Chile, Colombia, Fiji, Hungary, Indonesia, Malaysia, New Zealand, the Philippines, Thailand, and Uruguay). When this issue was deadlocked at the December 1988 ministerial meeting in Montreal, pressure from members of this group was instrumental in forcing discussion of a possible compromise between the EC and the United States. Unfortunately, the dispute between the United States and the European Communities was not resolved satisfactorily, and this eventually caused the negotiations to be suspended in late 1990.

Other Influences

Aside from these broad policy issues, specific problems can have a major impact on developing countries' views of the relative merits of the unilateral and multilateral approaches to trade policy reform. Among these are the credit issue (that is, the extent to which developing countries can use previously enacted reforms to negotiate concessions from other parties), the value of tariff bindings in the negotiations, and the perceived costs of joining the GATT.

One question is whether the unilateral liberalizations that have recently occurred in a number of countries will prejudice their bargaining position in the Uruguay Round negotiations. In recognition of the depth of the developing countries' concern about this matter, a statement was issued at the Montreal ministerial meeting that they should receive appropriate credit for past unilateral trade reforms. The statement was so vague, however, that it failed to clarify important issues.

The question is being addressed by several negotiating groups in the Round (including the Functioning of the GATT System group) but it is not clear which, if any, credit mechanism will be adopted. Box 8-1 illustrates some of the problems relating to this point and also indicates the kind of information needed to decide between a unilateral and a multilateral approach.[15] Unfortunately, much of the required information is missing or incomplete because of different concerns during past multilateral trade negotiations.[16] Based on the criteria explained in box 8-1, however, it is clear that countries with little bargaining power or that face relatively low external barriers to their exports (most Sub-Saharan African countries fit both categories) have little to gain from waiting. For other developing countries, preliminary evidence favors the unilateral approach as well; projections indicate that the economic losses resulting from internal trade barriers exceed those from external barriers.[17] One point is very clear: if credit is given for unilateral action, there is nothing to be gained from deferring reform.

An issue related to the credit question concerns the value of tariff bindings in the multilateral trade negotiations. Finger and Holmes argue that legally binding tariffs were a primary objective in previous multilateral negotiations and that such legal bindings were used to extract reciprocal concessions.[18] If the same importance is attached to legal bindings in the Uruguay Round, developing countries could adopt unilateral tariff reforms at any time and then offer to bind these reductions legally in the multilateral trade negotiations. If these bindings are viewed by trading partners as major concessions, this strategy will resolve the credit issue. When Mexico joined the GATT, it bound its top rate at 50 percent. Even though its actual top rate is currently 20 percent, it may use the 50 percent rate as the basis of future negotiated reductions. But the developing countries have potentially easy recourse to article XVIII, which has been used to justify trade barriers for balance of payments purposes. This approach could reduce the value of such bindings.

Another potentially important influence on developing countries' views of the unilateral and multilateral approaches to trade policy re-

Box 8-1.   *The Gains from Unilateral and Multilateral Liberalization of Trade Barriers under Alternative Time Paths*

The figure below illustrates some of the parameters that can influence the decision whether to pursue unilateral liberalization or to wait for multilateral negotiations. The lines in the graph show the time path of the natural logarithm of GDP growing at a constant rate. At time t_0 a decision needs to be made as to whether to liberalize or wait until time t_1, when a multilateral agreement will be negotiated. Waiting involves a true cost (in losses of domestic economic efficiency) and an uncertain benefit (the country cannot be sure what it will gain in the multilateral negotiations). Two types of gains are represented in the graph: the shift from A to B at t_0 represents the efficiency gains (increase in GDP) associated with the unilateral liberalization; the shift from D to C' at t_1 represents the efficiency gains plus the gains from the increased market access associated with participation in the negotiations. Two assumptions are made: that the unilateral and multilateral liberalizations are equal whether done unilaterally or multilaterally, and that the country receives no credit for its unilateral liberalization at time t_1 in the multilateral negotiations.

The net economic return of a multilateral liberalization strategy is given by the difference between the present value (at time t_0) of (a) the area $ABCD$ and (b) the gain $CC'I'I$ carried out to infinity. If the former is larger, the unilateral approach is optimal in an economic sense, and if the latter is larger, the multilateral approach is optimal. Although simplistic, the graph highlights several

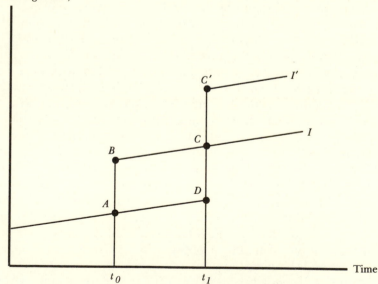

GDP (natural logarithm)

points about the economics of taking a unilateral or a multilateral approach to liberalization:

- The credit issue can be of key importance: the greater the credit for a unilateral reduction, the stronger the economic argument in favor of a unilateral reduction. If full credit is given, the gains for a country liberalizing at time t_0 would be the present value of $ABCD$ plus $CC'I'I$ to infinity. In this case the unilateral strategy is clearly optimal.
- Another factor affecting the economics of the liberalization decision is the relative costs to the country of its own trade barriers (AB) versus the costs of other countries' barriers to its exports (CC'). The greater the relative cost from other countries' trade barriers, the more likely the country is to favor a multilateral approach.
- A country's bargaining power and the amount of concessions it can extract from other countries are uncertain, so holding off until t_1 is something of a gamble, particularly when the country has a relatively good idea of the immediate gains from a unilateral liberalization.
- The time of the multilateral agreement may be important because the country may have an incentive to delay a unilateral liberalization if the time between t_0 and t_1 is short.
- The discount rate is a factor influencing the present value of present (unilateral) versus future (multilateral) gains. The higher the interest rate, the greater the incentive for a unilateral liberalization.

Source: Julio Nogués, "The Choice between Unilateral and Multilateral Trade Liberalization Strategies," Policy, Planning, and Research Working Paper no. 239, International Economics Department, World Bank (Washington, D.C., 1989).

forms is the perceived burden of the obligations they will incur in joining the GATT. There is some indication that new developing country entrants face more extensive obligations than did those developing countries that joined earlier.[19] Perhaps even more important would be a shift from what many see as the GATT's "no-obligation" policy toward developing countries to a policy requiring developing countries to accept roughly the same obligations as those imposed on developed countries.[20] Eliminating developing countries' ability to impose restrictions based on justifications not available to other GATT signatories would limit their policy options, but it would also make joining the GATT a more credible signal of the future direction of trade policy and help to resolve the credit issue by increasing the value of bindings.

Foreign Direct Investment

Historically, outward-oriented countries have encouraged and benefited from foreign direct investment (FDI). FDI has had important benefits in improving access to export markets, transferring technology and management skills, training the labor force, creating employment, and increasing production efficiency and competition. One World Bank study found that foreign majority-owned firms in Mexico were most efficient in eighteen of forty-one sectors in which they competed, with the reverse true in only two sectors. These benefits may be mitigated, however—if not entirely offset—when the investment "tariff hops" and enters heavily protected sectors or takes place in response to other artificial incentives. Consequently, FDI is most effective in promoting growth in economies characterized by relatively liberal trade regimes.

Foreign direct investment has attracted renewed interest recently as a potential source of finance to replace commercial bank lending. Its benefits in this respect, however, are not as large as sometimes thought; net foreign exchange flows from FDI to nonoil-exporting developing countries in 1987 were only SDR3 billion. In 1984–87, four developing economies (Brazil, China, Mexico, and Singapore) accounted for 60 percent of FDI in developing countries. Other economies such as Hong Kong, Indonesia, Malaysia, the Philippines, and Thailand have historically relied upon FDI for a significant share of their total investment. Furthermore, the distribution of FDI among countries and sectors has varied substantially over time. Much of this volatility is the result of fluctuations in the oil market. For nonoil-exporting developing countries, gross FDI peaked in 1981 at SDR15 billion, then stayed around SDR11 billion in 1982–86 before recovering to SDR14 billion in 1987. Gross FDI flows to all developing countries peaked at SDR25 billion in 1982, then fell to SDR13 billion in 1987.

The most significant factor in encouraging FDI is domestic economic and political stability. This has been the key to East Asia's success in attracting FDI, and Brazil's failure to maintain macroeconomic stability was a major factor in the decline of FDI in that country in the 1980s. A second set of factors relates to general protection of property rights (including intellectual property rights, particularly for high-technology industries) and respect for private sector activities. Fears of pressure to indigenize ownership, or of outright nationalization, discourage prospective investors. Regulations governing FDI should be transparent and stable. It is particularly important to allow liberal access to foreign exchange for profit remittances and imported inputs. Policies that create a good climate for investment in general are likely to be better than special incentives to attract FDI, such as tax holidays, which may attract footloose industries that leave when the holiday is over. One special incentive, debt-equity swaps, may be worthwhile and has apparently played a role in increasing FDI in some countries such as Chile and, more notably, Mexico.[21] Swaps may have adverse macroeconomic effects, however, and they are not necessarily better for attracting FDI than the alternative policies discussed above.

Trade Policy Issues in Regional Integration

Over the past several decades, a large number of schemes have promoted the goal of regional integration or cooperation among developing countries, including about twenty countries in Africa and nearly as many elsewhere. The steps taken by various groups of countries have included cooperation in services and infrastructure (for example, education and training, telecommunications, agricultural research, tourism, marketing, water, and transport development projects); abolition of virtually all trade barriers among members; establishment of a common external tariff; and the forging of joint positions in international negotiations. The most recent plan along these lines is the ambitious Global System of Trade Preferences among developing countries, which became effective with fifteen signatories in April 1989. Yet, despite numerous attempts, most of these schemes have disintegrated or failed to achieve their objective, and intraregional trade has fallen or remained constant in almost all cases (see table 8-2).

Benefits and Costs of Regional Integration

The benefits anticipated from integration, at least with respect to trade policy measures, are supported by three main arguments. One is the gain that comes from more efficient production when producers specialize in what they can make most cheaply. Another concerns the possibilities for the development of import-substitution industries involving economies of scale that could not be set up economically in any individual member country but can be justified by the larger regional market. The third is based on the learning and other benefits of competition among the generally high-cost industries already established in countries of the region. Integration is seen as a halfway house on the path leading to the full benefits of trade liberalization and wider markets. The experience expected to be gained in exporting manufactured goods to other member countries is seen as particularly useful in moving toward this goal.

Several disadvantages to integration must be weighed against these prospective benefits. First, the production of regional exports drains resources that could otherwise be devoted to exporting to world markets. Second, it is costly to divert trade, that is, to import from high-cost

Table 8-2. Characteristics of Trade among Members of Selected Economic Integration and Cooperation Schemes

Group	Major trade-related characteristics[a]	Exports among members in 1989 (millions of U.S. dollars)	Intrascheme exports as a percentage of total exports					
			1970	1975	1980	1985	1987	1989
Association of Southeast Asian Nations	6,7	22,648[b]	14.7	15.7	17.8	16.8	17.7	18.6
Latin American Integration Association	6	9,348	10.2	13.5	13.5	8.9	10.7	9.7
Economic Community of West African States	—	1,513	2.1	3.1	3.9	4.2	5.5	7.2
Regional Cooperation and Development (Iran, Pakistan, and Turkey)	—	1,305[c]	1.0	0.8	5.3[d]	9.9	5.2	—
Andean Group	1,2,7	1,157	2.8	5.4	3.3[d]	3.1	3.2	4.7
Central American Common Market	1,2,7	570	26.8	23.4	22.0	15.0	11.9	12.5
Caribbean Community	1	426	7.3	7.2	6.4	8.0	10.5	12.9

West African Economic Community	2,3,4	383[c]	9.1	6.7	6.9	8.9	7.7	—
Economic and Customs Union of Central Africa	1,2,4	184	3.4	3.9	4.1	0.7	0.9	3.9
East African Common Market	5	142[c]	16.9	12.6	7.8[d]	6.7	7.4	—
Memorandum item								
European Economic Community	—	852,600	48.9	49.4	52.8	54.9	58.8	62.5

— Not available.

a. 1 = free trade among members; 2 = common external tariff; 3 = redistribution of proceeds from tariff to settle payments imbalances among members; 4 = common currency; 5 = now defunct; 6 = some preferential trade treatment among members; 7 = joint positions in international trade negotiations.

b. This total and the shares do not include Singapore's exports to Indonesia, which, by mutual agreement, are not reported.

Source: Andras Inotai, *Regional Integrations in the New World Economic Environment* (Budapest: Akademiai Kiado, 1986), table 1, p. 44; Peter Robson, *The Economics of International Integration* (London: Allen & Unwin, 1987); OECD, *Foreign Trade Statistics* (Paris, various issues); IMF, *Direction of Trade Yearbook* (Washington, D.C., 1988); and Andras Inotai, "Regional Integration among Developing Countries, Revisited," Policy, Planning, and Research Working Paper no. 643, Country Economics Department, World Bank (Washington, D.C., 1991).

c. Data are for 1987.

d. Data are for 1981.

regional producers instead of low-cost international producers when regional tariffs are reduced below extraregional tariffs.[22] There are other costs as well, since integration requires complex negotiations that may deflect the time and energies of decisionmakers from other pressing tasks.[23]

Theory offers no presumptions about the outcome of the cost-benefit calculus in integration schemes, which depends on the particulars of each case. The benefits from trade creation will tend to be greater the larger the reduction of tariffs among members, the more members differ with respect to resource endowment and other factors affecting their cost of producing the goods they can produce most efficiently, and the lower the barriers to intraregional trade (for example, transport cost) relative to the barriers to extraregional trade (for example, transport cost, tariff, or nontariff barriers). The costs of diversion will tend to be greater the greater the postintegration disparity between intraregional and extraregional tariffs.

In practice, many of the industries established as a result of integration schemes among developing countries have had high production costs. This fact, together with high regional transportation costs and substantial barriers to extraregional trade, has meant that member countries have often ended up paying a substantial premium over the prices of comparable imports from outside the region. Thus the costs of diversion have been high. Furthermore, the goods and marketing channels employed in trade with neighbors are generally so different from those required for exporting to industrial market economies that the experience is not transferable to exports outside the region. In sum, the expected benefits have failed to materialize, and structural inefficiencies have been created or exacerbated.

The schemes have foundered on a number of practical problems in implementation as well. The most serious has been payments: how to settle the net balances among member countries when some have inconvertible currencies or severe balance of payments difficulties in their overall trade. Typically, some members would persistently run deficits but have no means to pay, and others perforce would become their creditors and then eventually stop giving them credit. Balance of payments difficulties have been a main reason for the sharp decline of intraregional trade in the Central American Common Market (CACM). Similar difficulties led to a breakdown of trade in the Andean Group and now plague the Economic and Customs Union of Central Africa (UDEAC), despite a common currency, because some countries run chronic deficits and others surpluses.

Other difficulties with regard to implementation have been encountered in integration schemes that have tried to negotiate a structure of uniform external protection with preferential treatment for regional trade. For one thing, many developing countries rely heavily on quantitative import restrictions and foreign exchange controls, which makes it inherently impossible to find a general formula for ensuring systematic preferential treatment among partners. Apart from this, harmonization of tariffs among more and less protected countries at different levels of development not only has required fractious and prolonged negotiation, but also has frequently led to increased protection in several member countries. A tendency to view any product made in a neighboring country as a good candidate for national import substitution has aggravated these difficulties. Because of these problems, as well as the chronic balance of payments difficulties of some countries, member states sooner or later increase protection against external trading partners and sometimes against other members. In some cases, the relatively high common external tariff became an obstacle to later trade liberalization by some members, such as Guatemala and Costa Rica in the CACM and Colombia and Bolivia in the Andean Group. Indeed, to carry out its trade policy reforms, Chile had to leave the Andean Group. The net effect of many integration efforts, then, has been a reduction in the level and efficiency of trade.

A final serious problem with integration efforts has been that industries have gravitated disproportionately to certain countries in the specific groups, generally to those with the best-developed industries and infrastructures. This has, at least in the short run, magnified disparities among countries and created friction. It has also brought about a demand for complex compensation arrangements.

On balance, integration based on trade policy measures has generated benefits for countries that have generally outward-oriented economies and that are already well developed, such as the members of the Association of Southeast Asian Nations (ASEAN) and, earlier, the European Communities. The countries in these groups have dynamic productive sectors, with products that are competitive on world markets. They are thus able to respond to increased regional trade opportunities. Integration efforts have been much less successful in economies, such as those in many African countries, with a limited product mix and economic agents unaccustomed to responding to market opportunities. Thus, in practice, the rationale for integration based upon its benefits as a training ground has been turned on its head: international competition has been necessary to train producers for regional trade, rather than the reverse.

Lessons from Experience

It is clear that the potential benefits from expanded trade among neighboring developing countries are currently quite limited. Such countries are likely to have similar factor endowments and production costs (relative to potential trading partners among developed countries). The gains from trade, therefore, are generally small, even under ideal circumstances. These gains are further limited by poor transportation and communication infrastructure among members. Significant gains from trade may be possible for some products—such as those for which economies of scale are important and which can be produced regionally at a cost that is competitive with imports; bulky items for which high transport costs make importation from outside the region relatively expensive; and those whose exports to traditional markets are artificially limited. But overall, the biggest gains from enhanced trade opportunities will come not from regional trade but from broader external trade.

Two important corollaries follow from this conclusion. First, measures in areas other than trade policy should generally be used to move toward greater regional cooperation or integration. Recent efforts have emphasized steps to increase factor (mainly labor) movements or to improve the infrastructure linking member countries. In the Middle East, for example, plans are being made to link national electrical grids to improve reliability of delivery. Some joint water supply projects are also being planned. In regions such as Africa, where the markets of individual countries are too small to support efficient construction firms, coordination of the public sector's procurement regulations would encourage the development of firms serving regional markets. As a natural byproduct of such coordination, improved infrastructure and factor movement will support the expansion of both interregional and intraregional trade by eliminating some of the biggest bottlenecks. Another potentially beneficial use for cooperative arrangements is to forge unified positions and increase leverage in negotiations with other countries. The members of ASEAN have used their association in this way (although not in the GATT negotiations), and other groups have followed this example, although with less success.

The second corollary, equally important, is that in the trade policy area the top priority of any integration effort must be to emphasize outward orientation and trade creation, rather than diversion. This generally requires making the currencies of all members convertible. It may also involve reducing existing artificial nontariff impediments to neighboring markets (for example, regulatory requirements and paperwork). In some cases there is considerable scope for this kind of action. Some African countries have easier access to the EC markets than to those of their African neighbors (up to seventy administrative steps are involved in legally moving goods across some African borders).[24] But above all, the integration should accelerate, or at least should not interfere with, liberalization of member countries' trade policies and reduction of their external trade barriers. (The CACM has recently announced explicitly that its members are not constrained by their commitments to the CACM when they reduce external barriers.)

This argument implies that if the goal is a common external tariff, the target rate should be the level of the least protective member, rather than either the most protective level or a regional average, as was the case in some schemes in the past.[25] This level should be reduced over time, while the levels of the more protective members should decline faster, so that they eventually catch up. If any preference is granted to members, it should be modest, on the order of 10 to 20 percent, and should be reduced according to a preannounced schedule.[26] This would allow the realization in a temporarily protected environment of the potential gains from learning, while limiting the potential losses from excessive protection and trade diversion.

Regional integration, in other words, should be viewed as a transitional stage in a process of integrating all the member countries into the world economy. The end result would be uniformly low barriers to trade, with no preferences for member countries. This goal should be announced at the beginning of the process, and a reasonable schedule (no longer than, say, five to seven years) should be set to reach it. This kind of agreement would be hard to negotiate, especially because some economies (the most protected) would have to adjust more than others. This difficulty notwithstanding, such a unified reform effort may have advantages over individual, uncoordinated reform in each country. Reforms carried out jointly with neighbors through a regional agreement may be more politically acceptable, credible, and sustainable. This was the experience of the members of the European Communities as they began to reduce barriers to trade with the outside world in the 1950s. In today's world, where developing countries may be more willing to undertake a liberalization program as part of an integration package than on their own, multilateral lending organizations or international donors might usefully provide support.

Summary and Conclusion

Declining tariff rates, expanding international markets, and preferential arrangements for some countries have provided new trade opportunities for developing countries in recent years. Their export prospects, however, have been adversely affected by rising protectionism in industrial countries in the 1980s. Many developing countries have a major incentive to participate in multilateral trade negotiations, but there are important differences in the bargaining power and interests of various countries. Many fear that unilateral trade policy reforms would prejudice their negotiating positions. Unilateral reformers could in theory reduce tariffs while also binding them at higher levels, and thereby maintain their bargaining position in the GATT negotiations. This strategy, however, implies a threat to raise tariffs back to their bound level, which may hurt the credibility of the tariff reform or, conversely, may be met with skepticism if, for example, the country has a commitment to the World Bank to maintain low tariffs. Consequently, an unambiguous clarification is needed by negotiating parties in the GATT that unilateral reforms will be credited in the negotiations. In the meantime, economic arguments suggest that developing countries should continue to liberalize unilaterally. Industrial countries should reduce their trade barriers.

In the past, the potential for expanding trade with neighbors has led countries to form regionally integrated groups. The benefits of these schemes are most likely to be realized when integration takes place among countries with complementary but dissimilar production conditions in goods they can produce efficiently and when the various schemes are accompanied by large tariff reductions and only modest regional preferences. In practice, few integration schemes have been carried out along these lines, and the benefits have proved illusory. The biggest gains from integration will come not from direct trade policy measures, but from cooperation to develop physical and human infrastructure and services. Any formation of customs unions should be based on lowering external barriers to extraregional trade.

Notes

1. Sam Laird and Alexander Yeats, "Nontariff Barriers of Developed Countries, 1966–1986," *Finance and Development* 26 (March 1988):12–13. For an overview of the evolution of industrial countries' trade policies, see Margaret Kelly and others, *Issues and Developments in International Trade Policy*, IMF Occasional Paper no. 63 (Washington, D.C.: IMF 1988).

2. See World Bank, *World Development Report 1986* (New York: Oxford University Press, 1986).

3. See Refik Erzan and others, *The Profile of Protection in Developing Countries*, UNCTAD Discussion Paper no. 21 (New York: United Nations Conference on Trade and Development, 1988). For an overview of major agricultural policies in industrial countries, including their main features, costs, and effects, see OECD, *National Policies and Agricultural Trade* (Paris, 1987). The OECD has also produced a number of detailed studies of individual countries' agricultural trade policies that quantify their external effects; see OECD, *National Policies and Agricultural Trade: Country Study, Japan* (Paris, 1987); and OECD, *National Policies and Agricultural Trade: Study on European Economic Community* (Paris, 1987). Sam Laird and Alexander Yeats survey and evaluate studies that have attempted to quantify the effects of agricultural trade barriers in OECD countries (*Quantitative Methods for Trade Barrier Analysis* [London: Macmillan, 1989]).

4. Alexander Yeats, "Agricultural Protectionism: An Analysis of Its International Economic Effects and Options for Institutional Reform," *Trade and Development*, no. 3 (Winter 1981).

5. Alberto Valdés and Joachim Zietz, *Agricultural Protection in OECD Countries: Its Costs to Less Developed Countries* (Washington, D.C.: International Food Policy Research Institute, 1980).

6. J. M. Finger and P. A. Messerlin, *The Effects of Industrial Countries' Policies on Developing Countries*, Policy and Research Series no. 3 (Washington, D.C.: World Bank, 1989).

7. UNCTAD, *Protectionism and Structural Adjustment, Introduction and Part I*, TD/B/1081 (Geneva, 1986).

8. John Whalley, *Trade Liberalization among Major World Trading Areas* (Cambridge, Mass.: MIT Press, 1985).

9. J. I. Haaland and V. D. Norman, *EFTA and the World Economy: Comparative Advantage and Trade Policy*, EFTA Occasional Paper no. 19 (Geneva: European Free Trade Association, 1987).

10. For a thorough survey of the issues, see Junichi Goto, "Effects of the Multifibre Arrangement on Developing Countries: A Survey," Policy, Planning, and Research Working Paper no. 102, International Economics Department, World Bank (Washington, D.C., 1988).

11. Robert E. Hudec, *Developing Countries in the GATT Legal System* (London: Gower Press, for the Trade Policy Research Centre, 1987).

12. A subject that deserves further attention is whether the newly industrialized developing economies could enhance their bargaining power by negotiating as a group or through a regional association like the Association of Southeast Asian Nations (ASEAN). For example, the combined exports of Brazil, China, Hong Kong, Korea, and Taiwan (US$146 billion) are almost 30 percent larger than those of France. It should also be noted that the EC countries have found it advantageous to negotiate in common in the Uruguay Round and in previous multilateral trade negotiations, and so a joint approach might be useful for developing countries as well.

13. J. M. Finger and Andrzej Olechowski, eds., *The Uruguay Round: A Handbook for the Multilateral Trade Negotiations* (Washington, D.C.: World Bank, 1987), p. 260.

14. The total value of manufactured exports of all Sub-Saharan African developing countries to developed countries, for example, was approximately one-tenth that of Korea (US$33 billion), while the total value of their nonoil exports was less than that of Mexico (US$19 billion).

15. Box 8-1 refers only to the *economics* of unilateral versus multilateral liberalizations. There are various reasons for believing that political factors in some situations may favor the multilateral approach. Note, for example, the almost total reliance of developed countries on the multilateral approach during the past four decades.

16. The basic difficulty is that developing countries adopted a position of nonreciprocity in previous multilateral trade negotiations, arguing that their special economic situation precluded the direct exchange of trade concessions. Consequently, there is little factual information that bears directly on

such issues as the credit problem, and it is difficult to speculate how this will be handled in the GATT negotiations.

17. The evidence is far from complete, but existing data do seem to come down in favor of the economics of a unilateral liberalization. For example, in the case of Argentina, the net present value of exports under immediate unilateral liberalization is estimated to exceed that under a delayed multilateral approach by US$23 billion. See J. Nogués, "The Choice between Unilateral and Multilateral Trade Liberalization Strategies," Policy, Planning, and Research Working Paper no. 239, International Economics Department, World Bank (Washington, D.C., 1989).

18. J. M. Finger and Paula Holmes, "Unilateral Liberalization and the MTNs," in Finger and Olechowski, *The Uruguay Round.*

19. See, for example, the description of the conditions of Morocco's accession to the GATT in GATT, *Report of the Working Party on the Accession of Morocco,* L/5967 (Geneva, 1986). In contrast, many African and Caribbean countries that were former colonies gained immediate membership in the GATT under article XXVI by being sponsored by the developed country with which they were associated.

20. See Hudec, *Developing Countries in the GATT Legal System* (chap. 9) for an analysis of specific GATT articles and regulations that might be applied to developing countries. Hudec specifically notes that GATT article XVIII "has lain rusting and unused for several decades" (p. 173). Developing countries have stopped asking for permission when they impose new trade barriers under this article, mainly because developed countries have stopped challenging them. The reason for the developed countries' lack of interest has been the seeming impossibility of the task, given the almost perpetual balance of payments problems and other development-related excuses in the developing countries. And if developed countries begin to increase regulatory pressure on the balance of payment applications of article XVIII, the article's infant industry provisions would still be available as an alternative legal defense of new tariff barriers.

21. Some evidence indicates that such swaps increase investment, as opposed to just subsidizing investment that would have been made anyway.

22. To illustrate the principle of diversion, suppose country A originally imposes a tariff of 40 percent on all imports of widgets. Importers in country A buy the widgets from world markets at a cost of $1.00 plus the $0.40 tariff, which is revenue for the government and not a real resource cost. Country B could potentially produce and sell widgets to A for $1.20, plus the $0.48 tariff, but because this is more expensive than prices on the world market, B cannot sell widgets and so devotes its resources to producing other things. Suppose A and B agree to drop all tariffs between themselves, leaving tariffs toward other countries unchanged. B finds it profitable to produce widgets at a real resource cost of $1.20 and sell them to importers in A, who now find it cheaper to buy from B than from world markets. But the real cost of acquiring a widget has risen from $1.00 to $1.20. The cost of trade diversion is 20 percent of the value of widget imports.

23. Bela Balassa and A. Stoutjesdijk, "Economic Integration among Developing Countries," *Journal of Common Market Studies* 14 (April 1978):37–55.

24. See World Bank, "Intra-Regional Trade in Sub-Saharan Africa," Trade and Finance Division, Africa Technical Department, World Bank (Washington, D.C., 1988), p. 51.

25. Article XXIV of the GATT makes explicit provisions for integration schemes. Although the conditions are rather vague, some of them seem to be intended to make it more likely that, on balance, trade will be created rather than diverted. These include a condition that extraregional trade barriers on the whole should not be raised, while barriers must be eliminated on virtually all trade among members. See Ulrich Lachler, "Regional Integration and Economic Development," Industry and Energy Department Working Paper no. 14, World Bank (Washington, D.C., 1989).

26. Other schemes could in principle improve welfare, but they would have to be evaluated on a case-by-case basis according to their costs and benefits. Any scheme that involves significant increases in the extraregional tariff of some members or large differences between regional and extraregional tariffs should be viewed with caution.

9
Assessing the Experience of Trade Policy Reform

Reform of trade policy is essential to link the economies of developing countries to worldwide technological advances and enable them to compete in an increasingly integrated world. In consequence, trade policy has been high on the agenda of reforms in these countries in the past decade, although it has been unclear what has actually been done and what the results have been.

The evidence in this book suggests that reforms in trade policy have, by and large, contributed to improved economic performance in developing countries. The book shows that countries that reformed are more open and their trade regimes more efficient than a decade ago. But the commitment to implement reform has been weaker than expected, and results have often been disappointing. Stronger and more comprehensive improvements in policy and institutions are needed to enhance the effectiveness of the reforms, among them measures to reduce the protection of domestic industry in competition with imports.

It is noteworthy that the supply response to reforms has been stronger in countries where institutions and infrastructure have supported changes in policy and where the linkage between trade and other policies has been recognized. This argues that more attention should be paid to actions that complement trade policy reforms in order to derive the greatest possible benefit from them.

Trade Policy Reforms and Their Effects

Most trade policy reforms of the 1980s in the developing countries were supported by the World Bank's adjustment lending, in conjunction with assistance from the IMF.[1] (A few countries, notably Bolivia, reformed their trade policies without explicit World Bank support.) The most common reform proposals concerned the exchange rate, export promotion, import restrictions, and studies of protection. Proposals regarding policy on exports and quantitative restrictions on imports were generally stronger than those concerned with the level and dispersion of tariffs.

The Extent of Policy Change

Many countries corrected misaligned exchange rates and reduced impediments to exports, including restrictions on imports needed for export production. Several countries substituted tariffs for quantitative restrictions on imports. Fewer countries significantly reduced both quantitative restrictions and tariff levels, but several have made good progress, including Bolivia, Costa Rica, Chile, Ghana, Korea, Mexico, and, until recently, Turkey. In nearly all these countries the bias against trade, especially exportables, declined in part as a result of a reduction in import protection.[2]

But progress in lowering import protection levels across countries has been slower than expected.[3] Also, implementation of reform has varied considerably among recipients of trade loans. Some countries achieved substantial reform (Chile, Mexico, and Turkey), while others made little progress or reversed their reforms (Guyana, Yugoslavia, Zambia, and Zimbabwe).

Four sets of domestic factors constrain stronger and more sustained reforms:

- The opposition of vested interests and inadequate conviction about the benefits of the reforms have weakened the commitment to reform (in Kenya, Peru, Yugoslavia, and Zimbabwe, for example).
- Administrative and institutional insufficiencies have contributed to setbacks in implementing reform (in Bangladesh, Côte d'Ivoire, and Malawi, for example) and reforms to strengthen institutions in the public sector have received inadequate attention.
- Weak macroeconomic performance and conflicts between policy reform and stabilization goals have sometimes slowed trade liberalization (as in Morocco and the Philippines) or even reversed it (as in Argentina and Zambia).
- Lags in the supply response to policy reform, by reducing its apparent benefits, have dampened enthusiasm, especially in low-income Africa.

The Effect on Performance

Assessing the impact of reforms on economic performance is made difficult by the incomplete nature of the reforms and the simultaneous presence of other contributing factors. Nonetheless, the evidence suggests that policy reforms have contributed positively to growth in output and exports. Both the additional financing from adjustment lending and the policy reforms themselves have contributed to a mild, relative improvement in GDP, exports, and other variables in the loan recipient countries—especially among the early and intensive recipients (those that received three or more adjustment loans).[4] The results are much stronger and are statistically more significant when the comparison is between trade policy reformers and nonreformers rather than simply between trade loan recipients and nonrecipients.[5]

The response of output to policy change has varied considerably. Studies of a number of countries identify several factors that constrain the supply response.

- The institutional and infrastructural needs of exporters are often insufficiently addressed because of weak systems for providing duty-free and restriction-free access to imported inputs; inadequate port, transport, and telecommunications facilities; and poor information and market services for exporters.
- Domestic regulatory policies are allowed to interfere with the change in incentives in response to reform (price controls) and to reduce the mobility of factors of production through labor market interventions, market entry and exit regulations, and foreign investment controls.
- Growing protectionism in international markets in the 1980s has depressed world prices and blocked access to markets, thereby reducing the response of exports, especially in agriculture. Lower tariffs for manufactured exports make the markets of industrial countries more promising, although the nontariff barriers they impose in some important product categories (such as textiles, clothing, and steel) have hurt the growth of exports in developing countries.
- The credibility of the reforms, which affects their sustainability, depends on a country's track record in policy reform, the forcefulness of its initial reform steps, its macroeconomic stability, and the consistency of its trade policy reforms with its reforms in other areas such as the financial sector or agricultural pricing.
- Underdeveloped entrepreneurial and managerial capacity inevitably slows the supply response. Shortages of trained labor and poorly developed input supply lines have also been serious problems.

The Sequencing and Timing of Trade Policy Reforms

Tariff reform may cause revenue losses, devaluation may increase inflation, and liberalization may aggravate balance of payments problems. Does this mean that trade liberalization is inconsistent with stabilization efforts? Indeed, there is little doubt that macroeconomic instability makes trade policy (and some other) reforms more difficult to implement successfully. For this reason some analysts have argued that the fiscal deficit and inflation should be reduced before trade policy reforms are introduced.

Stabilization and Trade Policy Reforms

In practice, the strong practitioners of trade policy reform in the sample have generally also managed to reduce their inflation and fiscal and balance of payments deficits more than have the weaker reformers. One reason is that some reforms increase revenue and thus reduce the fiscal deficit. Furthermore, in cases in which the fiscal deficit has been reduced sufficiently and the real exchange rate depreciated, the current account deficit has also declined despite the liberalization of imports. In these circumstances, import liberalization can reduce inflation and contribute to stabilization by providing much needed competition in domestic markets. Although devaluation raises the domestic prices of tradables and can fuel inflation, inflation can be lowered even with a devaluation if the fiscal deficit is lowered sufficiently.

But trade policy reforms are unlikely to be productive under conditions of severe and continuing macroeconomic instability. When inflation is very high and variable, leads and lags in the movement of individual prices mean that the resulting pattern of relative prices is a poor guide for economic decisions. Also, if the authorities use the exchange rate (instead of adequate macroeconomic policies) as a brake on inflation, the real exchange rate is likely to appreciate and thus reduce the effectiveness of the reform. Under these conditions the trade policy reform in question should be delayed until the very high rates of inflation are brought down.

Fiscal Reforms and Trade Policy Reforms

Eliminating nontariff barriers (especially by converting them to tariffs), eliminating tariff exemptions, and raising the lowest rates to make the structure more uniform are revenue-enhancing measures (which were used in Jamaica, Kenya, and Mauritius, for example). In a sample of countries that reformed primarily nontariff barriers, tariff revenue increased from 2.7 percent of GDP to 3.4 percent of GDP. Revenues can also be kept constant or raised in domestic currency if lowered rates are accompanied by a sufficiently depreciated exchange rate. And reducing very high tariff rates can increase trade tax revenue if tariff evasion rates fall as a result or if import demand is price elastic.

But an increase in tariff revenue cannot always be relied on. In a sample of countries that reduced tariffs as well as implemented other reforms—among them Mexico, Morocco, the Philippines, and Thailand—revenue fell on average from 2.8 percent of GDP to 2.3 percent of GDP. The fiscal effects of a devaluation also vary depending in general on whether the government is a net buyer of foreign exchange (Ghana, Sierra Leone, Somalia, Uganda, and Zaire, for example) or a net seller (Nigeria, for example). When import liberalization is likely to worsen an already large fiscal deficit, measures to reduce expenditure or increase revenue from other sources will need to be implemented along with the tariff reforms. Mexico generated additional revenue through tax reform when its trade taxes fell, whereas Morocco took no compensatory measures when tariff revenue fell (and did not reduce nontariff barriers to increase revenue while reducing tariffs), and in consequence experienced a partial reversal of reform.

The Sequencing of Domestic Reforms and Trade Policy Reforms

In general, the benefits of trade policy reforms are greater when accompanied by domestic economic reforms. Hence, trade policy and domestic reforms are best carried out simultaneously. But in practice not all actions can be taken at the same time and so the issue of sequencing becomes relevant. Initiating trade policy reforms often exposes the need for domestic reforms and investments (as was the case in Madagascar, Mexico, Tanzania, and Zaire). It also exposes unforeseen infrastructural needs of industries that are based almost entirely on foreign demand (such as fresh fruit and salmon in Chile, cut flowers in Colombia, and cutlery and television sets in Korea). And sometimes domestic reforms should be deferred until the business and financial communities clearly understand that the protection of imports will be reduced. Otherwise, when investment or price controls are removed in highly protected sectors, increased investment and production might be encouraged in the wrong sectors. At other times, trade policy reform may need to wait until a domestic control is relaxed. For example, a processed product (such as textiles) may see its effective protection vanish or become negative if its tariffs are reduced while the price of its basic input (cotton), which is set by a monopolistic parastatal, remains high.

The Order and Pacing of Trade Policy Reforms

If all reforms cannot be carried out simultaneously, priority should be placed on removing or counteracting the most important and binding constraints to better performance. If a country has a substantially overvalued exchange rate, the first step should be to achieve and maintain a real devaluation and to unify any multiple exchange rates. Because a real devaluation can make quantitative import restrictions redundant and facilitate their removal, large devaluations have often preceded or accompanied the rapid removal of these restrictions (as in Bolivia, Chile, Ghana, Laos, Mexico, Nigeria, Sri Lanka, and Zaire). Such a shift from commercial policy protection to "exchange rate protection" constitutes a major step toward establishing neutral incentives between and among exportables and import substitutes.

Introducing some export policy reforms shortly before, or at least at the same time as, import reforms stimulates a more rapid export supply response and can insulate exporters from any adverse effects of tariff unification by exempting them from paying higher rates on imported inputs. Import policy reform often starts by replacing non-tariff barriers with tariffs that provide roughly the same protection. This step not only eliminates tariff exemptions but also improves re-source allocation, increases transparency, reduces rent-seeking, and improves the fiscal situation. Reducing the dispersion of tariff rates ought to follow, in order to move toward a uniform incentive struc-ture. It should usually be accompanied or followed by a reduction in the average tariff rates so as to reduce protection levels. At the same time, any potentially harmful effects on the fiscal deficit should be offset. If revenue is not a serious concern, nontariff barriers could be phased out without introducing equivalent tariffs.

Expeditious reform avoids a drawn-out process that gives opponents time to organize and lobby for a reversal. It also avoids difficulties in importing intermediate and capital goods that would interfere with the restructuring that liberalization is expected to set in motion. Also, the sooner the benefits of reform begin, the better the prospects for sus-tainability. Some successful reforms have been comprehensive, inten-sive, and fast, as in Bolivia. Mexico quickly reduced the coverage of quantitative restrictions and reduced tariffs in about two years. Chile's phasing out of quantitative restrictions was rapid, but tariff reductions took place over five years. Korea carried out its comprehensive re-forms over twenty years, with substantial import liberalization occur-ring only after 1980. When implementation of tariff reform is spread over several years to give affected activities time to adjust, it is desirable to announce the trade policy reforms in advance, as Chile did.

Experience suggests that substantial and comprehensive liberalization can be completed in less than five to seven years from the start of the ad-justment program, although the decision on the pace of reform ulti-mately depends on the specific circumstances of the country involved. This should allow time for quantitative restrictions to be phased out and for tariffs to be reduced to, say, 15 to 25 percent. Later stages of reform might reduce the tariffs further. But even when reforms are drawn out over this period, major and decisive actions in the first years are important to signal commitment and give the reform credibility.

Trade Policy Measures

A real devaluation improves the incentives for producing exports and efficient import substitutes.[6] Devaluation needs to be accompanied by macroeconomic policies to restrain inflation and maintain the real exchange rate. In addition to sound exchange rate and macroeconomic policies, there are some cost-effective means to support export development. More fundamentally, export development is assisted indirectly by policies to reduce import protection that contribute to a more appropriate real exchange rate and to a smaller antiexport bias.

Export Development

East Asia's economic success has rested on macroeconomic stability—low fiscal deficits and inflation rates, and stable and adequate exchange rates. Relatively low protection of import substitutes helps to sustain a more depreciated real exchange rate than would otherwise be the case. Low protection rates also make it easier to administer schemes that exempt exporters from restrictions and tariffs on their imported inputs. Although Korea and Taiwan were successful in using protective import policies by avoiding exchange rate overvaluation and offsetting the antiexport bias of import protection, their approach would be difficult to replicate in today's world economy. Korea's approach during the 1960s and 1970s included export subsidies, which other countries would countervail today, and on vigorous government intervention to suppress rent-seeking activities viewed as incompatible with export growth.

Giving direct and indirect exporters restriction-free access to inputs at duty- and tax-free international prices is particularly effective in developing manufactured exports.[7] One method is to have no tariffs or restrictions on imports (as in Hong Kong and Singapore). Where import protection remains, however, the bias against exports needs to be reduced through schemes that reduce import costs. One approach that can be used for large export-oriented firms that import inputs is to provide duty waivers (and exemptions from other import restrictions) or temporary admissions of imported inputs (as in India, Indonesia, Mexico, Morocco, and Turkey). For small or occasional exporters, for which waivers or temporary admission schemes are impractical, a quick, reliable method is to use drawbacks or rebates of duties and indirect taxes actually paid (as in Korea, Taiwan, and Thailand). But collecting and refunding duties is less efficient than waiving duties, and drawbacks do not offset nontariff barriers. Other duty-free schemes allow in-bond or duty-exempt export manufacturing plants to locate almost anywhere (as in Mauritius and Mexico) or establish physically separate export processing zones (as in more than thirty developing countries). But many export processing zones have proved to be poor investments as a result of unwise location, high investment costs, mediocre management, or uncooperative customs officials. Duty-free schemes for exporters do, however, involve costs. For example, they may temporarily increase a fiscal deficit,[8] penalize domestic suppliers of importable inputs, and create new opportunities for rent-seeking.

Manufactured exports must meet special requirements of quality and timeliness if they are to be competitive. Exporters require efficient infrastructure and telecommunications, readily available export credit, and support in technology development, quality control, production planning, and trade logistics. The East Asian experience suggests the value of relaxing regulations on layoffs, fringe benefits, minimum wages, and collective action in order to reduce labor costs and increase the flexibility of the enterprises.[9] Policies regarding industrial location and regional development may also need to be changed, because exports on a large scale cannot be expected from undeveloped areas with poor infrastructure. Helping exporters secure technical assistance services from consultants and information suppliers of their choice may also be useful. Foreign firms can be a valuable source of technology and capital and can provide a link to world markets. Foreign investors are attracted to countries with macroeconomic stability, strong protection of property rights (including intellectual property rights), a stable and transparent regulatory environment, and liberal access to foreign exchange for profit remittances and imported inputs and services. This kind of good climate for investment is likely to produce better results than special incentives, such as tax holidays, which may attract footloose industries that leave when the holiday is over.

Import Policy

Nontariff barriers make the system less transparent and less predictable and encourage lobbying, rent-seeking, and corruption. Even with little or no decrease in protection levels, therefore, a reduction of nontariff barriers can have major salutary effects. One simple reform is to switch from a list of permitted imports to a list of forbidden imports and allow unlicensed import of all items that are not listed—the first step in Korea's liberalization in 1967. Auction systems can sometimes be substituted for administrative rationing, with good results. Quotas can be auctioned, with the quota amount increased until its protective value falls to zero, at which point it can be abolished. Alternatively, tariffs providing approximately equivalent protection can be imposed on product categories as nontariff controls are eliminated. This change reestablishes the link between domestic and international prices and ensures that they move in the same direction and diverge by no more than the amount of the tariff.

Because tariffs are usually higher on finished products than on intermediates and raw materials, and tariff exemptions are common, effective protection varies greatly across industries. To achieve efficiency in production, effective protection must be reduced and protection levels among imports must be made more uniform, while the protective effect of the domestic tax system is taken into account. Coordinating tariff reform with domestic tax reform permits deeper reductions in tariffs than would otherwise be fiscally acceptable. Reductions should eventually result in a low, equal rate of tax of imports and domestic production for each product. Raising low tariff rates (usually on inputs) also raises revenue, allowing high rates to be reduced further, and makes effective protection more uniform between inputs and finished goods.

On efficiency and political economy grounds, a relatively low and relatively uniform tariff structure is the best option. Uniformity minimizes distortions in production incentives for a given level of overall protection, subject to the qualification that exporters should be insulated from paying prices above world levels for their protected imported inputs. In general, such a tariff structure has the further advantage of being less likely to encourage lobbying. Bolivia, Chile, and Mexico have converged their tariff structures toward 15 percent, in addition to nearly eliminating quantitative restrictions, and other countries have reduced tariffs to below 30 percent.

An industry-by-industry approach to tariff reform is difficult to implement because changes in one industry have repercussions in others. What seems to work better is the concertina approach, whereby at each stage all the top rates are collapsed to the next highest level. Even better is a radial reduction, in which all rates at each step are cut to an equal fraction of their previous level, thereby consistently reducing protection at each stage. Although radial tariff reduction promises faster gains in production efficiency than does the concertina approach, it is more likely to reduce revenue in its first stages.[10] A combined approach—collapsing the very high rates and radially reducing all others subject to the revenue constraint—should be the best alternative because it combines the advantages of each of the other schemes.

Policies toward Trading Partners

Should developing countries reduce barriers unilaterally or delay re-forms in hopes of gaining concessions in multilateral negotiations? The issue could be resolved if all parties in multilateral negotiations were to declare unambiguously that credit would be granted for unilateral re-ductions of barriers. An alternative is for developing countries to bind tariffs at a level higher than the actual level and to offer to reduce the bound level at negotiations. This approach requires a credible threat to raise tariffs to the bound level if negotiations fail, as well as a credible commitment not to raise the tariffs if negotiations succeed. For most countries the costs imposed by their own trade policies are likely to be higher than the costs imposed by other countries' barriers. This situa-tion argues for unilateral reforms.

Industrial countries have reduced tariffs from an average of approxi-mately 40 percent in the late 1940s to less than 5.5 percent today. The markets of industrial countries remain attractive for a wide range of manufactured exports from developing countries. But nontariff barri-ers have increased, and the proportion of imports of developed coun-tries affected by nontariff barriers nearly doubled between 1966 and 1986. More than 90 percent of OECD imports of foodstuffs are now af-fected by some type of nontariff barrier. This change, coupled with the surpluses resulting from high OECD agricultural support prices, has dis-torted and destabilized agricultural markets. The nontariff barriers and agricultural policies of industrial countries reduce the potential benefits of reform in developing countries, reduce consumer welfare in industrial countries, and threaten the world trading system. It is in the interest of all countries that industrial countries reform their trade policies.

Some countries have formed regional trade groups, expecting to real-ize gains from increased trade, to take advantage of economies of scale by producing for a larger regional market, and to gain initial exporting experience under protection. But intraregional trade has grown little or has even declined. Industries established in response to integration usu-ally had high production costs, and the experience firms gained in mar-keting to neighbors proved irrelevant for exporting to wider markets. Most regional groups also raised barriers against extraregional trade, thereby discouraging integration into the world economy, where the gains from trade are likely to be greater. The costs of this diversion of trade from efficient world markets to high-cost regional producers were also great.

Success in integration has been greater among countries with gener-ally outward-oriented economies (such as the Southeast Asian coun-tries or the European countries). Two lessons from the experience with integration efforts are noteworthy. First, integration schemes should focus more on improving infrastructure and factor mobility than on direct trade policy measures. Increased trade would follow naturally. Second, trade policy measures ought to focus on reducing barriers to all trade, not just trade among members. The Central American Common Market, for example, has explicitly recognized the need to avoid impeding the progress of its member countries in overall trade reform.

Policies Complementary to Trade Policy Reform

Fiscal policy can complement trade policy reform in several ways. Domestic taxes can be used to equalize the price of domestically produced final goods and the tariff-inclusive price of imports, thereby reducing protection, raising revenue, and allowing tariff rates to be lowered more than they otherwise could be (as Malawi, Nigeria, and Togo are beginning to do). Fiscal policy can also be used to direct public investment in ways that support the trade policy reforms. Efficient investments in infrastructure and expenditures for research and extension services are important to take full advantage of increased trade incentives. Cuts in expenditure designed to achieve fiscal policy goals have, however, caused public investment budgets to fall in many countries (such as Côte d'Ivoire, Mexico, Morocco, and the Philippines). Some successful reformers have raised the share of public investment (Chile, Korea, and Turkey, for example); in other countries, the share has declined. In either case, the key is to ensure that the investments are efficient and appropriate to support the adjustment to policy reforms.

Public sector reform is an important complement to trade policy reform. Protection of state-owned manufacturing enterprises has sometimes interfered with trade liberalization (as in Argentina, Bangladesh, Chile, and Peru). Even when governments have privatized unprofitable firms (Togo's steel mill, for example), buyers have insisted on guarantees of high protection. Liquidation would probably be preferable to privatization in these cases. In socialist countries trade liberalization needs to be accompanied by a phasing out of the central planning and allocation mechanisms, so that the new market signals can be effective at the firm or farm level (in Poland, for example). Domination of crop output markets by state enterprises might mean that the effects of devaluation on producer prices are realized very slowly while input prices rise quickly. Or a state monopoly in input markets (seeds and agro-chemicals, for example) may mean that farmers lack high-quality inputs to use in responding to the liberalization of output markets. Meaningful trade liberalization in such cases may require abolition of the state enterprise (as in Nigeria) or elimination of its legal monopoly in the import market (as in Mexico). A corrupt or inefficient customs service can also reduce the supply response to reform; hence, as greater reliance is placed on tariffs, the customs service might need to be upgraded.

Reform of regulatory policies is another area that supports trade policy reform. If exit from or entry to the market is difficult, inefficient firms may hang on and new firms may never start up. Regulations that make it costly for firms to restructure or shut down have been a factor in failed liberalization attempts in Poland, Turkey (in the early 1970s), and Yugoslavia. In Mexico until 1988, regulations governing entry of new firms and expansion of established firms apparently slowed the pace of adjustment. The absence of such inhibiting controls was important for the success of Chile's trade policy reforms in 1974–79, which were carried out concurrently with the reduction or elimination of many regulations. Price or wage controls are incompatible with trade policy reforms whose purpose is to alter relative prices.

Financial sector regulations that encourage or enable banks to continue to lend to bankrupt enterprises (which must close down if the economy is to reap the efficiency gains from trade policy reform) may reduce the supply of new credit available for firms that should be expanding in the wake of the reforms. Regulatory reform, combined with support for restructuring in the financial and industrial sectors, could magnify the benefits of trade policy reforms.

Credibility and Sustainability

If the private sector is to invest in new sectors, it must believe that the new pattern of incentives will be sustained. If not, firms in previously protected sectors may invest in lobbying efforts and go deeply into debt trying to ride out the storm until their protection is restored. To be credible, the first steps of reform should be clear and decisive: reforms begun with tentative steps have often been reversed. A strong, well-publicized announcement of the program that demonstrates the head of state's commitment to the reforms can also be important in establishing credibility. In addition, a general interest agency (the central bank or finance ministry) is usually more reliable in executing a reform program than is an agency with specific interests to protect (such as the ministries of trade or industry).

Credible announcement of a timetable—although it carries the risk of giving the opposition time to mobilize against the reform—can usually strengthen the reform process. Reforms are generally easier to introduce after a crisis that discredits old policies. Since the crisis is often related to the balance of payments, a strong devaluation and macroeconomic adjustment are probably necessary and may be useful in sending a signal to producers, whose supply response will help to justify the program. Sustainability may also be enhanced by an external commitment to maintain reforms—such as joining the GATT—that raises the costs of reversal.[11] In some cases reforms may be politically more acceptable, credible, and sustainable if they are carried out under regional auspices, as was the case when the European Communities began to lower external trade barriers in the 1950s. This approach has yet to be tried in the developing world, however.

Successful trade policy reform can also have short-term transitional costs because some groups are made worse off as a result of shifts in resources. Taking steps to partially compensate losers may increase the odds that the reforms will be sustained and may have other benefits as well. Some compensatory measures, such as retraining workers, can improve factor mobility and thereby speed up the intersectoral adjustment process. Other measures, such as antidumping procedures (set up in Chile and Mexico, for example), may reduce resistance to the reduction of more costly forms of protection. Devaluation can also be viewed as a measure to partially compensate for the loss of protection and thereby reduce political resistance.

Other steps, such as targeted food assistance programs and employment programs, may offset any transitional effects of adjustment measures on real wages or employment. Often, however, workers displaced from protected industries are not among the poorest groups in the society. Moreover, new programs run the risk of creating new distortions and worsening the fiscal deficit. But the compensation issue needs to be addressed, and pragmatic and effective means must be found to target the programs well.[12]

Implications for Trade Policy Reform

This book strongly supports further reform of trade policies. It recommends that future programs seek to improve the design and implementation of reforms. In addition to ensuring an appropriate exchange rate and removing export restrictions, well-designed trade policy reform will reflect the following considerations:

- The main initial priority will be to reduce quantitative restrictions.
- Strong action needs to be taken to reduce import protection through tariff reductions and reforms.
- Relatively low and relatively uniform tariffs are preferable for reasons of efficiency and political economy, even though uniformity of import tariffs cannot be demonstrated in theory to be optimal in many circumstances.
- Studies of the economic costs of existing policies and evaluations of the expected benefits of reform are useful in improving the accept-

ability of trade policy reform. The lack of adequate data on indicators and measures of nominal and effective protection is a deficiency that needs to be remedied.

- A strong commitment to monitor and evaluate results is essential. The capacity of reforming countries to assess their own policies needs to be strengthened.
- Although the main focus in this book has, by intent, been developing countries, the urgency of the need for industrial countries to reform their trade policies is recognized.

Lessons have emerged from the experience with trade policy reform that should help address concerns regarding the interaction between such reform and other priorities.

- If all reforms cannot be carried out simultaneously, careful sequencing of the reforms can usually avoid conflicts among them. With respect to macroeconomic stability, it is necessary to consider the likely consequences of trade liberalization for the fiscal deficit and ways to offset adverse effects, if they are judged likely to be serious. When the inflation rate is very high and variable, stabilization efforts can precede other reforms.
- Greater emphasis on complementary policies, investments, and institutional reform will improve the payoff to trade policy reform. Where domestic market problems are severe, deregulation, infrastructural improvements, and institutional reforms are essential for the success of trade policy reforms.

Thus, although many governments have already taken the initial steps, much remains to be done to prepare for and implement trade policy reforms. It is hoped that the lessons discussed in this book will help these countries, and others that have not yet begun reforms, to design and implement programs to liberalize their trade regimes significantly. The eventual outcome of widespread reforms would be a more open global trading system and an enhanced standard of living in all countries.

Notes

1. As of June 1989, a total of ninety-eight loans to forty-four countries contained significant trade policy components.
2. Usually the estimates of bias compare the real effective exchange rates (taking into account import tariffs and export subsidies) for exportables with those for importables, in addition to comparing domestic relative prices.
3. Implementation data were available for twenty-four of the forty trade loan recipients. Detailed findings on implementation refer to the twenty-four

recipients. Aggregate data were also considered for the forty recipients, as well as for forty-seven nonrecipients.

4. Accordingly, the results measured for all recipients are likely to understate the benefits because they include the early stages of what is a continuing, cumulative process in some cases.

5. Real exchange rate adjustment and export-related reform had the greatest beneficial effect in some of the cases examined (Pakistan and Thailand, for instance). Most examples of import liberalization during the 1980s also involved a real exchange rate depreciation, and this combination was beneficial (in Chile, Jamaica, and Mexico, for example).

6. A devaluation, of course, should not be carried out simply as an export promotion measure. Competitive devaluations designed to undercut competitors on world markets should be avoided. Rather, devaluation should be considered a means to restore equilibrium in internal and external markets and to encourage long-run growth.

7. This approach avoids the wide variations in effective incentives that arise when different exports use inputs subject to different import controls and tariffs. It is not subject to the countervailing measures that importing countries are increasingly applying to direct or indirect export subsidies.

8. Short-run negative revenue effects may occur when protection of inputs is provided principally by tariffs. Tariff revenue should increase, however, as expanding exports increase the supply of foreign exchange for imports.

9. Another ambitious but effective strategy used by Korea and Taiwan is to establish a full range of industries, characterized by highly efficient technology, location, scale, and production operations, that provide intermediate inputs at low prices.

10. In contrast, the concertina approach concentrates initial reductions on very high rates, some of which may be so high that reducing them will increase import volume and tariff revenues.

11. However, the value of this commitment is decreased by the easy access developing countries have to GATT provisions that allow them to impose barriers for purposes of correcting balance of payments disequilibria or protecting infant industries.

12. A UNDP-World Bank program for trade expansion is providing technical assistance to a number of countries in this and other key areas of implementation of trade policy reform.

Index

Adjustment (structural), reform and, 1–5
Adjustment lending. *See* Loans
Administration: reform and, 174; weakness in, 40
Africa, 41, 113, 191, 195, 196; agricultural exports and, 144–45; agriculture and prorural reform bias in, 82; devaluation and, 158; intervention and, 50–51; lack of entrepreneurs in, 75; primary exports and, 142; reform bias in, 82; reform commitment and, 40; reform resistance and, 86; stabilization and, 99. *See also names of specific African countries*
Agriculture, 75, 85, 86, 142, 146, 181, 182; exports and, 51, 143, 144–45; prorural reform bias in Africa and, 82; protection of (Korea), 132
American Economic Association, 80
Andean Group, 194, 195
Antidumping, 41, 162, 214
Antiexport bias, 4, 31, 33, 37, 65, 76, 142, 158, 163, 203, 208
Argentina, 35, 41, 47, 83, 103, 106, 126, 140, 141, 143, 171, 186, 203, 212
Association of Southeast Asian Nations (ASEAN), 195, 196
Auction: foreign exchange, 91; systems of, 210

Australia, 158, 159, 169, 185, 186

Balance of payments, 1, 32, 51, 99, 157, 194; constraints on reform and, 39; Mexico and, 66
Balassa, Bela, 50
Baldwin, R. E., 92
Bangladesh, 27, 28, 40, 83, 126, 135, 142, 143, 171, 203, 212; reform resistance in, 90
Banking, 110
Bankruptcy, 74, 81, 170, 213
Barbados, 182
Betancur government, 88
Blum, R., 84
Bolivia, 56, 143, 195, 203, 210; devaluation and, 157; reform and, 202; tariff reform and, 164
Bonded factories, 138
Botswana, 182
Brazil, 28, 47, 106, 109, 110, 126, 141, 159, 185, 186, 190, 207; private sector in, 111

Canada, 186
Central American Common Market (CACM), 194, 195, 197, 212
Central planning, 30–31, 75; liberalization and, 111; phasing out of, 212
Chenery, Hollis, 50
Chile, 4, 34, 35, 37, 39, 42, 47, 59, 83, 87, 89, 90, 92, 93, 97, 107,

Chile *(continued)*
110, 141, 143, 146, 160, 175,
186, 191, 195, 203, 206, 207,
210, 212, 213, 214; crawling peg
system and, 102; devaluation
and, 157; growth in, 13; imports
and, 69, 155, 169; import
substitution and, 68; import tax
and, 113; infant industries and,
154; investment and, 69;
liberalization and, 68–69, 169;
output performance and, 81;
protection and, 68, 69; protection reduction and, 81–82,
170; quantitative restrictions
and, 156; revenue stabilization
and, 150; tariff reform and,
164; tariffs and, 68; trade
liberalization and manufacturing
in, 68–69; trade restrictiveness
and, 25, 31
China, 111, 126, 128, 138, 190;
export growth in, 140, 185
Choksi, Armeane, 72, 74
Colombia, 28, 34, 35, 37, 40, 47,
59, 87, 91, 107, 126, 159, 182,
186, 195; crawling peg system
and, 102; Dutch disease and,
149–50; exchange rate and, 28;
export of cut flowers and, 82–83,
175, 206; liberalization in, 88;
protection and, 84; reform
resistance in, 84
Competition, 47, 175; domestic,
29; imports and, 160, 170
Concentration ratio (Chilean
manufacturing), 69
Consultants, 141
Costa Rica, 27, 39, 73, 126, 168,
195, 203
Côte d'Ivoire, 37, 39, 40, 65, 107,
142, 143, 145, 157, 161, 203,
212; currency and, 70, 71, 157;
debt and, 71; devaluation and,
70; exchange rate and, 70–71;
exports and, 70–71; tariffs and,
70; trade policy in, 70–71
Country samples, 14–15
Credibility (of reforms), 40, 74,

117–18, 155–56, 204, 208, 213
Credit, 146; export, 141; Korea's
exporters and, 130; Mexico and,
66; subsidies, 134, 140
Crisis, 87–89, 93, 96, 213
Currency, 30; Côte d'Ivoire and,
70, 71, 157; depreciation, 35, 71
Customs service, 142; valuation
and, 41
Cyprus, 126

Data, 43; country experience,
59–65; country groupings,
16–18; cross country, 14–15;
economic indicator, 6–7
Debt, 116, 171; complication of,
116; Côte d'Ivoire and, 71;
fiscal reform and, 110, 111;
performance and loans and, 59
Deficits (current account), 89;
trade, 65
Deficits (fiscal), 1, 19, 118, 214; in
developing countries, 99; in Côte
d'Ivoire, 71; revenue effects on,
114–16; stabilization, 97, 205;
trade restrictions and fiscal, 99
Denmark, 185, 186
Depreciation: currency, 35, 71;
exchange rate, 32–34, 54, 65,
66, 76, 92, 102, 205; Mexico
and, 67. *See also* Devaluation
Devaluation (exchange rate), 12,
20, 34, 65, 75, 83, 142, 214;
agriculture and, 158; Bolivia and,
157; Chile and, 157; Côte
d'Ivoire and, 70, 71; depreciation, 32–34, 54, 65, 66, 76,
92, 102, 205; exports and,
90–91, 110; import prices and,
102; imports and, 157–58; Latin
America and, 72–73; Mexico
and, 66–67; Poland's trade
promotion and, 30, 31; real
exchange rate and, 101–03. *See
also* Depreciation; Exchange rate
Developing countries: fiscal deficits
in, 99; manufactured exports
and, 125; Multifibre
Arrangement and, 183;

negotiating differences among, 185–86, 197; structural adjustment and, 1; tariffs and rates for, 25–27; trade restrictions and, 25–27

Domestic reforms, 169–76, 203, 206

Dominican Republic, 126, 138

Dutch disease, 89; Colombia and, 149–50; exports and, 89, 148–50; foreign exchange and, 148; government expenditures (Colombia) and, 149; policy response to, 148–50

Duty drawbacks, 28, 42, 65, 83, 135, 136–37, 142, 147, 153, 163, 165, 167, 209; exports (Taiwan) and, 136–37.

Economic and Customs Union of Central Africa (UDEAC), 194

Economic growth. *See* Growth

Education, 174

Effective rate of protection. *See* Protection

Efficiency, allocative, 176

Egypt, 47, 126

Eisenhower, Dwight, 92

El Salvador, 126

Emergency Committee for American Trade, 90

Employment, 170, 174, 214; exports and, 72, 73; import substitution and, 72; inward orientation and, 73–74; labor regulations in Madagascar and, 172–73; manufacturing and, 72, 73; outward performance and, 72, 74; trade policy reform and, 67–74

European Economic Community (EEC), 158, 181, 182, 183, 184, 186, 195, 196, 214

Exchange rate, 19, 20, 21, 42, 82, 83, 89, 99, 115, 140; adjustment in real, 34–35; Chile and, 105–06; Colombia and, 28; Côte d'Ivoire and, 70, 71; country experiences and, 59, 65; Dutch disease (Colombia) and, 149;

exports and, 123, 129, 133; fiscal sector reform and, 110, 111; imports and, 157–58, 165, 168; indexes for, 36; Latin America and, 72; Mexico and, 67; policy and, 66; primary exports and, 143, 146; protection and, 207; real, 101–06, 118; stabilization and real, 117–18; trade policy reform and, 2, 4. *See also* Devaluation (exchange rate)

Exports, 1, 19, 41; Africa and, 142; agricultural, 51, 143, 144–45; causal relation with GDP and, 47, 54; Côte d'Ivoire and, 70, 71; of cut flowers (Colombia), 82–83, 175, 206; devaluation and, 90–91, 110; developing countries and manufactured, 125; documentation delays and, 75; Dutch disease and, 89, 148–50; duty rebates (Taiwan) and, 136–37; effects of restrictions on, 51–54; employment and, 72, 73; exchange rates and, 123, 129, 133; expansion and, 46; foodstuff, 186; foreign buyers and, 128; growth and, 13; Hong Kong and, 125, 126, 129, 148, 185, 208; implementation and, 32, 39; import reform and, 37, 207; Korean experience and, 125, 126, 129, 130–34, 135, 136, 139, 140, 141, 142, 147; manufactured, 123, 125, 126, 128, 129, 131, 138, 139, 142, 147, 171, 185, 209; Mexico and, 66, 67; Multifibre Arrangement and, 182, 183; neutrality versus liberalization and, 11–12; in *1980*s, 125–28; output performance and, 46–47, 48–49; performance and loans and, 58, 59, 65; Poland's trade promotion and, 30, 31; policy implications of reform and, 65, 66, 124–25; primary sector, 123, 125, 142–47; promotion and imports and, 135; protection (of imports)

Exports *(continued)*
and, 123, 129; quantitative
restrictions and, 2; reduction of
imports and, 123; reform and
expansion of, 46, 208–09;
schemes for, 42; requirements
for development of, 129–39;
technical assistance and, 141–42;
trade restrictiveness and, 28;
unsatisfactory methods for
increasing, 139–40; voluntary
restraints on, 182–83. *See also*
Antiexport bias
Export subsidies. *See* Subsidies
Export tax, 12, 32, 102, 114, 143
External shocks, 1; costs of
protection and, 8
Extraregional trade, 194, 211

Fiji, 186
Financial sector, 171; reform and,
54–58, 110–11
Finger, J. M., 182, 187
Finland, 185
Fiscal reform, 205–06; debt and
110, 111; exchange rate and,
110, 111
Foreign exchange, 8, 54, 87, 88,
115, 129, 140, 143, 158, 209;
auction, 91; controls on, 99,
195; Dutch disease, and 148;
Madagascar and, 172; overvalued
exchange rate and, 102; restrictions, 100–01
Foreign investment. *See* Investment
France, 71

Gambia, 109
García regime, 89
General Agreement on Trade and
Tariffs (GATT), 13, 20, 27, 41,
162, 196, 198, 214; liberalization
and, 184; Mexico and, 66, 187;
protection and, 93; unilateral
reform and, 184–89
Germany, 82
Ghana, 13, 27, 32, 34, 47, 82, 102,
103, 114, 115, 141, 143, 146,
157, 203, 206, 207
Global System of Trade
Preferences, 191
Government: Dutch disease and
expenditures of (Colombia), 149;
reform and, 83–86; reform
commitment and, 40; spending
of, 50, 70
Gross domestic product (GDP), 4;
Chilean trade in, 68–69;
export-GDP ratios and, 37;
export growth and, 50; growth
and reform and, 9, 54–58;
import-GDP ratios and, 35;
supply response and, 74
Growth: in Chile, 140, 185; exports
and 13; in Hong Kong, 13; in
Korea, 13; liberalization and, 13;
reform and outward orientation
and, 9; supply response and, 74;
trade policy reform and, 8–9,
46–54
Guatemala, 126, 168, 195
Guinea, 32, 102, 157, 171, 174
Guyana, 28, 56, 65, 203

Haiti, 56, 126, 138
Holmes, Paula, 187
Honduras, 41
Hong Kong, 190; exports and, 125,
126, 129, 147, 185, 208; growth
in, 13; imports and, 155
Hoover, Herbert, 80
Hungary, 126, 186

Import licensing, 87, 91, 129, 135,
159–60
Imports, 20, 41, 99; Chile and, 69,
155, 169; competition and, 160,
170; devaluation and prices of,
102; documentation delays and,
75; domestic reforms and,
169–76; effects of restrictions on,
51–54; exchange rate and,
157–58, 165, 168; export
promotion and, 135; exports and
protection of, 123; foodstuff,
181, 211; Hong Kong and, 155;

Korea and, 154, 155, 156, 169;
liberalization and, 35, 39, 43, 65,
67, 76, 90, 92, 134, 160, 171,
175; Mexico and, 66, 67;
neutrality versus liberalization
and, 11–12; output performance
and, 54; performance and loans
and, 58; policy and reform and,
65, 66, 67; protection and, 5,
35–37, 51, 130, 162, 163, 165,
166, 203, 206, 209–10; quantitative restrictions and, 2,
156–62; reform and, 4, 153–55,
209–10; reform implications and,
32, 39; reform program components and, 155–56; Singapore and, 155; stabilization
and, 113; structural adjustment
and, 1; tariff rate reform and,
25–27, 161–69; trade
restrictiveness and, 28
Import substitution, 39, 50, 65,
110, 134, 158, 176, 191, 208;
Chile and, 68; employment and,
72; protection and, 170, 208;
protection reduction and, 81;
reform resistance and, 85; tariffs
and, 161–69
Import tax, 112–14, 116, 163, 173
Incentives, 19, 67, 75, 169, 213;
direct export, 65; Poland's trade
promotion and export, 31;
production, 210; trade reform
and, 4, 5; trade reform
implementation and, 31–35
Income, 80, 87, 148
Income distribution, 73, 80; reform
resistance and, 85
India, 8, 27, 40, 47, 87, 126, 135,
136, 141, 154, 156, 170, 186, 208
Indigenization (local content)
programs, 160
Indonesia, 13, 41, 42, 84, 89, 90,
91, 129, 135, 136, 141, 143,
186, 190, 208
Infant industries, 153–54
Inflation, 19, 39, 71, 87, 89, 101,
102, 205; real exchange rate

and, 106; stabilization and, 96–97
Infrastructure, 70, 97, 107, 109,
128, 138, 184, 196, 204, 209,
212; improvements in, 174–75;
inadequacies in, 172–74;
investment and, 175, 212;
Madagascar and, 173
Institutional reform, 40, 86, 204
Integration, regional. *See* regional
integration
Interest rates, 19; real, 107, 118;
stabilization and real, 107
International Monetary Fund
(IMF), 1, 15, 27, 160, 202
Intraregional trade, 194, 211
Investment, 9, 50, 169, 174, 206;
Chile and, 69; foreign, 42,
74–75, 142, 190–91; infrastructure, 175, 212; Korea's
exports and, 130–31; performance and loans and, 59;
primary exports and, 142;
private sector, 213; public,
107–09; reform and, 117–18;
stabilization and, 97; trade policy
reform and foreign direct, 190–91
Inward orientation, 10, 37;
economic performance and, 47;
employment and, 73–74
Israel, 47, 106

Jamaica, 27–28, 32, 39, 87, 102,
114, 126, 141, 205
Japan, 129, 140, 181; infant
industry programs and, 154
Jordan, 126

Kennedy Round, 90, 92
Kenya, 35, 37, 39, 40, 41, 42, 59,
102, 142, 148, 203, 205; import
tax in, 113
Korea, 4, 35, 37, 42, 47, 59, 92,
97, 107, 203, 206, 207, 210,
212; antiexport bias and, 31;
credit and exports and, 130;
exchange rate depreciation and,
33, 34; exports and, 125, 126,
129, 130–34, 135, 136, 139, 140,

Korea *(continued)*
141, 147, 185, 208; growth in,
13; imports and, 154, 155, 156,
169; import tax in, 113; infant
industries and, 154; liberalization and, 37, 133, 154, 210;
protection of agriculture and,
132; resource allocation and,
132–33; trade restrictiveness and,
25

Labor regulations (Madagascar),
172–73
Lake, David, 80, 85
Laos, 157, 207
Latin America, 41; devaluation
and, 72–73, 158; exchange rates
and, 72; export promotion and,
139, 140; primary exports and,
143–44; protection of manufacturing and, 86; stabilization and, 99; trade restrictiveness and, 28; wages in, 72–
73. *See also names of specific
countries*
Liberalization, 20, 21, 156;
attempts at, 80; Bangladesh and,
90; benefits from, 83; central
planning and, 111; Chile and,
68–69, 169; Colombia and,
88; commercial, 32, 59; compensation and, 92–93; concerns about trade, 5; costs of
protection and, 8; domestic
reforms and, 169, 175–76;
export, 51; GATT and, 184;
growth and, 13; import, 35, 39,
43, 65, 67, 76, 90, 92, 134, 160,
169, 171, 175, 209–10; Korea
and, 37, 133, 154, 210;
manufacturing (Korean) and,
169; neutrality and, 11–12;
opposition to, 86; Peru and,
89; price and, 31; regional
integration and, 191; revenue
effects of, 109–16; socialist
countries and, 212; stabilization
and, 102, 103; tariffs and, 118;
time period for, 207; trade policy

reform and, 10; transitional costs
of, 47; unilateral, 179, 187,
188–89; United States and,
84–85, 90. *See also* Trade policy
reform
Licensing (import), 87, 91, 129,
135, 159–60
Loans: economic indicators and
adjustment, 6–7; export expansion and, 46; financing and
adjustment, 54–58; performance
related to adjustment, 58–59;
sectoral adjustment, 26; structural adjustment, 26; text
approach to, 14–15; trade policy
adjustment, 4, 26; trade proposals and adjustment, 27–31;
trade restrictiveness at outset of
adjustment, 25–27
Local content programs, 160
Lopez Michelsen administration, 88

Madagascar, 32, 143, 145, 146,
171; foreign exchange and, 172;
labor regulations in, 172–73;
infrastructure and, 173
Malawi, 32, 42, 73, 109, 114, 143,
163, 203
Malaysia, 73, 110, 111, 126, 129,
138, 143, 186, 190
Malta, 126
Manufacturing: benefits from
reform and, 82; employment
and, 72, 73; exports and, 123,
125, 126, 128, 129, 131, 138,
139, 142, 147, 171, 185, 209;
Korean liberalization and, 169;
protection of, 86; reform
resistance and, 85; trade
liberalization in Chile and, 68–69
Maquila plants, 138
Marketing boards, 143–46, 147
Mauritius, 28, 32, 102, 114, 126,
139, 182, 205, 209
McKinley, William H., 85
Messerlin, P. A., 182
Mexico, 4, 13, 28, 32, 34, 35, 37,
41, 42, 47, 59, 87, 88, 89, 91,
92, 93, 97, 107, 109, 114, 126,

143, 157, 160, 175, 185, 186, 203, 206, 207, 208, 209, 210, 212, 213, 214; balance of payments and, 66; bonded factories in, 138; credit and, 66; devaluation and, 66–67; domestic regulation and, 170, 171; exchange rate and, 66, 67; exports and, 66, 67; GATT and, 187; imports and, 66, 67; import tax in, 113; protection and, 66, 67; quantitative restrictions and, 154, 156, 168; reform opposition in, 84; reform policy and performance in, 66–67; revolving fund arrangements in, 141; stabilization and, 103; tariffs and, 66

Michaely, Michael, 72, 74
Morocco, 35, 39, 41, 42, 59, 73, 89, 102, 107, 114, 115, 126, 141, 143, 169, 172, 203, 206, 208, 212
Mozambique, 102
Multifibre Arrangement, 182, 183

Nationalization, 190
Nelson, J. M., 91
Nepal, 141
Neutrality, 11–12
New Zealand, 158, 159, 186
Nicaragua, 85
Nigeria, 41, 42, 82, 87, 143, 144, 146, 148, 157, 161, 163, 173, 206, 207, 212
Nominal rates of protection, 2–4
Nontariff barriers, 27, 28, 41, 93, 125, 142, 153, 160, 181, 205, 206, 207, 211
Norway, 185

Openness, policy and, 9
Organisation for Economic Co-operation and Development (OECD) 27, 73, 181, 185, 186, 211
Output performance: exports and, 46–47, 48–49; imports and, 54
Outward orientation, 37; approach to, 13; Chile and, 81; economic

performance and, 46, 47; employment and, 72, 74; growth and reform and, 9; performance and, 46, 47; policy reform and, 9–10

Pakistan, 27, 28, 34, 35, 37, 40, 59, 114, 125, 126, 135, 142
Panama, 32
Papageorgiou, Demetris, 72, 74
Papua New Guinea, 146, 150
Parastatal distortions of crop output markets, 171. *See also* Public sector
Performance: adjustment loans and, 58–59, 65; inward orientation and, 47; outward orientation and, 46, 47; reform and, 203–04. *See also* Output performance
Peru, 73, 81, 84, 89, 90, 91, 171, 203, 212
Philippines, 32, 33, 35, 37, 39, 47, 59, 85, 107, 126, 143, 161, 186, 190, 203, 206, 212; import tax in, 113
Pinto, Brian, 148
Poland, 126, 158, 170, 171, 212, 213; trade promotion and, 29, 30–31
Policy. *See* Trade policy reform
Politics, 19, 92; gains and losses from reform and, 81–82; import policies and, 174; opposition to reform and, 80–81, 86, 87; role of, 93; tariffs and, 162–63
Portugal, 126
Price controls, 29, 74, 170, 177, 213
Price indexes, 2
Prices, 19, 143, 144, 153; coffee and cocoa, 70, 71; costs of protection and, 5, 8; devaluation and import, 102; domestic, 176; Dutch disease and, 148, 149; liberalization and, 31; neutrality and, 11; Poland's trade promotion and, 31; support for domestic, 181; trade policy reform and, 2
Private sector, 67, 75; in Brazil,

Private sector *(continued)*
111; hostile policies toward, 174;
investment and, 213
Privatization, 171, 212
Productivity, 147; Chilean
manufacturing, 68; growth and
reform and, 9
Profitability, 69, 170
Profits, 31, 169
Property rights, 190
Protection, 81, 153, 168, 204;
agriculture and, 132; Chile and,
68, 69; Colombia and, 84; costs
of cross country comparisons
and, 35; effective rate of (ERP),
3–4, 167; exchange rate and,
207; exports and, 129; exports
and reduction of imports, 123;
implementation and effective, 32;
imports and, 5, 35–37, 51, 130,
162, 163, 165, 166, 203, 206,
210; import substitutions and,
170, 208; infant industry,
153–54; international agreements
and, 93; of manufacturing and
Latin America, 86; Mexico and,
66, 67; nominal rates of (NRPs),
2–4; policy reform and costs of,
5–8; prices and, 5, 8; reduction
and Chile and, 81–82, 170;
reduction and import substitution
and, 81; reformers and, 86;
supply response and, 75; tariffs
and costs of, 8; temporary, 154;
trade policy and external, 179–82
Public sector, 75; desire to protect,
171; liberalization and, 90;
reform of, 212; reform resistance
and, 83–84

Quantitative restrictions, 19, 32,
42, 68, 86, 93, 115, 118, 176;
Chile and, 156; eliminating, 92,
161–62; exports and, 2; imports
and, 2, 154, 156–62; Mexico
and, 66, 154, 156, 168; policy
change extent and, 203; reform
implementation and, 33–35;

tariffs and, 158–59, 161–62;
trade reform and, 2; trade
restrictiveness and, 28–29;
variations in, 37
Quotas, 19, 157, 158, 210

Recession, 39
Reciprocal Trade Act (U.S.), 85, 87
Reform. *See* Trade policy reform
Regional integration, 191–97,
211–12
Regional trade groups, 211
Regulation, 29, 170, 174, 175, 204;
bottlenecks created by, 41;
complementary policies to trade
reform and, 213; labor
(Madagascar) and, 172; supply
response and, 74; wages and, 74
Rent-seeking, 133, 159, 173, 209;
costs of protection and, 8
Resource allocation, 30, 165; Korea
and, 132–33; socialist countries
and, 140
Resource reallocation, 9, 75, 94, 103
Revenue. *See* Taxes
Rodriguez, C., 84
Romer, P. M., 50
Roosevelt, Franklin D., 87
Rubio, L., 84

Salinas, President, 88
Savings, 9, 54
Scully, G. W., 51
Sector adjustment loans (SALs). *See*
Loans
Sectoral programs, 40–42
Self-sufficiency (importables) 164,
166
Senegal, 32, 141, 143, 148
Shortages, 30
Sierra Leone, 102, 206
Singapore, 47, 190; exports and,
125, 126, 129, 139, 147, 208;
imports and, 155
Smoot-Hawley tariff act (U.S.), 80,
87
Smuggling, 167
Socialist countries, 212, resource

allocation and, 140. *See also*
Central planning
Somalia, 102, 206
Sri Lanka, 84, 87, 126, 140, 157, 207
Stabilization, 19, 21, 32, 39, 215;
Africa and, 99; Chile and
revenue, 150; imports and, 113;
inflation and, 96–97; investment
and, 97; Latin America and, 99;
liberalization and, 102, 103;
Mexico and, 103; in *1980s*,
96–97; public investment and,
107–09; real exchange rate and,
101–06, 117–18; real interest
rates and, 107; trade policy
reform and, 97–109, 118, 205;
trade restrictions and, 99
State-owned enterprises. *See also*
Marketing boards, Parastatal
distortions of crop output markets
Structural adjustment, 1–5
Structural adjustment loans.
See Loans
Subsidies, 13, 128, 150, 166;
credit, 134, 140; export, 65, 70,
140, 141, 142, 181, 208
Supply response, 21, 43, 202, 204;
constraints on, 74–75; GDP
growth and, 74; protection and,
75; regulation and, 74; sustained,
109
Sustainability, 93, 96, 117–18, 156,
214
Swaziland, 163

Taiwan, 4, 47, 73; exports and,
125, 126, 129, 135, 136, 138,
140, 185, 208; growth in, 13;
infant industries and, 154
Tanzania, 102, 109, 143, 146;
import tax in, 113
Tariffs: Chile and, 68; classification
of, 41–42; concertina cuts in,
113, 168, 169; costs of protection and, 8; Côte d'Ivoire
and, 70; exemptions from, 210;
fiscal reform and, 205–06;
frequent changes in, 153;

implementation and, 32, 39;
imports and, 161–69; international agreements and,
93; liberalization and, 118;
Mexico and, 66; OECD countries
and, 181; politics and, 162–63;
quantitative restrictions and,
158–59, 161–62; rates for
developing countries and, 25–27;
rebating, 42, 135, 136–37, 147;
reform and Chile and, 164; text
approach to, 19–20; trade
restrictiveness and, 28, 29;
trading partners and, 211;
uniform, 92, 163–64, 165, 167,
207; U.S. and, 87. *See also* Duty
drawbacks
Taxes, 31, 50, 212; agricultural
exports and, 143; export, 12, 32,
102, 114, 143; import, 112–14,
116, 163, 166, 173; primary
exports and, 143; reform
programs and, 42; revenue
effects of reform and, 109–16;
revenue effects on fiscal deficits
and, 114–16; trade, 39, 171,
205; VAT, 114–15, 116
Technical assistance, 141–42
Technological change, 9
Technology, 147, 209
Temporary admissions, 42, 135
Thailand, 35, 59, 113, 114, 126,
129, 135, 136, 143, 186, 190
Time periods, 14–15
Togo, 41–42, 163
Tokyo Round, 186
Tourism, 125
Tradables and nontradables, 11,
32, 65, 72, 74, 88
Trade Act (U.S.), 92
Trade policy reform: Bolivia and,
202; changes in external
protection and, 179–82;
commitment and, 90–91;
commitment and Africa and, 40;
costs of protection and, 5–8; in
Côte d'Ivoire, 70–71; crisis and
change and, 87–89, 93; data on

Trade policy reform *(continued)*
country experiences and, 59–65;
debt burden and, 116; defining,
12; discriminatory trade
measures and, 182–84;
distortionary interventions and,
50–51; domestic, 169–76;
domestic factors and, 203;
economic performance and,
203–4; employment and, 67–74;
exchange rate and, 2, 4, 66;
expansion of exports and, 46,
208–09; export and import
restrictions and, 51–54;
financing, 54; fiscal reform and,
205–16; foreign direct
investment and, 190–91; GATT
negotiations and unilateral,
184–89; GDP growth and,
54–58; government and, 83–86;
growth and, 8–9, 46–54; ideas
and, 89–90; impact of, 47–50;
implementation of, 31–35,
91–93, 203; implications for,
214–15; imports and, 65, 66, 67;
liberalization and, 10; measures
included in, 9–13; need for, 80;
new trade theory and, 10–11;
obstacles to, 80–86; outward
performance and, 9–10;
performance related to loans
and, 58–59, 65; policies
complementary to, 65–67,
212–13; political will and
opposition to, 80–81; potential
gains and losses from 81–83;
prices and, 2; progress and
constraints and, 37–42; proposals
for, 27–31; of public sector, 212;
regional integration and, 191–97,
211–12; resistance and, 86;
revenue effects of, 109–16;
sectoral programs for, 40–42;
sequencing and timing of,
204–08; stabilization and,
97–109, 118, 205; structural
adjustment programs and, 1–5;
supply response and, 21, 43,
74–75, 109, 202, 204; text
outline and, 15–20; themes of,
20–21; trade restrictiveness
and, 25–27, 31, 32, 51; trading
partners and, 211–12, wages and,
72–73. *See also* Exchange rate;
Exports; Imports; Liberalization;
Protection Tariffs; *names of
specific countries*
Trade promotion policies (Poland),
30–31
Trade theory, 10–11
Transport sector, 41, 171, 191, 196
Tunisia, 41, 126, 141
Turkey, 8, 13, 28, 32, 34, 35, 37,
42, 47, 59, 107, 109, 110, 111,
114, 125, 135, 140, 141, 142,
143, 170, 203, 208, 212, 213

Unemployment, 72; import reforms
and, 155; in Madagascar, 172–73
United States, 84–85, 86, 87, 90,
92, 93, 133, 181, 182, 186
Uruguay, 103, 126, 141, 143, 182,
186
Uruguay Round, 179, 182, 184, 187

Venezuela, 91

Wage controls, 29, 213
Wages, 170, 214; Latin America
and, 72–73; Poland's trade
promotion and, 31; regulation
and, 74; trade reform and, 72–73
Wilson, Woodrow, 87
World Bank, 1, 14, 27, 42, 43, 59,
89, 96, 135, 140, 142, 145, 156,
160, 164, 172, 174, 182, 202

Yemen, 125
Yugoslavia, 28, 37, 40, 47, 56, 65,
126, 140, 170, 203, 213

Zaire, 102, 103, 157, 206, 207
Zambia, 34, 37, 39, 40, 56, 65, 87,
88, 102, 103, 141, 203; tax
measures in, 115
Zimbabwe, 40, 56, 126, 141, 203